Yonder Come the Blues combines three influential and much-quoted books: *Savannah Syncopators; Blacks, Whites and Blues*; and *Recording the Blues*. Updated with additional new essays, the book discusses the crucial early development of the blues as a music of Blacks in the United States, explaining some of the most significant factors that shaped this music. Together, these three texts emphasise the significance of the African heritage, the mutuality of much white and black music and the role of recording in consolidating the blues, thus demonstrating the importance of these formative elements in its complex but combined socio-musical history. Redressing some of the misconceptions that persist in writing on African American music, this book will be essential reading for all enthusiasts of blues, jazz and country music and will be important for students of African American studies and music, popular music and popular culture.

PAUL OLIVER is Director of the Centre for Vernacular Architecture Studies at the School of Architecture, Oxford Brookes University. As well as having published works on architecture, he has researched and published extensively on blues and African American music, including *Blues Fell This Morning*, *Conversation with the Blues* and *Songsters and Saints*, also published by Cambridge University Press.

TONY RUSSELL is a freelance writer on blues, jazz and country music. He was editor for many years of the journals *Old Time Music* and *Jazz Express* and was the compiler and author of the compact disc series *The Blues Collection*. He is the author of *The Blues, from Robert Johnson to Robert Cray* (1997).

ROBERT M. W. DIXON is Director of the Research Centre for Linguistic Typology, La Trobe University, Victoria, Australia, and has published several books with Cambridge University Press, including *Ergativity* and *The Rise and Fall of Languages*. The fourth edition of his *Blues and Gospel Records 1890–1943* was published in 1997.

JOHN GODRICH, who died in 1991, published discographies of the blues in specialist journals. He was co-author with Robert M. W. Dixon of *Blues and Gospel Records* in its first three editions. A noted discographer, HOWARD RYE, joined the team for the fourth edition and contributes an essay for this book.

YONDER COME THE BLUES
The Evolution of a Genre

Paul Oliver
Tony Russell
Robert M. W. Dixon
John Godrich
and Howard Rye

PUBLISHED BY THE PRESS SYNDICATE OF THE UNIVERSITY OF CAMBRIDGE
The Pitt Building, Trumpington Street, Cambridge, United Kingdom

CAMBRIDGE UNIVERSITY PRESS
The Edinburgh Building, Cambridge CB2 2RU, UK   www.cup.cam.ac.uk
40 West 20th Street, New York, NY 10011–4211, USA   www.cup.org
10 Stamford Road, Oakleigh, Melbourne 3166, Australia
Ruiz de Alarcón 13, 28014 Madrid, Spain

First published as three volumes by Studio Vista 1970 and in the USA by Stein and Day Publishers
(November Books) 1970

Printed in the United Kingdom at the University Press, Cambridge

Typeface 11.5/14.5pt Ehrhardt MT   [GC]

A catalogue record for this book is available from the British Library

Library of Congress Cataloguing in Publication data
Yonder come the blues: the evolution of a genre / Paul Oliver . . . [*et al.*].
      p.   cm.
   Includes index.
   Discography
   Contents: Yonder come the blues: introduction / Paul Oliver – Savannah syncopators: African
retentions in the blues / Paul Oliver – Blacks, Whites and blues / Tony Russell – Recording the
blues / Robert M. W. Dixon & John Godrich – Afterword / Howard Rye.
   ISBN 0 521 78259 7 (hardback); 0 521 78777 7 (paperback)
      1. Blues (Music) – History and criticism. 2. Afro-Americans – Music – History and criticism.
   I. Oliver, Paul, 1927–

ML3521.Y66 2001
781.643–dc21

                                                                              00-028917

ISBN 0 521 78259 7   hardback
ISBN 0 521 78777 7   paperback

CONTENTS

ILLUSTRATIONS

Book three: Recording the blues
Dixon, Godrich & Rye

INTRODUCTION: YONDER COME THE BLUES

Paul Oliver

Collecting blues and jazz records in Britain before the 1950s was by no means easy, and some enterprising collectors who had picked up a rare Paramount or two would reissue them for like-minded enthusiasts on 78 rpm discs – Colin Pomeroy on Jazz Collector and James Asman on his Jazz label. I was desperate to buy Jimmy Asman's first item, which was 'Ma' Rainey's *Stack O'Lee Blues* on Jazz 5001. It delighted me, but I found myself increasingly attracted to the 'B' side – *Yonder Come the Blues*. As I tried to unravel the tangled skeins of myth, fiction, anecdotes and interviews which passed for blues history, I identified with her words:

> I get disgusted and all confused,
> Every time I look around, yonder come the blues.

'Ma' Rainey was doubtless singing of the blues as a feeling of despair, but for me her lines increasingly represented the first intimations of the blues as a new idiom, made all the more remarkable by her recollections of a tent show in a Missouri township in 1902. She told John W. Work and the poet Sterling Brown how 'a girl from the town came to her tent one morning and began to sing about the "man" who had left her. The song was so strange and poignant that it attracted much attention.' 'Ma' Rainey used it as an encore to her act and 'many times she was asked what kind of song it was, and one day she replied, in a moment of inspiration, "It's the *Blues*"' (Work, 1940).

Blues had come from way back, but no one knew then, or even knows now, quite where, when or how they sounded. To many blues enthusiasts Charley Patton represents the earliest phase of the blues, and his recordings their most archaic form. It wasn't always so. His first record, made in June 1929, was *Mississippi Boweavil Blues*, issued by Paramount under the pseudonym of 'The Masked Marvel'. When Harry Smith included it in his celebrated 'Anthology of American Folk Music' in 1952 it was still under this name. It was a long-forgotten collector, James McKune, who identified the singer and first drew attention to Patton's powerful blues, and a noted guitarist of the 'Blues Revival' years, John Fahey, who, in 1958, made the first field trip to Mississippi to research his life and music. Fahey's monograph, *Charley Patton*, was one of the innovatory studies in the Blues Paperbacks Series published by Studio Vista, in 1970–1 (Fahey, 1970).

Eventually, John Fahey's book was superseded by two later studies: an extended paper on the singer by David Evans, included in the proceedings of an international conference organised in Liège, Belgium (Sacré, 1987), and a subsequent work on the 'King of the Delta Blues Singers' written by critic Stephen Calt and field researcher Gayle Wardlow (1988). The heat generated by the historical data, contentious claims and disputed lyric transcriptions in these works are illustration enough of the problems of blues historiography. David Evans was the author of another in the Blues Series, *Tommy Johnson*, about the influential Mississippi singer and guitarist who was a contemporary of Patton (1971). After further field research Johnson and his circle were examined later in Evans's *Big Road Blues*, an exhaustive work on a regional tradition (Evans, 1982).

Seminal rural bluesmen like Patton and Johnson were not the earliest blues singers on record, however. For me, one of the initial four monographs in the Blues Series just had to be on Gertrude 'Ma' Rainey. After some persuasion the late Derrick Stewart-Baxter, arguably the first regular columnist on the blues in any country, agreed to write it. His book *Ma Rainey and the Classic Blues Singers* (1970) was devoted to the singing of the generation of women professional artists who, in the early 1920s, did make the earliest recordings. A decade after Derrick's book a study of Gertrude 'Ma' Rainey was written by Sandra Lieb (Lieb, 1981). Surprisingly, in view of their former popularity, a more extensive overview of the so-called 'classic blues' singers did not exist until 1988 when Daphne Duval Harrison's *Black Pearls: Blues Queens of the 1920s* was published.

Among the earlier blues pianists was Eurreal 'Little Brother' Montgomery, who, in fact, both accompanied some of the women singers, and recorded before Patton and Johnson. He was befriended by a German researcher, Karl Gert zur Heide, whose book in the Series, *Deep South Piano* (1970), was the story of Montgomery and his associates in New Orleans and Chicago. Another regional tradition was examined in *Crying for the Carolines* by Bruce Bastin, who conducted research in the Carolinas and the East Coast states, eventually producing a comprehensive study of the southeastern blues tradition (Bastin, 1971, 1988). These were broadly historical works; William Ferris, Jr. concentrated on the blues that were currently played and sung in Mississippi in the 1970s, in *Blues From the Delta*, which was later expanded (Ferris, 1970). *The Devil's Son-in-Law* was about pianist and guitarist William Bunch, known also as 'Peetie Wheatstraw'. Written by Paul Garon, an advocate of surrealism, it discussed the singer's personality and blues imagery (Garon, 1971). Bengt Olsson from Sweden contributed a study entitled *Memphis Blues and Jug Bands*, a pioneering work in this subject (1971). Subsequent articles in *Storyville* magazine by other authors on the history of the jug bands were promised in book form, but this never materialised.

By the 1970s blues appreciation had become truly international, as the authorship of a number of the books in the Blues Series demonstrates. This was in part due to the 'Folk Blues Festivals' which, under the direction of the late Horst Lippmann and Fritz Rau, toured Europe in the 1960s. Bob Groom, English editor of one of the first blues journals, described the phenomenon in *The Blues Revival* (1971). One European writer, however, anticipated the revival by many years. He was the youthful Dutch blues collector Frank Boom, who drafted his book on satirical blues, *Laughing to Keep From Crying*, as early as 1943. He died in Indonesia a decade later, and on hearing of the work, as Editor of the Blues Series, I hoped to include it in a subsequent batch, which would also include David Evans's *Big Road Blues*. Frank Boom's family, however, declined to give permission for its publication at that time. In the 1990s the Dutch blues lexicographer, Wim Verbei, traced three versions of Boom's text which, at the time of this writing, are being prepared for publication.

So how did the Blues Series come about? Back in 1964 I had been invited to prepare a large exhibition at the American Embassy, London, which included some 500 photographs and large-scale reproductions of ephemera. For several years after, I worked on a book based on the material I had gathered, which was eventually published under the same title, as *The Story of the Blues*. Book designer and producer Ian Cameron of November Books was enthusiastic about it and asked me if I had anything else 'on the stocks'? I told him about a short book which I had been planning, which stemmed from my experiences in West Africa in 1964. Discussing this, and other studies that I knew about, led to our devising a series of short paperback books which would reflect current research in the blues. Studio Vista were interested, agreeing to publish a series of books of 112 pages each, and to issue them also in hardback form, but under the same series title. It was clear that the books should comprise new and focussed studies in aspects of the blues, and in particular in those that had not received much attention in the previous decade of blues writing. They might include biographies, local traditions, historical and theoretical studies which could therefore appeal to a cross-section of the potential readership. *Savannah Syncopators* (1970), an examination of possible 'African retentions in the blues', was to be one of the first batch, as it would consider issues that were scarcely touched upon in *Story of the Blues*.

American music authority Tony Russell had been talking for some time about the similarity between recordings of the white country singers in whom he was interested and those of his first passion, the blues singers. Here, without doubt, was a subject which had been largely ignored in the literature to date, and one which would well represent the intentions of the Blues Series; *Blacks, Whites and Blues* was one of the first four books (1970). Robert M. W. Dixon had organised the Blues Recording Project to raise loans for me to do recordings in the United States while I was conducting field research in 1960. His discographical partnership with John Godrich produced their unrivalled listing *Blues and Gospel Records, 1902–1942*, and during the 1960s they worked on a revised edition which was published in 1969. Apart from the discographical data it included summaries of the principal 'Race labels', but a fuller history was undoubtedly needed; *Recording the Blues* by the compilers was the outcome. In the week of its publication Dixon left for the antipodes, to take up a post in linguistics at the Australian National University, Canberra.

Another book was also included in the first group of four monographs, but, as already noted, Derrick Stewart-Baxter's work on 'Ma' Rainey and her contemporaries was largely incorporated in, and superseded by, later studies. This has not been the case with the other three books that initiated the series, which are reprinted together in the present collection. The three were the first to go out of print, and though they have been the most frequently cited, they have not been generally available since the early 1980s. During that time blues has changed, becoming an international popular music genre which has been largely detached from the milieu of its progenitors.

This increasing distance may account for some of the mistakes that have appeared in blues and related histories which could have been avoided. For instance, '*Juke* is an African retention, a word meaning "evil, disorderly, wicked" in Bambara, a language spoken in parts of the Congo. Absorbed into English via Gullah, the language of Blacks in the Georgia Islands' (Davis, 1995, p. 7). Bambara, however, is not spoken in the Congo, but 2,000 miles away in the West African Savannah, so the implications of the origins of the word are profoundly different. Or again, Morgan and Barlow state that the origins of slave secular song 'can be traced back to West African *griots*' who 'were also the "living libraries" of the region's Bantu-language tribes' (Morgan and Barlow, 1992, p. 8). The *griots* are not Bantu-speaking, the nearest living over 500 miles from the western limits of the Bantu region.

Such errors could have been avoided if *Savannah Syncopators* had been read, and their appearance, among a number of others in recent books, is seriously misleading – especially so at a time when, as the twentieth century has drawn to a close, there has been an increasing awareness of the most intractable problem in the history of the blues: how it began. Though a book which brought together these three studies might not answer all the questions that arise concerning the beginnings of the blues, it seemed that such a work, augmented in the light of recent research, might further illumine some aspects of the problem. Less clear to the authors was how the three thirty-year-old studies should be presented. There was an argument for full revision of the books, though this might extend them considerably, while the new material would obscure the original texts. Another possibility was to reprint them in their entirety, but to amend errors and adjust the presentation where this may be viewed as 'politically incorrect'. Such a partial revision was thought to be undesirable, in that it was at best an uneasy compromise.

Considered by the authors to be the most honest solution, and the one which we have adopted, is the republication of the three books as they were originally written, with just a few inconsistencies and errors corrected; not without difficulties, nonetheless. For instance, there was the problem of nomenclature. At the time of writing the authors used the then acceptable term of 'Negro', with 'black' as an alternative. Subsequently, 'Afro-American' became the preferred term, later (in the 1990s) to be supplanted by 'African American'. 'Black' and 'Blacks', though once regarded as being somewhat derogatory, have been reinstated. They are used here, with the 'lower case' form being employed as an adjective. After due consideration the authors have chosen to retain all terms in the original texts that were acceptable at the time of writing, and to employ current usage in the new supplementary chapters.

There were some problems with illustrations, especially where photographs or ephemera are now missing, or former owners untraced, so they have been somewhat reduced in number. Where the original texts cited LP recordings which have now been replaced by compact discs the LP issue numbers have been deleted and reference made to CDs on which the titles mentioned are currently available. The nature of the references being very different for each works, they have not been brought together in one bibliography, but are separately listed. Likewise, this applies to the references for the supplementary chapters.

In the case of the supplementary chapter to *Savannah Syncopators* I have found it necessary to exercise some control on the references cited, for there has been a plethora of writing on the relationship between African American culture and its African antecedents or counterparts. Much of this has been on the sources of slaves. Linguistic studies have been numerous, while several papers on African music have also been published. In this chapter I discuss how these subjects may bear on African American music in slavery and after, and in particular how they may have been sustained in the blues. Though there has been a notable increase in writing on blackface minstrelsy, its origins, popularity, repertory and practice by both white and black troupes, this has not been paralleled by a similar volume of works on the commonality and exchange of the respective folk traditions. As researcher and writer in both blues and country music, as the compiler of a comprehensive discography of the latter, and as editor of the journal *Old Time Music*, Tony Russell has been uniquely placed to collect and collate such further material on their interaction as it has become available. His chapter supplementing *Blacks, Whites and Blues* considers this, especially where the formative years of the blues are concerned.

A major factor in the spread and popularisation of the blues was the development of the phonograph record, as R. M. W. Dixon and John Godrich documented in *Recording the Blues*. Since writing this book they saw the publication of a revised and expanded edition of their *Blues and Gospel Records* discography, its time span increased to 1890–1943. A fourth edition, having a broader perception of 'blues and gospel', was published in 1997, with Howard Rye being added as a third member of the team. A very experienced writer, researcher and discographer in jazz and blues, Howard Rye, on behalf of all three compilers, contributes the chapter which takes these changes, and further research on the activities of recording companies, into account.

It cannot be claimed that the questions concerning the origins of the blues have been answered in full. Nevertheless, the evidence offered herein is drawn from an extended period, 60 to 200 years ago, from whence, way back yonder, come the blues. These studies document the major, and largely consecutive, mediators in the emergence and evolution of this music.

REFERENCES

Bastin, Bruce. 1971. *Crying for the Carolines*. London: Studio Vista.
  1986. *Red River Blues: The Blues Tradition in the South-East*. University of Illinois Press.

Boom, Frank (Verbei, Wim, editor). 'Laughing to Keep From Crying'. Unpublished manuscript.

Calt, Stephen, and Wardlow, Gayle. 1988. *King of the Delta Blues. The Life and Music of Charlie Patton*. Newton, NJ: Rock Chapel Press.

Davis, Francis. 1995. *The History of the Blues. The Roots, the Music, the People, from Charley Patton to Robert Cray*. London: Secker and Warburg.

Dixon, Robert M. W., and Godrich, John. 1970. *Recording the Blues*. London: Studio Vista.

Dixon, Robert M. W., Godrich, John, and Rye, Howard. 1997. *Blues and Gospel Records 1890–1943*. (4th edn) Oxford: Clarendon Press.

Evans, David. 1971. *Tommy Johnson*. London: Studio Vista.
  1982. *Big Road Blues. Tradition and Creativity in the Folk Blues*. Berkeley: University of California Press.

Fahey, John. 1970. *Charley Patton*. London: Studio Vista.

Ferris, William, Jr. 1970. *Blues From the Delta*. London: Studio Vista. Revised and enlarged edn, 1984. New York: Da Capo Press.

Garon, Paul. 1971. *The Devil's Son-in-Law. The Story of Peetie Wheatstraw and his Songs*. London: Studio Vista.

Godrich, John, and Dixon, Robert M. W. 1969. *Blues and Gospel Records, 1902–1943*. (2nd edn) Chigwell, Essex: Storyville Publications.

Groom, Bob. 1971. *The Blues Revival*. London: Studio Vista.

Harrison, Daphne Duval. 1988. *Black Pearls: Blues Queens of the 1920s*. New Brunswick, NJ: Rutgers University Press.

Lieb, Sandra R. 1981. *Mother of the Blues: A Study of Ma Rainey*. Boston: University of Massachusetts Press.

Morgan, Thomas L., and Barlow, William. 1992. *From Cakewalks to Concert Halls: An Illustrated History of African American Popular Music from 1895 to 1930*. Washington DC: Elliott and Clark Publishing.

Oliver, Paul. 1969. *The Story of the Blues*. London: Barrie and Jenkins, The Cressett Press.
  1970. *Savannah Syncopators: African Retentions in the Blues*. London: Studio Vista.

Olsson, Bengt. 1970. *Memphis Blues and Jug Bands*. London: Studio Vista.

Russell, Tony. 1970. *Blacks, Whites and Blues*. London: Studio Vista.

Sacre, Robert (ed.). 1987. *The Voice of the Delta. Charley Patton and the Mississippi Blues Traditions*. Liège: Presses Universitaires Liège.

Stewart-Baxter, Derrick. 1970. *Ma Rainey and the Classic Blues Singers*. London, Studio Vista.

Work, John W. 1940. *American Negro Songs and Spirituals*. New York: Bonanza Books (reprint, n.d.).

zur Heide, Karl Gert. 1970. *Deep South Piano. The Story of Little Brother Montgomery*. London: Studio Vista.

1 SAVANNAH SYNCOPATORS

African retentions in the blues

Paul Oliver

1 · AFTERNOON – NANGODI

Kunaal was a Fra–Fra, a member of a tiny sub-tribe in the Awuna complex of Grunshi tribes – though only the long scar that ran from the side of his nose to his jawline indicated it to those who could recognise the scarifications. His long features and high, broad cheekbones, the long upper lip and the shrewd eyes, emphasised his savannah heritage, though his clothes were adapted European. An ill-fitting grey suit jacket, which he had marked out in large tacking stitches, a pair of khaki shorts and a hat completed the outfit. Made of translucent green plastic, the mock trilby hat allowed no ventilation and the perspiration streamed down his face from under the brim, as he threw from one hand to the other at great speed a calabash rattle filled with beans. By agitating the rattle between fingers, palms and the fleshier parts of the hand, he produced a succession of rapid and extraordinarily loud rhythms. His companion, Sosira, also bore the Grunshi scar on his face for he, too, was a Fra–Fra. Sosira wore the loose, coarsely woven smock made up from bands of indigo and white striped cotton cloth that was fairly common among the men of the region. His head was bound in a close turban and he looked cooler and more comfortable than Kunaal. More serious, too, for it was evident that Kunaal wore his modified European clothes with humour, conscious of the curious figure that he cut. Both men sang, but the burden of the singing was carried by Sosira whose slightly hoarse high phrases were placed against those of the two-stringed fiddle that he played at waist level. Fashioned from a small gourd over which a skin membrane had

1 Fra-Fra musicians, Nangodi, Ghana: Kunaal (*left*) and Sosira

been tightly drawn, and with an arm to which the strings were held in tension by hide tuning rings, the fiddle was decorated with strips of coloured cloth, fragments of skins and a cow's tail. With a small semi-circular bow of animal hair, Sosira played an accompaniment of repeated melodic-rhythmic phrases, stopping the strings with fingers that slid momentarily along them to produce subtly wailing, whining notes.

A crowd of men gathered to listen from the neighbouring compounds of cylindrical mud houses sculptured on the dusty laterite land. They sat beneath a shady tree, some nearly naked, some in shirts and trousers imported to the market from the coast 400 miles to the south. For the village of Nangodi where Kunaal and Sosira were playing that day in May 1964 was in the extreme north of Ghana, just 5 miles from the border with Upper Volta, deep in the savannah parkland belt which gives way to the desert, another couple of hundred miles to the north. I was there with a specific purpose: to gain information on the problems of communication with the Grunshi tribes, whose minimal economy and agriculture at bare subsistence level in the hot, arid zone was to be the subject of a resettlement programme. Eventually I was to instruct African architectural and planning students from the southern Akan tribes in techniques which might establish basic communication systems. But I was also engaged in recording the music of the peoples with whom I was working and in conducting lines of research which had arisen from my studies in Afro-American music. For me the hours in which the unflagging Kunaal and Sosira played that afternoon as we passed around calabashes of millet beer were immensely exciting. It wasn't only the heady brew which made my brain sing in the heat of the overhead sun; it was also the thrill of making what was for me a discovery which gave the first inkling of an answer to a fundamental problem that I had encountered a while before.

Although I was a visiting lecturer in the Faculty of Architecture at the University of Science and Technology in Kumasi, the capital of the Ashanti region, I had also spent a month as a visiting lecturer in the Department of African Studies at the University of Ghana in Legon near Accra, a hundred-odd miles to the south, close to the coast. There I had given daily lectures in Afro-American music, with particular emphasis on the blues, American Negro folk song, gospel music and early jazz, and held regular seminars with a group of students who were engaged in studies of Ghanaian music. The opportunity to do some field work in this area of study had been an exciting one and the facilities at Legon were exceptional. Under the guidance of Professor Kwabena Nketia, the most erudite African writer and student of African music, the work being undertaken was varied and serious. Visiting musicians from many parts of the country stayed on the campus and demonstrated their music which was thus available for the analysis of the students. Ga, Ewe, Ashanti, Fanti, Nzima and other Akan tribes were accessible and their many musical traditions were still much alive within miles of the coast.

The seminars with the students of the Department, almost all of whom came from the Akan tribes, and particularly from Ashanti, proved to be very perplexing. Accustomed as they were to the music of their own peoples but trained, too, in Western techniques of recording and analysis, they were in an ideal position both to detect and to identify 'African' retentions in jazz. But seldom was there more than a ripple of positive response, and even when there was it was generally conceded that the differences vastly outweighed any points of similarity. By examining some West Indian musical forms where the retentions were clear and identifiable and relating these to examples of New Orleans jazz by veteran musicians, it was possible to agree on generalities concerning the rhythmic use of front line instruments, or the polyrhythmic texture of piano, guitar, bass and drums. Eventually some of the generalisations made concerning the relationships of African music to jazz could be substantiated in outline, but the positive evidence that I had sought and hoped for was elusive.

If this applied to jazz, it applied with even greater disparity to the blues. Interested as I had been in African arts, building and music for many years, I had long been puzzled by the gulf between African music, as represented by the drum orchestras, and the blues. African work songs seemed to supply some tangible link with the American Negro vocal traditions, and in the hand-clapping 'praise shouting' of congregations in Negro churches echoes of Africa could be heard. By extension from these one could trace uncertainly some tenuous threads which linked African vocal approaches with the blues, but I could not share the confidence of those who could detect pure Africanisms in the singing of Blind Willie

2 The slave compound, Elmina Castle, Ghana

Johnson or Charley Patton. Still more perplexing was the music that could be heard in the villages of the rain forest and coastal belts in Ghana and the neighbouring territories of Ivory Coast and Dahomey, and, to the east, Nigeria. Drum orchestras with *atumpan* 'talking' drums and tunable tension drums produced no sounds comparable with the instrumental techniques and traditions of the blues singers, the songsters, the ragtime banjoists and guitarists, or, as far as one could determine, their antecedents.

Yet along the coast could be seen the great stone castles of Christians-borg, Anomabu, Elmina, Dixcove and many others; storybook castles bristling with ancient black cannon between the castellations of their white walls and keeps, still trained on the beaches and the approaches. Charming monuments now; but down low near the water-level can still be seen the dank, evil-smelling dungeons where slaves were herded to await shipment to the Americas on the Middle Passage. And running through the massive walls, dripping and slime-covered, remain the tunnels that led straight to the holds of the ships, down which the slaves took their last steps in Africa. This was the Guinea Coast, the Slave Coast that stretched by way of Whydah and the lagoons of Lagos round the bend of Africa, south to the Gabon. This was the land from which the slaves were shipped; if there were any surviving links with the blues, surely they should be here? This was the problem and it was not until I made the trip to Bolgatanga, Navrongo and Nangodi that a possible line of enquiry that might eventually lead to a solution presented itself. Later, after a while in the Yoruba country of eastern Nigeria, I travelled to Kano, the great Hausa city in the northern region of Nigeria from which the camel trains set off to cross the Sahara. Here, too, I found further support for a new approach to the question of African retentions in the blues.

Both before and since my stay in West Africa, I had been engaged in a project with the Houston folklorist, Mack McCormick. This was, and is, a detailed study of the blues and related Negro secular music in Texas and adjacent territories. Thorough research in a vast and little-studied area – as far as blues is concerned – had involved us in a far more lengthy and complex work than we had anticipated. During the course of it, many problems presented themselves, some common to blues history as a whole, some peculiar to Texas. Texas was settled late in the history of the South, and much of its population did not arrive until the Civil War. On the other hand, a small but not insignificant body of planters and slave-owners had been in the bottomlands of the Texas rivers for many years before. The question arose of how many of the slaves that they held, and that were in Texas at the time of Emancipation, had come directly from Africa; or were they the sons and daughters of slaves whose memories of Africa still survived? What retentions were there of African traditions in the blues in Texas? It was in anticipation of finding some answer to these questions from the African end that I journeyed so eagerly to Ghana. However, the drum orchestras, the music of the funerals, the festivals and the 'fetish' dances in Ashanti only added to the confusion which a study of the writings of jazz historians had already created.

I cannot claim to have solved the problems surrounding the question of African retentions in the blues. Only after detailed research both in the United States and in West Africa might a positive conclusion be reached. This monograph does no more than attempt to lay out some aspects of the questions arising for reexamination, and perhaps serve as a guide to future research. Basically, it may be summarised as a prelude to a study of African retentions in jazz and the blues, for it attempts to raise the fundamental questions: What is meant by 'Africa'? Where in Africa can musical forms related to the blues be found? Is there any justification for assuming that slaves came from these regions, if they exist? Can African peoples be considered as homogeneous, or do they divide into specific groups? Can African music be considered as homogeneous, or does its character vary over the territories which supplied the slaves? Are there any characteristics of music and instrumentation that do, or do not, accord with those in North America? If musical forms related to the blues can be found, is there any basis for the assumption that slaves came from these regions? Were there circumstances in North America that would inhibit African retentions and were there any that would promote them?

In general this book looks in outline and approximately in this order at these questions. But much has been written already by anthropologists, ethnomusicologists and jazz historians on African retentions in North American music, especially jazz, and it is necessary therefore to look at some of these writings and the questions that they, too, raise. And all this discussion is based on the assumption that retentions of African culture, or a part of it, do exist and can be established. But if they are proven, by what means were they transmitted? This, perhaps, is the first question that should be examined. If there seemed to be, in the music of Kunaal and Sosira, some fragile link with the music of the blues, was it by accident, was it coincidence, was it a direct ancestral tradition shared in Africa and by the slaves in America, or was it an innate capacity for producing music of a particular kind? It was the question that presented itself then, and it was one to which there is as yet no definitive answer. But the following is a sketch of the lines of research that might be pursued, and which, given the opportunity, I hope one day to undertake.

2 · AFRICA AND THE JAZZ HISTORIAN

In a monument to racial prejudice, Madison Grant stated in 1916 that 'whether we like to admit it or not, the result of the mixture of two races, in the long run, gives us a race reverting to the more ancient, generalized and lower type. The cross between a white man and an Indian is an Indian; the cross between a white man and a Negro is a Negro.' *The Passing of the Great Race* summed up unequivocally the American attitude to the identity of the black man. Within the world of blues and blues singers there are those who sing and those who listen who represent every shade from black to near white, whose designation, legally or by custom, is Negro. Notwithstanding the illogicality and the lack of any scientific basis in the belief, a man is a Negro if he has any perceptible or known Negro blood in him. Yet pure-blood Negro stock in the United States is exceptionally rare today and some white ancestry is known in the family tree of a large proportion of Negro families. When the anthropologist Melville Herskovits prepared his *Anthropometry of the American Negro*, he concluded that over seventy per cent of his informants had knowledge of white persons in their ancestry. This and other evidence was sifted by the team led by Gunnar Myrdal who substantially agreed with his findings and with the general conclusion that the majority of 'Negroes' so designated have perhaps one-third white blood, while some have considerably more and others much less.

It is popularly assumed that the Negro has an innate sense of rhythm; that his capacity for music and dance, for athletic performance and even sexual performance relates to inherent abilities. Whether these are diminished or diluted by the presence of more or less white blood is seldom questioned in the folk myth, for the Negro is a Negro and the question does not arise. The belief that cultural traits can be inherited is generally discounted by the anthropologist. Though he was dedicated to Negro studies, Herskovits questioned von Hornbostel's earlier propositions on this point. 'It has been claimed by Professor von Hornbostel that the spirituals of the United States are essentially European folk-songs created by the innate musical genius of the African, and that only the motor behaviour which biologically determines the manner in which they are sung is African. But would this type of motor behaviour persist in crossing? For the appearance of the mixed Negroes and the pure ones when singing these songs is quite the same', he commented, posing the fundamental question, 'what is innate and what is cultural?'

If the present studies which pursue the nature of biological rhythms in animals are extended to mankind's creative capacities, it is feasible that one day the evidence may again substantiate the belief that rhythm may be transmitted culturally. Even if this does turn out to be the case, Herskovits' question as to whether it would survive transmission through ethnic dilution still stands. At present such a view is not favoured by anthropologists, who would generally support the argument that cultural traits are learned rather than inherent. The process of enculturation through which the habits of one generation, its values and its customs, are passed on to subsequent ones may account for the persistence of some cultural elements, while the process of acculturation, whereby the meeting of cultures may lead to the evolution of a new one, is also accepted. To these may be added the process of cultural diffusion, or the spread of culture by imitation and influence. These together may indicate the manner in which Negro cultural patterns have taken the forms that they have in the United States. In the persistence of mannerisms of song, or musical technique; in the continuance of traditional modes of expression and vehicles of creativity – as for instance, the church songs or the work songs – enculturation is seen at work. As the African's music met that of his American masters; as his language became modified and adapted to a new language to persist in some ways of phrasing in a culturally distinct argot; or in the way in which the ballads have assumed the western structure and the blues have been constructed upon the European tetrachord, the process of acculturation is witnessed. And as the blues spread, or the gospel songs moved from city churches to country congregations, just as the earlier shouting services had been transmitted from the rural to the urban places of worship; as jazz moved upriver or fanned out across the southern and the northern states, the principle of diffusion is repeatedly demonstrated.

In a sense, this might suffice as evidence of process. But it does not explain what is transmitted, welded or diffused, nor does it explain where the origins of the elements that have been so passed on actually lie. If certain of these characteristics in Negro music, and in the blues of the present century, are above all characteristic of the 'Negro', it is appropriate to question where and how they arose. Few jazz historians, at any rate, have been in doubt that 'Africa' is the source of most of these cultural characteristics which have shaped Negro jazz. In his pioneering *Shining Trumpets*, Rudi Blesh devoted a chapter to African origins, with many other references to African elements throughout his study of traditional jazz. To support his thesis, he drew extensively on the recordings made by the Herskovitses in Dahomey in 1931, and on Mieczyslaw Kolinksi's analysis of them. In *The Story of Jazz*, Marshall Stearns devoted three chapters to African origins and survivals, again making extensive use of Herskovits' writings and adding earlier documentary evidence in the writings of George Washington Cable and others, notably the former's much-quoted 'The Dance in the Place Congo'. More recently, among numerous jazz histories, Gunther Schuller has, in *Early Jazz*, followed this line of argument, but has used as his principal source the Reverend A. M. Jones's *Studies in African Music* which is based mainly on a group of dances of the Ewe people of eastern Ghana.

As these writers were primarily concerned with the history of jazz, and with its New Orleans origins specifically, the quotations from Cable or Latrobe which described Congo Square, or, as in Robert Goffin's *Jazz – From the Congo to the Metropolitan*, the descriptive writings of Lafcadio Hearn also, are entirely appropriate to the context. These emphasise the drumming that was long a tourist attraction in Congo Square, New Orleans, and the conclusions that may be drawn as to the influence of African derived music on military brass and parade music, when jazz began to emerge as a musical form of distinctive character at the close of the nineteenth century. For their arguments, the studies made by Herskovits in Dahomey or the West Indies, of Harold Courlander in Haiti or Father Jones in Ghana amply supported the contention that the rhythmic character of New Orleans jazz, the multi-lineal structure of its instrumentation and the melodic–rhythmic nature of jazz improvisation were essentially 'African' in origin. These contentions could be borne out and can be explained readily enough in terms of enculturation and acculturation.

When it comes to the blues, the jazz historians are generally shorter on detailed analysis, although the assumption that the blues pre-dated jazz ('the more we learn the earlier it seems to have been', wrote Stearns) has necessitated the ascribing of African origins. 'The blues harmony, like that of its source, the spiritual, combines with melodies of a pentatonic character. These melodies do not extend beyond the five-note span of the tetrachord and in their formation clearly refer to West African melody', Rudi Blesh stated. Marshall Stearns took a different view: comparing Leadbelly's holler, *Ain't Goin' Down To The Well No More*, he stated that 'identical melodic phrases occur in a 1947 recording by Chano Pozo, who belonged to a Nigerian cult in Havana'. But for Stearns, 'the harmony employed in the blues is another matter. It is pretty clearly derived from European music although colored by the tonality of the cry. At its simplest the harmony of the blues consists of the three basic chords of our musical language.'

A comparison of observations on the nature of the 'blue note', or flattened seventh, in the blues underlines the confusion and disagreement among writers as to the extent of African influence. Winthrop Sargeant, who argued a 'blues scale' in *Jazz Hot and Hybrid*, studied a number of African recordings to conclude that 'though the blues scale is not indicated anywhere, the preference for one of its components – the flat seventh – is quite marked'. He added that 'among the crude harmonic combinations used one of the most prominent – the dominant seventh, or ninth chord – points strikingly toward certain peculiarities of blues harmonization'. It was not a view shared by André Hodeir. 'Compared with the singers of the Dark Continent, the most authentic of the blues singers would be considered "Europeanized". Don't the blues themselves, with their blue notes, represent quite a deviation from African songs?' he asked, stating confidently 'as we know, these blue notes resulted from the difficulty experienced by the Negro when the hymns taught him by the missionaries made him sing the third and seventh degrees of the scale used in European music, since these degrees do not occur in the primitive five-note scale'. Perhaps the most original proposition of all is Gunther Schuller's, when he considers it 'worth mentioning that Indo-Pakistani music is divided into six principal modes, three of which – afternoon modes – are nothing but the blues scale. To establish a possible historic link between these modes and the American Negro's blues scale might be an interesting project for a future student of jazz.' In view of his dependence on the work of A. M. Jones, it is surprising that he was unaware of the studies made by Jones on the influence of Polynesian and Melanesian music on that of Africa through the employment of the gapped heptatonic scale in the Oceanic and African xylophone.

Gunther Schuller discards as untenable Ernest Borneman's position that 'the only true jazz is Spanish- or Latin-American-influenced jazz,' and states that he is 'on shaky ground when he attempts to develop a theory that, as early as the Middle Ages, African music had a strong influence on Arabic music' and that 'there were all kinds of African strains in the music of Spain which the Negro slaves on arrival in the Caribbean recognised immediately as a sort of musical second cousin'. Developed in his article 'Creole Echoes' and in *Just Jazz 3*, Borneman's theory argued that jazz derived in New Orleans from a Creole source which the African and Spanish acculturation in the West Indies had inspired. In earlier writings Borneman, who had studied with Erich von Hornbostel, had advanced this theory to some extent but had laid greater emphasis in *An Anthropologist Looks at Jazz*, and, subsequently, in 'The Roots of Jazz', on the West African influence on jazz. For Borneman 'the complex structure of all traditional twelve-bar blues could hardly have been evolved without the survival of a third Africanism – rhythmic variations on a metric theme'. Borneman gave more attention to African elements in blues than have most writers on jazz, though his references were largely concerned with instrumental blues in jazz. Speaking of the tonic, subdominant, dominant sequence of the blues he generalised that in African singing this progression 'will add the diminished seventh to the tonic in his first line, to the sub-dominant in the second and to the dominant in the third. Thus he arrives at the peculiar harmonic structure of the blues.' Neat – but he gave no indication that this experiment had ever been carried out by 'an African'. He did, however, give due attention to the characteristics of African singing and their relationship to blues vocals.

Unfortunately, the connections between African music and the blues have been little researched or considered by anthropologists, especially those with experience in the field in both Africa and the United States. Harold Courlander could have been the exception, but, though he is instructive on the relationship of African work song to Negro work song in the United States in his *Negro Folk Music* of 1963, his chapter on the blues might have been written two decades before, so little does it take into consideration the research undertaken on the subject. So it happens that a paper written by Richard Alan Waterman on 'African Influence on the Music of the Americas' as far back as 1952 has not been super-seded. In his paper, Waterman identified a number of characteristics of African music which 'set it off markedly from that of Europe'. These included: dominance of percussion; polymeter; off-beat phrasing of melodic accents; overlapping call and response patterns and, above all, what Waterman has termed the 'metronome sense'. These elements could be identified in the music of many countries with Negro populations. In 'Brazil all traits of African music have been retained, and many songs are sung in West African languages. Negro songs of Dutch Guiana exhibit all listed traits of West African music; they are, however, sung in a cre-olized language, compounded for the most part of English vocabulary and West African phonetics and grammar.' He goes on to list the presence of these 'five basic African traits' in the songs of the *Voudun* cult in Haiti, the sacred and secular music of the Port Morant district in Jamaica, and the 'religious songs of the Shango Cult of Port-of-Spain, conceived in purely African style' in Trinidad. Certain elements in the music of Puerto Rico, Guatemala, Vera Cruz and elsewhere are also identified with these aspects of African music.

These observations are borne out by the work of Waterman himself in Cuba, Alan P. Merriam in Bahia, Joseph G. Moore in Jamaica, Harold

Courlander in Haiti and many other researchers. When it comes to the United States, Waterman notes fewer elements present: 'One of the main African components, polymeter, is usually absent except by implication, and there is a dearth of African-type musical instruments. Metronism, however, is present in all Negro sacred and secular styles, as is the importance of percussion (wherever percussion instruments or effects are not proscribed by circumstances) and the overlapping call-and-response pattern.' Waterman makes no reference to the blues, but notes that in the urban gospel hymns 'percussion effects are stressed even in the absence of actual instruments, and the instruments (sometimes, but rarely, the pipe-organ, usually the piano, and frequently the guitar and tambourine) used are, in general, exploited to the full extent of their percussive possibilities.' This analysis substantially agreed with Melville Herskovits's conclusions on retentions of African culture in the Americas. In 1945 he published a 'Scale of Intensity of New World Africanisms' in which he broke down the possible areas into 'Technology', 'Economic', 'Social Organization', 'Non-kinship Institutions', 'Religion', 'Magic', 'Art', 'Folklore', 'Music' and 'Language'. In the award of degrees of Africanisms, the Bush Negroes of Guiana rated highest among the score of categories which he identified. These were principally subdivisions of Guiana, Haiti, Brazil, Jamaica, Trinidad and the United States, with Cuba, Honduras, Mexico, Colombia and the Virgin Islands also rated. In his chart the Negroes of the Gullah Islands rated higher than those of the US rural South and US urban north, as might be expected, but overall the United States rated lowest in his assessment of African retentions. Musically, however, all three regions were rated 'b' – 'quite African'; an assessment which would not be shared by some researchers. But as early as 1935 he had contended in *New Republic* that in the Negro churches and in jazz, 'in the work songs and songs of derision, love songs and dance songs [at this date he did not specify blues] that have come down into American life as jazz, rather than the spirituals, it is in their rhythms, their melodic progressions, their seeming cacophonies, that we must look for the heritage that has been given musical America by the Africans who sang and, singing, inspired those to whom their song eventually passed down.'

Lengthy yet necessarily summary though this outline of views expressed by critics, jazz authorities and anthropologists on the African derivations of North American Negro music has been, it serves to emphasise a number of points. In the first place there is little doubt in the minds of most authorities that Africanisms of a kind have persisted in American Negro folk music and jazz. These, it is accepted, are less than those present in the Latin-American countries, but are present in sufficient quantity in North America to account for the specific nature of jazz when it emerged at the turn of the century. The hiatus between the cessation of slavery and the commencement of jazz is accounted for by the persistence of the drumming and dancing in Congo Square, the popularity of street parades and the continued interest in military brass band music, and the unbroken traditions of music at funerals and other functions which are accounted as African in origin. The strong survivals in *Voudun* (Voodoo) of Haiti which perpetuated a Dahomean cult, or the Shango cult of Bahia and Trinidad directly derived from the cult of Sàngo, the Thunder god of the Yoruba, are confirmation enough of the direct transference of African custom to the Americas. The fact that Voodoo is also practised in the United States and particularly in New Orleans is taken as evidence that other survivals in music can be expected. These contentions are supported by authoritative anthropological evidence and therefore need not be held in question.

A second point that is evident from the writings of jazz historians is that Africa is the most frequent source quoted: not any part of Africa, or even a region, but simply the continent itself. The characteristics that are deemed 'African' are not further identified in many cases. In others, where more specific derivations are sought, West Africa and the Congo are cited. Some writers accept that in North America at any rate the slaves were principally from West African sources, and where these are more specifically identified, Dahomey figures prominently, Yorubaland and Ashanti rate next and further particularisation is rare. This presupposes that there are elements in common in the musics of the tribes and peoples who were enslaved to an extent where generalisations can be made about African music. Though the survivals of the customs and rites of particular cults in individual tribes are identified, the survivals in the music are assumed to be universally applicable in Africa, or else in West Africa.

Thirdly, the comments are generally made from the point of view of the anthropologist, or from that of the jazz historian. In the former case, the survivals in the Americas as a whole are generally classified with special reference to the West Indies; in the latter, the viewpoint is conditioned by the need to seek and identify retentions in instrumental jazz, and any reference to them in blues is secondary. Blues, in jazz histories, is usually seen as a precursor of jazz and an influence upon it, rather than as a music with parallel development. It therefore appears as a link between the slavery period and the end of the nineteenth century. In order to fulfil this selected role it must represent certain aspects of the African heritage. Emphasis is placed on the quality of blues singing and the 'vocalised tone' of jazz instrumentation.

It is not the purpose of the present study to attempt to discredit these conclusions or to dispute them. Ample data supporting these contentions have been presented in the works cited as in others. However, the question remains as to whether these 'African' elements persist in the *blues* in the manner they describe. Again, it may be questioned whether the image of the blues as portrayed in these writings is in any way accurate, and whether any survivals from Africa exist in the music which have not been identified in them. If the arguments in support of African retentions are applicable to jazz in New Orleans, they are not necessarily equally applicable to blues. Though from the jazz historian's point of view the relationship between the two musical forms exists, there is nevertheless a great deal of difference between them. Jazz, at least in its early phases, was primarily a group music, using brass and wind instruments with rhythm background, employing improvisational techniques both collectively and in solo. If the histories are correct, solos on clarinet or trumpet were relatively rare in the early phase and the emphasis was on collective improvisation in a polyphonic organisation of a three-part 'front line' against a 'rhythm section'. All instruments tended to play rhythmically, although the role of the front line instruments was to state the theme and improvise upon it. Such jazz bands performed a social function and were used both for street parades and for dances or balls. According to William Russell, the 'brass bands' played for parades and were fully augmented with French horns, trombones and sousaphones, side and snare

3 King Oliver's Creole Jazz Band, San Francisco, 1921. Minor Hall, drums, Honore Dutrey (trombone), King Joe Oliver (trumpet), Lil Hardin (pianist)

drums, etc., following a military brass band pattern, while the 'string bands' played for dances and had a trumpet–clarinet–trombone front line, but with the rhythm filled out with guitar or banjo (in some reports with the guitar *preceding* the banjo), string bass and one or two violins.

From this it will be seen that the complex structure of the front line music is not a part of the blues as normally executed, while the brass band music has only the most tenuous links with blues. String bands playing jazz came somewhat closer, in view of their instrumentation; but the blues uses stringed instruments in a melodic–rhythmic manner with a fairly complex finger-picking, whereas the use of guitars and banjos in jazz was almost exclusively used for rhythmic purposes. Much has been made of the vocalised techniques of cornet and trumpet playing and of the use of mutes to achieve crying and choked vocal effects. This has been compared with the use of 'talking drums' in Africa, though these have as their basis pitch and tone elements of language and are not 'vocalised' in the jazz sense. In the use of mutes in jazz, the vocal sounds tend to be imitative and the blues content abstract. In the blues, as a separate music, both the voice and the literal content of the sung lyric are fundamentally important and instruments frequently supply a support to the vocal to extend its content.

It is not to be denied that blues has been a continuing influence on jazz, but it must also be recognised that the influence of jazz on blues has been relatively small. Blues has had an independent life of its own which has met jazz tangentially many times and has provided a source of inspiration, and even fundamental character, to jazz. Nevertheless, the blues has not had an especially important history in New Orleans, but throughout its life has had a far wider distribution. Histories of jazz have always laid emphasis on the origins of the music in New Orleans, but adequate and parallel investigation of jazz in other regions – Florida or the south-west for instance – has not been undertaken. But the case for New Orleans is apparently well established and has had a wealth of documentation in its support. As blues was far more widely distributed, it would seem that either the stimulus of blues on instrumental music was less appreciated elsewhere in the early years of jazz, or that the course of the two musical forms was really very different: the one localised and concentrated, the other diffuse and growing steadily in many parts of the South. So it seems that we are considering not one tradition which had blues preceding and leading to jazz, but two fairly distinct but contiguous traditions. Jazz had origins rooted in parade music, ragtime and dance music, and blues had origins rooted vocally in work songs, and instrumentally in stringed traditions: fiddle, banjo and guitar in particular.

Henry A. Kmen, in his exceptionally well documented *Music in New Orleans*, clearly demonstrated that the stringed traditions existed even in New Orleans in the early decades of the history of the city's slaves. 'As early as 1799 fifes and fiddles were used', he reported, 'and in time banjos, triangles, jews harps and tambourines were added. Moreover observers tell of seeing jigs, fandangoes, and Virginia breakdowns in the square', though from the tunes they played he concluded that 'however much of the primitive there was in the Congo Square dances, it seems apparent that they were borrowing rapidly from the culture around them'. Examples given of Negro dances make frequent mention of violins and banjos, and one of the first of the New Orleans balls described as early as 1802 had an orchestra of six Negro musicians mainly playing fiddles. We read of slaves supplying an orchestra of violins, a flute, triangle and tambourine for a plantation party just outside the city; or fiddle, fife, and flute for a New Year's serenade; or 'Virginia breakdown music' for one of their own Christmas parties. It is not surprising, then, to find references to musical ability in the advertisements of slaves who had escaped or who were up for sale. A random dozen of these notices from 1810 to 1820 show that most played violin, but the tambourine, fife and drums are also mentioned. To read of a slave escaping with only his clothing and a violin, or attempting to carry with him both a violin and tambourine, reveals much. Gabriel, who ran away in 1814, was described as 'fond of playing upon the fiddle' while Abraham's master broadcast that 'he played well on the violin'. A mulatto, offered for sale in 1811, was said to play 'superbly on the tambourine and a little on the fife, beats the drum better than any other in this city, very intelligent, sober and faithful'.

These, among many other references, emphasise that, though the drums were played, the violin and the fife were extremely popular with Negro musicians and slaves within the city of New Orleans half a century before the abolition of slavery. That many – perhaps most – of the slaves mentioned in this period had been imported from Africa seems undeniable and the question inevitably arises whether their fondness for and skill with the violin or simple woodwind owed anything to capacities acquired before enslavement. In these reports the banjo figures much less frequently than the fiddle. 'The banjo', wrote George Washington Cable in the 1880s, 'is not the favourite musical instrument of the Negroes of the Southern States of America. Uncle Remus says truly that this is the fiddle; but for the true African dance . . . there was wanted the dark inspiration of African drums and the banjo's thrump and strum.'

Such a record of Negro fiddles and fiddle players can be echoed throughout the old South, where banjos were also noted at an early date. Nearly 200 years ago, in May 1774, Nicholas Cresswell from England witnessed a Negro dance in Nanjemoy, Maryland. In his *Journal* he wrote that the Negroes 'generally meet together and amuse themselves with dancing to the Banjo. This musical instrument (if it may be so called) is made of a Gourd something in the imitation of a Guitar with only four strings and played with the fingers in the same manner. Some of them sing to it, which is very droll music indeed. In their songs they generally relate the usage they have received from their Masters or Mistresses in a very satirical manner. Their poetry is like the Music – Rude and uncult-ivated. Their dancing is most violent exercise, but so irregular grotesque I am not able to describe it.' Ten years later, Thomas Jefferson in his *Notes on Virginia* endorsed these observations. In music 'they are more generally gifted than the Whites, with accurate ears for a tune and time, and they have been found capable of imagining a small catch' he wrote, noting particularly that 'the instrument proper to them is the *banjar*, which they brought thither from Africa'. It seems likely that when, seventy years after, the 'Big Four' of minstrelsy, Dick Pelham, Billy Whitlock, Frank Brower and Dan Emmett, formed The Virginia Minstrels, they did base their performance, for all its caricature, on Negro prototypes. Emmett played the fiddle, Whitlock the four-stringed banjo, Pelham the tam-bourine and Brower clacked the bones. Though minstrelsy was soon to follow a path which led the native American show far away from Negro music, in these earliest years the dramatic success of the Four may well have related directly to the effectiveness of their mimicry of Negro musi-cians, playing fiddle, banjo and rhythm instruments.

In the early 1840s, when Dan Emmett and his company were galvanis-ing audiences with their versions of Negro music and jigging, Thomas D. Rice, the originator of *Jim Crow*, sang his ditty and danced the shuffling steps that he had copied from a Negro stable-hand in Pittsburg. But Fanny Kemble, witnessing a ball on Pierce Butler's plantation in 1839, wrote: 'I have seen Jim Crow – the veritable James; all the contortions, and springs, and flings, and kicks, and capers you have been beguiled into accepting as indicative of him are spurious, faint, feeble, impotent – in

4 Dan Emmett and Billy Whitlock of the Virginia Minstrels, 1840s

a word, pale Northern reproductions of that ineffable black conception.'
She was fascinated by the dancing, 'the languishing elegance of some –
the painstaking laboriousness of others – above all . . . the feats of a certain
enthusiastic banjo player who seemed to me to thump his instrument
with every part of his body at once'. In these early days when slaves were
still pouring in from Africa – notwithstanding the illegality of the trade
– and Africa was a live memory for many on the plantations, reports of
plantation customs suggest the persistence of African practices. Kenneth
Stampp quotes a report that 'at Christmas in eastern North Carolina,
they begged pennies from the Whites as they went John Canoeing (or
"John Cunering") along the roads, wearing masks and outlandish cos-
tumes, blowing horns, tinkling tambourines, dancing and chanting'. He
quotes the *Farmers' Register* of 1838 which related a persimmon party
among Virginia slaves, where the banjo player had his chair atop a beer
barrel and 'a long white cowtail, queued with red ribbon ornamented his
head and hung gracefully down his back' and his tricorn hat was decorated with peacock feathers, a rose cockade, a bunch of ripe persimmons
and 'three pods of red pepper as a top-knot'. Slaves, noted Stampp,

5 Veteran banjo player, Happy Mose, 1911

'danced to the music of the fiddle or banjo, or they beat out their rhythms with sticks on tin pans or by clapping their hands or tapping their feet' and James Weldon Johnson stated that 'every plantation had its talented band that could crack jokes, and sing and dance to the accompaniment of the banjo and the "bones"; the bones being actual ribs of sheep or other small animal, cut the proper length, scraped clean and bleached in the sun. When the planter wished to entertain his guests, he needed only to call his troupe of black minstrels.'

Further elaboration is not necessary here, but detailed examination of plantation records and early writings would substantiate the evidence that the fiddle and the banjo were the most prominent of instruments used by the slaves and their immediate successors, with hand-drums, tambourines, bones, rattles made from jawbones of animals, triangles, and fifes, whistles and flutes also often played. Predominating in most accounts are the references to the stringed instruments, which themselves became fundamental to the effectiveness of minstrel-show parodies of Negro music: fiddle and banjo, tambo' and bones. Of course the fiddle was in itself a popular instrument of European immigrants and provided the music for the dance in folk gatherings of the white populace. Among the more devout of the latter, especially the Presbyterian Scots and the Methodists of the Great Awakening, the fiddle was the instrument of the Devil. There could have been relatively little opposition to the playing of the instrument by Negro slaves, whose very blackness would have accorded with the folk image of the fiddler.

Banjo player and fiddler alike developed techniques on their instruments that were copied by white musicians, but the Negro community was sufficiently separate for them to develop traditions which were distinct. Ultimately some elements of these were passed into the blues, even if the guitar, popularised at the close of the nineteenth century, largely replaced them. The sliding notes and *glissandi* of the fiddle were matched upon the guitar strings as fingers pressed them across the frets; the percussive 'thrump and strum' of the banjo was carried on the bass strings by the thumb. These techniques could conceivably have evolved solely on the North American continent, but their singularity suggests that some musical heritage was represented within them which was special to the Negro slave from Africa. But if so, where in those parts of Africa from which the slaves were drawn did such traditions exist? Few writers on jazz and blues – perhaps none – are as familiar with African music as they are with North American Negro music and must therefore depend on the available writings on the former with all their contradictions and perplexities.

Some of the problems that arise may be illustrated by one of the few blues studies to consider the African influence in any detail. In his book, *The Bluesmen*, Samuel Charters notes that the solo song forms of the Ila and Tonga people were 'closely related to the blues that were to develop on another continent more than a century later, not only musically, but also as a concept of an individual song style developing in the midst of a communal music tradition'. After describing them he notes that the widespread 'style of singing was one of the few areas of solo performance within a communal framework in West Africa'. In fact, however, the Ila and Tonga people are neither of them West African, but separated by vast terrains, culturally and linguistically, from that region, being of the Middle Zambesi 2,300 miles away. They were a people virtually untouched by the slave trade to the Americas and any links with the blues must therefore be demonstrative of both remarkably common factors in African music and great tenacity of tradition. 'There was also in Africa a strong tradition of guitar-like instruments, and most of the early accompaniment styles in the blues seem to have grown from the rhythmic finger picking styles that had been developed in West Africa' Charters continued; 'The instrument was introduced in Africa by the Portuguese in the fifteenth or sixteenth century in its earliest European form as the small "matchet" or rabequina. Using this as a model, the African musicians built crude guitars that were called rabekin, ramakienjo, ramakie, rabouquin or ramki.' His source for this data was *The Musical Instruments of the Native Races of South Africa* by Percival R. Kirby. Kirby makes it clear that the ramkie was essentially an instrument of the Cape and quotes O. F. Mentzel who was there between 1733 and 1741 and who gave a detailed description of the instrument. Mentzel stated that the instrument had been brought by slaves from Malabar – Portuguese India – to the Cape and there copied by Hottentot musicians. Other reporters noted the instrument among the Bantu and Bushmen, though Kirby agreed that it was originally developed by the Hottentot. Some 3,000 miles from West Africa it can in no way be associated with the music of that region and had no part to play in the slave trade to North America. This does not, of course, preclude the possibility that the music of the Cape Hottentots is in some way related to that of West Africa – as the xylophones of Madagascar, the Congo,

Cameroun or Mali are related – but greatly weakens any argument of direct influence.

Direct influence of the African xylophone on the marimba of the West Indies arises from the frequency with which this instrument is found in the West African countries. But it is inaccurate to say that 'three stringed instruments were common, but most of them had six, as well as the characteristic guitar finger board, sound box, and moveable pegs', and that it was 'clearly an influence on the American musical style', for in fact the remkie is not found in West Africa, six-stringed instruments are unusual even among examples of the ramkie and the characteristic guitar structure is not typical of West African instruments. The strings are usually tuned with adjustable rings, the arm that takes them is usually cylindrical and without frets, and moveable pegs are rare. The arched harp of *Central* Africa had both an approximate hour-glass shape and pegs, but the latter, as Sibyl Marcuse notes, 'are immovable, their purpose being to prevent the strings from slipping'.

Neither the Cape, the Middle Zambesi nor Central Africa had any significant part to play in the provision of slaves for North America. It seems important therefore to consider the music of the regions which did supply the slaves and to examine what relationship it may have to the development of Negro music in the United States in order to have some grounds for speculation on the possible influence it may ultimately have had upon the blues.

3 · MUSIC IN WEST AFRICA

Inland from the coast of Ghana the bush is dense for 150 miles. According
to the vegetation maps, the tropical rain forest thins out in Ghana, and,
compared with Sierra Leone or parts of Ivory Coast or Nigeria, is even
considered to be non-existent. But to the visitor, even though primal
forest probably survives nowhere in the country, the lush vegetation, the
huge leaves like elephants' ears, the soaring, unstable cotton trees combine to give an impression of congested and barely tamed growth. Laterite
roads, red and hard, raising clouds of choking dust under the wheels of
a 'mammy wagon' in the dry season, deeply rutted, saturated and often
impassably flooded in the rainy season, wind through the forest. Nar-
rower paths and twisting tracks lead off into the bush to villages of
laterite mud houses and thatched markets. From these can be heard the
rumble and thunder of the drums through the hours of the night and a
soft roar of village voices. Above them, clear and penetrating, the sharp
clacking of the 'gong-gong' strikes a persistent, unflagging pattern until
daybreak.

Driving through the bush one may happen upon a celebration; more
often it can be heard from a distant and hidden village unlocated in the
deceptive acoustics of the bush. Occasions like these are often the wakes
and successive celebrations which are held at intervals after the death
of a member of the community. In Ashanti the number of functions and
occasions when the villagers gather for dancing are numerous: puberty
festivals, meetings of hunter and warrior associations, religious festivals

6 Ashanti drum orchestra with gong players in foreground and *atum pan* drums, left.

and cult ceremonials, state assemblies and so on. And there are the social
occasions when the *adowa* bands play primarily for recreational purposes.
Every function has its special drum orchestras and often the drum groups
are named specifically for the one dance or celebration for which they
perform a limited number of instrumental pieces. To the untrained ear
the complex of rhythms is difficult to disentangle and the total sound
from one orchestra may seem very like that of another; to the Ashanti the
rhythms are distinct and the conjunction of patterns, the offsetting of the
rhythms of the different drums against the gongs and against each other,
sets up an exhilarating tension whose complexity he may interpret in his
dancing. And, while the rhythm patterns combine to produce a texture
of a complexity which defies analysis, the *atumpan*, the 'talking drums',
speak the traditional phrases in bursts, intermittent eruptions and rolls
of sound intelligible only to those who can hear their language.

The elders sit beneath shelters of palm leaves, while the young men
bring crates of locally brewed beer. Flaming orange cloths wrapped round
the body with one end thrown over the left shoulder proclaim that this

is a funeral. Purple cloths can be seen too, and very occasionally a black one, but it is the great splash of indian red, with the *adinkra* patterns stamped upon them, which gives a brave show of colour to the scene. In the clearing, dancers raise small spurts of dust from their sandalled feet as they twist and turn, descend to their knees or leap in the air, to imitate and interpret the occupations and the pleasures of the deceased and themselves. A chorus of women sings in chanting fashion, with one woman leading with vocal lines to which they respond, seemingly without relationship to the compelling rhythms of the *adowa* band. Shaded by an awning, the *adowa* band pours out its rhythms, the two players of the *donno* tension drums standing beside the *atumpan* drummer whose large instruments are raised before him on a stand. On his left sits the *apentemma* drummer with his alto drum, and the heavy-sounding *petia* drum is beside him. Behind are the players of the male and female 'gongs', banana-shaped tubes of metal struck with lengths of iron which create a ringing, unvarying rhythmic line against the complex of variations within the strict structure of the instrumental performance. If the excitement of the drumming and the spectacle of the dancing seem contrary to the grief of the bereaved, they find solace in the messages of sympathy addressed to them by the *atumpan* drums.

It was drumming like this which I heard at many functions through the kindness and grave courtesy of the elders and headmen of Ashanti villages. For me it was deeply exhilarating music and the occasions which I was privileged to attend, culminating in a cult or 'fetish' dance for a local *obosom*, or protective spirit, were simple and moving. But when I thought about the music being created here in the heart of the Ashanti region, the centre of slave trading on the Guinea coastal regions, it seemed far, far removed from jazz, still further from the blues. If the slaves came from here, what happened to their music to make so marked a transformation? Or were the slaves brought from other regions by the Ashanti and sold to the white traders at Winneba, or Sekondi or Bushwa? It seemed important to ascertain which music-producing cultures flourished in Africa and what bearing they could reasonably have on the music of the Deep South.

Alan P. Merriam has identified as distinct musical regions those of the Hottentot-Bushman; East Africa; East Horn; Central Africa; West Coast;

Sudan Desert; and the North Coast. Of these the Central African and West Coast regions are 'differentiated from each other perhaps more in terms of degree than of kind', he wrote, 'The West Coast area is distinguished by a strong emphasis on percussion instruments and especially by the use of "hot" rhythm.' The idea of 'hot rhythm' is one which Richard A. Waterman borrowed from jazz and applied to African drumming. In Merriam's view the 'hot' concept 'as well as the traditional use of the three-drum choir and the consistent use of drums in a majority of types of music, extends southward in the coastal regions of French Equatorial Africa and the Belgian Congo', but he points out that it 'seems to be nowhere in Africa as strong as it is along the Guinea Coast'. Merriam, however, questions Waterman's emphasis on 'drums, rattles and gongs' and the dependence of most African musicians on percussion instruments, noting that 'this excludes the large number of string and wind instruments as well as unaccompanied song. It would seem wiser to speak of African *music* as percussive, rather than to emphasize the use of percussion instruments exclusively.'

In the West African region identified by Merriam it is indisputable that the drum orchestra has always played the most important part in the music of the many peoples and tribes that come within its compass. 'We are almost a nation of dancers, musicians, and poets. Thus every great event, such as a triumphant return from battle, or other cause of public rejoicing, is celebrated in public dances, which are accompanied with songs and music suited to the occasion', wrote the Ibo slave Olaudah Equiano. Born in 1745 he was captured in a slaving expedition in 1756 and taken to Virginia. Later, he was taken to England and sold to Captain Henry Pascal, but he purchased his freedom in 1766. In later years he became an active member of the anti-slavery movement and his *Interesting Narrative* was published when he was forty-four. He described the dances and the music of his tribe, each representing 'some interesting aspect of real life, such as a great achievement, domestic employment, a pathetic story, or some rural sport; and, as the subject is generally founded on some recent event, it is therefore ever new. This gives our dances a spirit and variety which I have scarcely seen elsewhere. We have many musical instruments, particularly drums of different kinds, a piece of music which resembles a guitar, and another much like a stickado. These last are chiefly used by betrothed virgins, who play them on all grand festivals.' Equiano's description would be quite applicable to the dances and the music of the Akan, whose drumming orchestras play specific pieces of great rhythmic complexity but to which the dancers invent new and descriptive steps. His 'piece of music which resembles a guitar' was probably a chordophone such as is found among most West African coastal tribes, though not with the frequency of the drums.

Between the lands of the Ibo and those of the Ashanti (Akan) of the old Gold Coast (Ghana) lie the domains of the Yoruba of Nigeria and Dahomey, and those of the Ewe of Togoland and eastern Ghana. In these, as well as in the sub-tribes, the drums are of great importance. Their use is not static but shows both evolution and influence. So Anthony King identified the *Igbin* drum family as appropriate for the god Obàtálá, the *Bàta* drum family for the worship of Sàngo, *Ogìdàn* drums to worship Ogun and *Ipèsì* for the god Ifá, yet he observed in *Yoruba Sacred Music* that one drum family, *Dùndún*, 'serve, instead of those previously listed, in the worship of the gods concerned'. This adaptability and eventual dominance of one type may help to indicate how a multitude of drumming practices may have eventually been merged into a few basic ones on transplantation to the Americas, where, as has been noted, Sàngo and Ogun are still worshipped.

Further west among the Ewe, the Reverend A. M. Jones did the field work which led to his important *Studies in African Music*, in which he analysed in detail the structures of the *Nyayito, Sovu* and other funeral and ritual dances of the Ewe, with the expert guidance of the master drummer, Desmond Tay. 'Drumming', he contended in 'African Rhythm', 'is the very heart of African music. In it are exhibited all those features of rhythmic interplay wherein African music differs fundamentally from the West.' He identified many salient characteristics: that 'the main beats never coincide', that crossing the beats 'is absolutely fundamental to African music'. These are substantiated in detail by Kwabena Nketia, whose studies of *Drumming in Akan Communities* identify some sixty kinds of drum, more than a score of drum types and many specific functions for which the drum orchestras are indispensable. How pervasive the importance

7 An Ewe master drummer playing the five-foot long *atsimevu*

of drumming is, he indicates in great detail, but the passion for rhythm, drumming and rhythmic dancing of the people is everywhere manifest: 'Arising from the general conditioning for rhythm is a widespread passion for rhythm-making. Boxes, tins, pans, even mortars and pestles may be turned, especially temporarily, into instruments for rhythm making by young and old. There is usually in these excursions some indication of a grasp of the principles of pitch contrast, phrasing and "crossing of rhythms" that underline Akan drumming.' Between these tribes and the peoples of Dahomey, Togo and the Gold Coast there was influence and contact as the shared instruments, dances and tunings identified by Nketia in his paper, *The History and the Organisation of Music in West Africa*, indicate.

Similar important drum orchestras are to be found throughout the coastal rain forest belts of West Africa as the recordings of Gilbert Rouget, Charles Duvelle and Donald Thurlow among the Baule of Ivory Coast stress. Further details of the drum traditions in the tropical rain forest belt are superfluous, for the evidence of their number and pervasiveness is overwhelming. Comparison of the recordings reveals similarities of approach to rhythm and even, in some instances, similar rhythm patterns. Generally the master drum carries the burden of rhythmic complexity and the supporting drums, graded in size, pitch and tone, set up rhythms against it and each other. 'The crossing of the beat *must* be established; after that is done, additional drums may be added with main beats of the bar coinciding with one or other of those already beating', Father Jones has explained, 'but with a different rhythm-pattern; or, in the case of the master drum, once the first two drums have established a cross-rhythm, he may do just what he likes; he usually creates a series of rhythm-patterns whose main beat crosses at least one of the other drums.' Professor Nketia has pointed out that the rhythms are conceived either unilineally with the patterns 'assigned to one drum or a pair of drums played by one man, or to many drums played by different men. In the latter case, a number of the same type of drum or different drums may be playing the particular set of rhythms together'; or multilineally, where 'a number of rhythm patterns are assigned to two or more drums, each drum or group of drums beating different patterns or adopting different sequences of patterns in such a way as to offset some beats of their respective patterns.' Against these may be placed hand-claps, often by two or three individuals or groups of people, whose clap rhythms are also played against each other, while the 'gongs' or clapperless bells establish a metronomic time signal. The suggestion that the master drummer may 'do just what he likes' is rather misleading, for the length and character of the rhythm phrases is determined by the function, the nature of the dance and the 'piece' that is being performed. Improvisation, in fact, is very strictly controlled. As Nketia has pointed out in a paper on the music of the Ga people, 'the drummers of an ensemble cannot just drum what catches their fancy. They have to know what is required of them in respect of rhythm and tone. They have to know the basic parts assigned to each drum and how they are intended to be combined. For although the resources of drums are limited, they can be arranged in different ways so as to produce drum pieces which can be clearly distinguished from each other.'

To what extent is the West African approach to drum music and its rhythms reflected in jazz and the blues? To Harold Courlander, the links are direct. 'There is no doubt', he said, 'that drums were widely used in the African manner in the United States as late as seventy or eighty years ago. Literature on Louisiana is prolific with references to drums. A survey conducted in the Sea Islands of Georgia only a relatively few years ago produced evidence that persons then alive recalled the use of drums for dances and death rites. In Alabama in 1950 I found the remains of an old peg-type drum being used as a storage container for chicken feed. It is probable that the persistent use of the shallow tambourine or finger drum by certain Negro groups stems as much from African tradition as from European. In secular folk music, the wash-tub bass is played precisely in the manner of the African earth bow: the string is plucked and beaten by one player, while a second beats on the inverted tub as though it were a drum.' Harold Courlander has likewise compared the drum battery of Baby Dodds with aspects of African usage. 'Different tones are produced on the block by striking it in different spots and with different parts of the drumstick, as in the case of the African slit-log drum. The left-hand "hard" beats are called "mama" and the right-hand "soft" beats are called "daddy"' and he compares this with West Indian and West African terminology. Yet it must be acknowledged that, whatever the links with African drumming, and they may not be as numerous as this suggests, conceptually jazz music is very different.

To the ear accustomed to both jazz and African music, it is apparent that the fundamental opposition of rhythms and the multilinear rhythmic approach of African drumming is only marginally echoed in American jazz. Though Waterman has emphasised the 'hot' character of the drumming of both cultures, jazz does not get its impetus from the use of cross-rhythms, except in so far as the trombone, trumpet or clarinet may be said to be used rhythmically. The 'rhythm section' is controlled heavily by the 'beat' and this allows none of the tension to develop which is characteristic of the drum orchestras of the African rain forests. Instead, jazz developed a different kind of rhythmic feeling with a lifting movement between adjacent beats which the jazz musician identifies as 'rock' or 'swing'. Waterman relates this to the 'metronome sense': 'Musical terms like "rock" and "swing" express ideas of rhythm foreign to European folk tradition, and stem from African concepts, as does the extremely basic idea of the application of the word "hot" to musical rhythms. The development of a "feeling for the beat", so important in jazz musicianship, is neither more nor less than the development of the metronome sense.' But, if this is so, then nearly all the other African concepts of rhythm were discarded in its favour, for, in the jazz sense, West African drum orchestras simply do not 'swing'. The 'ride' of a New Orleans jazz band, the 'slow and easy' slow-drag of a country blues band, have no counterpart in the forceful thrust of the multilineal drum rhythms.

In jazz drumming the most African-seeming characteristic of its rhythms lies in the shifting of accents to the weak or 'off'-beats – syncopation in fact. But syncopation of this kind is not an element of African drumming, and only appears so through the filter of western notation. 'Any attempt to write African music in the European manner,' wrote Father Jones, 'with bar lines running right down the score and applying to all the contributing instruments simultaneously, is bound to lead to confusion. It gives the impression that all but one of the contributors is highly syncopated, and the multitude of tied notes and off-beat accents makes the mind reel. Looked at from the point of view of each player, African music is not syncopated nor is it complicated except for the master-drum rhythms.'

In addition to those problems which arise from the relation of the jazz approach in rhythm and syncopation to the West African concepts of drumming, there are similar difficulties stemming from the use of wind instruments and the nature of jazz improvisation. Though horns are used in parts of the rain forest, they are seldom employed with the drum orchestras and have relatively little flexibility. Improvisation on the theme, which is fundamental to jazz, also appears to owe little to improvisation within tight rhythmic patterns on the drums.

All these problems are present in a still more marked degree when the blues is considered. Largely a vocal music, it is also one which was, in its formative years, created by solo artists, or by pairs of musicians. The 'blues band' is seldom of more than four or five pieces at any event, and even when it is as large as this it is dominated by stringed instruments. Blues singers working solo with a guitar or with a piano are in the majority; combinations of two guitars, guitar and mandolin, or guitar and piano are fairly common; while guitar and fiddle, guitar and harmonica or, occasionally, piano and harmonica have all been popular in varying degrees. The use of string and tub basses, washboards, and jugs, with the rare survival of banjo and the infrequent use of the kazoo, more or less rounds out the customary use of instruments in the blues. When blues instrumentation, improvisation, rhythm and use of vocals are compared with the music of the rain forest drum orchestras they seem even further removed than jazz from this African tradition. It was precisely because of these considerations that the music of Kunaal and Sosira in the village of Nangodi seemed so important to me. For here was the combination of vocal, rhythm and stringed instrument which hinted at a link with the blues; here, too, I heard in person for the first time an African music which could be said to 'swing' in the jazz sense, where the singer and his accompanist seemed free to improvise and where the combination of instruments had a certain feeling of syncopation.

Sosira and Kunaal represented a different tradition in African music, and though they were on the southern fringe of it they were related to a body of song and musical expression which extended in a great belt across the sub-Saharan savannah regions. Although they are all of them Negro peoples, the tribes that inhabit this vast region are, in many ways, distinct from those of the rain forest. The history is complicated by the movement of peoples during the past five centuries, but certain generalisations can be made which are substantiated by linguistic evidence. Although virtually all the tribes of West Africa south of the Senegal River may be considered as speaking Sudanic languages, they may be grouped into major divisions which have been most exhaustively examined by Joseph H. Greenberg. Though some details are disputed, in general his African linguistic classification is accepted by scholars and may be briefly summarised. The coastal rain forest tribes, of which the Ashanti are a federation, come within the Kwa group which stretches from Liberia east to Ibo territory in Nigeria. Within this belt are included the Baule-, Twi- (Ashanti-), Ewe-, Yoruba- and Ibo-speaking peoples. North of them are the Gur group, taking in the Bobo, Mossi and Dogon peoples among many others, while to the north-west is the massive group of Manding- or Mande-speaking peoples, including the Malinke (Mandingo), Bambara

8 Chicago street band 1937, with guitar, banjo and tub bass; photo by Big Bill Broonzy

and Soninke. Along the coast from Senegal to Liberia are to be found the west Atlantic sub-family which includes the Wolof, Diola and the scattered groups of the Fulani.

Apart from the Kru-speaking peoples of Liberia, it will be seen that the peoples of the drum orchestras are within the Kwa group. This is partly due to the vegetation, which is dense tropical forest yielding large-boled woods suitable for the making of big drums. As one moves north from the rain forest and into the tropical woodlands and savannah mosaic regions, the trees become fewer and smaller. They are less suitable to the making of drums and are prized, when they do grow large, for the

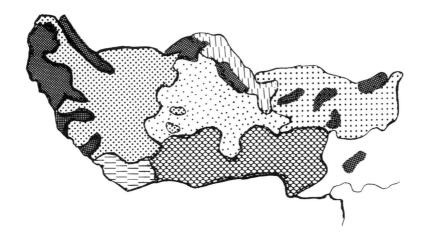

WEST AFRICA – *Linguistic areas*

(adapted from J. H. Greenberg and others)

West Atlantic: includes Wolof, Serer, Diola, Temne, and Fulani (the Fulani are pastoral–nomadic).

Mande (Mandingo): includes Soninke, Malinke, Mende, Vai, Kpele, Dan, Guere, Bambara, and Dyoula.

Kru: small region including Kru, Grebo, and Bakwe.

Gur: includes Senufo, Lobi, Dagomba, Grunshi, Gurensi, Mossi, Dogon, and Gurma. (With pockets of Mande Dyoula.)

Kwa: includes Baule, Anyi, Ashanti, Fanti, Ga, Brong, Yoruba, Nupe, and Ibo.

Songhai.

Chado-Hamitic: includes Hausa, Sokoto, Bede, Ngizim. (Tuareg are Berber, penetrating from the north. Also pockets of Fulani.)

9 West Africa: linguistic areas

shade they offer. Further north still, the savannah parklands give way to steppe and, eventually, to the desert. In the savannah regions the woods available for instruments are small-boled and they are more frequently fashioned into resonators for stringed instruments, or into strips for xylophones. But in these regions calabashes and gourds grow, providing other types of resonator, and the bodies for large calabash drums.

For many centuries the savannah and grassland peoples have been assailed by Muslims from the north, so that many of them have totally embraced Islam. Others have partially retained their pagan animism, while some tribes are divided between pagan and Muslim groups. To the south on the other hand, along the rain forest, the peoples have been exposed to Christianity and western missionaries, while their tribal religions are strongly animistic and in some cases, the Yoruba for instance, have a pantheon of gods. Contact with Islam has affected the savannah peoples culturally in a number of ways, the Muslim strictures against representational arts, for instance, resulting in sculpture that is more abstract in form than the more figurative sculptures of the rain forest; many of the Manding-speaking tribes produce little sculpture at all. Of course, the available woods again affect the artifacts, savannah sculptures tending towards 'pole' forms, while those of the rain forest are more fully realised in the round. The vegetation and climate also affect the crops; millet is the staple diet among the savannah peoples, yams and tree crops are staples in the coastal belt. Ethnically, the peoples are complex, but those on the coast include a large proportion with high counts of the sickle-cell gene making them resistant to malaria and able to withstand heat and high humidity; those in the savannah belt include large numbers of tribes with low sickle-cell counts and lower resistance to malaria, yet they are physically more suited to a dry atmosphere, high day temperatures and cool nights.

North of the rain forest there stretches a belt of savannah and semi-desert some 250 miles in depth and sweeping from Lake Chad in the interior eastwards for nearly 2,000 miles. It takes in the northern part of Nigeria, and the southern part of Niger; dips over Dahomey and Togo to take in part of Ghana; embraces the Republic of Upper Volta and the southern part of the Federation of Mali; and takes in the north of Guinea

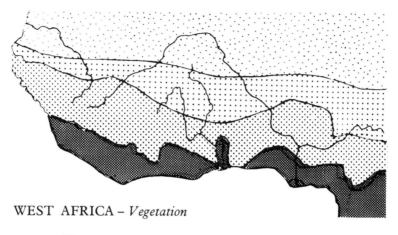

WEST AFRICA – *Vegetation*

Key

Semi-desert and desert

Savannah steppe

Savannah grasslands and woodlands

Tropical rain-forest

10 West Africa: vegetation

to Gambia and Senegal on the west Atlantic coast. Within this great belt live hundreds of tribes who are linguistically, culturally, climatically and environmentally distinct from the Kwa-speaking peoples of the coastal rain forest, even though they are all Negro and all speaking Sudanic languages. It is the latter (Kwa) who have been the subject of comparative studies concerning African retentions in jazz and the music of the Negro in the Americas: the drum-dominated tribes of the Ashanti, Yoruba and Ewe. North of them are peoples who also have drums and who also employ drum orchestras, but among whom are to be found a variety of stringed instruments, horns, flutes and xylophones, which together reveal a broader base to the African musical heritage. Is it to these regions that any African retentions in jazz can be traced? And, bearing in mind the combinations of lutes, harps and fiddles, are there any links with the blues and its antecedents to be found here?

It is probably true to say that nearly all African peoples have stringed instruments of some kind, but in those of the tropical rain forest they generally play a very small part in the musical expression of the people. The 'musical bow', which is the ordinary hunting bow plucked as a musical instrument, is to be found in most hunting societies, and there is a curious combination of bows, where each string has a separate stem, that together make the so-called 'West African harp'. Belly-harps and belly-lyres, with single strings held in tension across a bow fitted with a gourd resonator, are also frequently found. With the cup of the resonator placed against the stomach, they can be played by plucking or with a bow-string. Lyres are common, with the horns carrying a crosspiece to which the strings are attached, but monochords plucked, bowed or picked with a plectrum, and similar chordophones with two, three or more strings are even more familiar. In addition there are large harps and plucked lutes; some of the former, with as many as a score of strings on which extremely complex music can be played, are to be found in the western parts of the savannah regions. To the ear attuned to blues it is the manner of playing that impresses, with the moaned and wailing notes of the bowed instruments, the rapid fingering of the lutes and harps, and the combined interweaving of melodic-rhythmic lines when two or more musicians play together, offering some remarkable comparisons. The pentatonic and heptatonic scales often used by many of the savannah peoples do not preclude the inflections and shadings that come from rising to hit the notes, relaxing tension on the strings, or drawing the bow across them to make immediate parallels with the 'blue notes' – diminished thirds and sevenths – familiar in blues and jazz.

In the African countries where Islam has had a powerful influence and where chiefs exert considerable authority, much of the music-making is the province of the *griots*. These are traditional musicians who are employed as individuals, or in pairs, or even in very large groups and orchestras. In many savannah societies the *griots* are professional musicians, but in some – as in Senegal – they are part-time entertainers and may also be farmers, fishermen or follow some other occupation. The latter may be attached to a village and may have only a small, local reputation as song makers and instrumentalists, but in many regions the *griots* are employed by the sultans, emirs, chiefs or headmen. Others – the most famous – are free-ranging groups of professional musicians, unattached to any employer, who hire their services out to families, groups of workers or others who wish to hear and temporarily employ them. Many *griots* were slaves at one time and some, technically, still are. But the freely travelling, nomadic *griots* are totally independent and proud of it. 'The musical arts of the *griots*', wrote Tolia Nikiprowetzky when introducing a collection of their recordings in Niger, 'is rich and varied. The basis of their repertoire consists of songs of praise: the *griot* is attached to a chief and by custom flaunts the qualities of his master and perpetuates the memory of the members of his family who have preceded him in his ruling functions, or have singled themselves out by their efforts. When attached to a "professional body" (cultivators, fishermen, butchers, etc.) the *griot* praises the achievements of some members of the profession and encourages the efforts of the workers.' The *griots* play for important occasions like marriages, circumcisions and the like, and leave with considerable sums of money. It is stated that one celebrated *griot* in Senegal has a more substantial income than the highest-paid officials in the country.

Generally, indeed almost invariably, the *griots* are the sons and nephews of older *griots*, their role being hereditary. They are taught by their fathers and uncles and are trained over many years to learn the enormous quantity of traditional songs and to master the melodies and rhythms which are expected of them. A *griot* is required to sing on demand the history of a tribe or family for seven generations and, in particular areas, to be totally familiar with the songs of ritual necessary to summon spirits and gain the sympathy of the ancestors. Some of the *griots* are women, though they are generally the wives of the male singers, and they gather gossip and details which the *griot* may incorporate into his songs. For though he has to know many traditional songs without error he also must have the ability to extemporise on current events, chance incidents and the passing scene. Their wit can be devastating and their knowledge of local history formidable. As Curt Sachs noted, 'they importune the rich with either glorification or insults depending on whether their victims are open-handed or stingy. They often roam from village to village in gangs of about a dozen under a chief who is at the same time a seasoned historian and genealogist and knows to the last details the alliances, hostilities and conflicts that unite or oppose the families and villages of the country.' This puts the *griots* in a position of some power; they blackmail their listeners with their ridicule and are feared and despised for it, while being admired for their skill. The attitude of their audiences is ambivalent, for while they fear being the butt of their humour they want to hear the gossip and news they purvey, and listen to their music.

Arabic has been adopted by the learned among the cultures of the savannah regions and the Muslim schools have brought a degree of literacy. But it is primarily an oral culture and hence the *griot* plays an important role within it. He has a stock-in-trade of songs and words, he has a standard available repertoire of tunes, but he is also an innovator and a manipulator. He fits new words to old musical themes, models old phrases into new ideas, and rather than being a perpetuator of attitudes is, as Nikiprowetzky has pointed out, in Senegal at any rate, an instrument for social change. Nevertheless, these are slowly moving societies and the *griots* have been established for many centuries, and may well continue to be. Their position in the society is an ambiguous one: both privileged and un-privileged. They can acquire large fortunes and as the custom of giving and receiving gifts is prevalent among savannah peoples, with 'giving' gathering the higher esteem, the *griot* is often the recipient of gifts from his master. But they are a caste apart, as André Jolivet has explained, 'the last in the hierarchy with the smiths, the rope-makers and the weavers'. Among many tribes who venerate the earth and whose ancestors are intimately associated with them, the interment of a *griot* would be a desecration. Instead of being buried, therefore, their bodies are placed upright in the trunks of hollow baobab trees and allowed to putrefy.

In the pursuit of the profession, many *griots* achieve remarkable standards of virtuosity. The players of the great harp-lute, called the *kora*, for instance, combine melodic inventiveness with subtle and constantly moving rhythms, plucking the twenty-one strings of their instrument with the thumbs, while steadying their hands on two projecting wood horns.

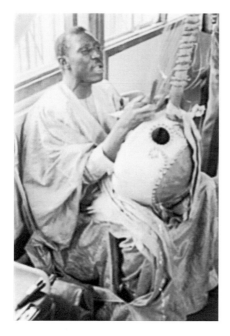

11 *Jali* Nyama Suso of Gambia, playing the 21-string *kora*, London, 1972

Or they may play a ground bass and play intricate patterns over it while singing in a third layer a praise song, or improvised market-place satire. Among the Mandingo sub-tribe of the Malinke, the *seron*, a variant of the *kora* with nineteen strings, is equally popular, while, in the Gambia, the *bulumbata* offers a further variant. Made like the others from a huge calabash and covered with a skin, it has a curving arm which carries the strings and which terminates in a metal plate festooned with rings that vibrate with every touch of the strings. These instruments have their strings held in place by tuning rings, or leather loops, which are slid when wet up the shaft of the arm and allowed to tighten on drying.

Some bands of *griots* comprise a large number of musicians, singers and praise-shouters – sometimes as many as twenty. But five or six is more usual and trios, or pairs, of musicians very common. In the larger orchestras there are many kinds of instrument; or alternatively there are those which have a large assembly of a single type – drums or horns – which are played for particular functions only. Some of the techniques employed are unusual, such as the calabash drum whose tones are constantly varied by piling up or clearing sand away from the bowl which is half immersed in it. Others show the borrowings of instrumental techniques from nearby peoples: the floating calabashes of the Tuareg for example. Rhythms are important in the music of the *griots*, but, as Nikiprowetzky has observed, 'Contrary to the usual belief that African music is above all rhythm and percussion, we have observed "melody lines" which spontaneously spring to life and unfold according to their own internal nature without being subjected to any rhythmic straightjacket.' It is hard to generalise about a musical culture and tradition which is shared by so many tribes over so vast a region. The *griots'* orchestras are numerous and there is evidence of their increasingly widening influence.

Writing in 1931, William Seabrook noted the presence of *griots* among the Dan and Guere of the Ivory Coast rain forest. 'These are a special class' he wrote, 'and divide further into two separate specialized functions. One type of *griot* is like the subsidized poet or minstrel who was attached to a European Court in the Middle Ages. He is an improvising singer, shouter, orator, whose duty is to flatter and glorify his master. The second type of *griot* corresponds even more precisely to the medieval king's jester. He is a comic fellow to whom every outrageous licence is permitted.' His reports and photographs reveal that the *griots* did not accompany themselves on stringed instruments, or apparently on any musical instrument at all. Thirty years later, Hugo Zemp explained that, in general, any Dan might play an instrument and that 'any one of the boys can learn to play the drum or transverse trumpet. In contrast to these non-professionals, the musicians of the Malinke (the neighbouring tribe in the North) belong to a professional caste of musicians. Some of these *griots* have settled with the Dan and live near the headmen as musicians and leather workers.' Contact with the Malinke was evident in other ways: 'The Northern Dan of the Savannah have adopted the Malinke practice of maintaining permanent hunting groups, and also the musical instrument which the hunters take with them, the *ko* (hunter's harp). This instrument has six or seven strings, arranged in two parallel rows.' Hugo Zemp also found the six-stringed harp-lute among the Senufo whose lands are in the savannah region. They had 'undoubtedly taken over the harp-lute from their Western neighbours, the Malinke. Among the latter it is called *koni* and played by hunters, also to the accompaniment of iron rasps.'

Though the Senufo hunters wore similar attire and played rasps, 'on no occasion known to us was the principal singer able to play the harp-lute. However the instrument is always carried about and although never sounded, and perhaps for this very reason, has a special significance for the singer.'

Further west among the Wolof of Senegal and Gambia the *griots*, known as the *gewel*, occupy a lowly social position, as Sachs has observed. Their status is below that of the descendants of the slaves of blacksmiths and leather workers and the praise-singers, minstrels, jesters and musicians, and the descendants of their slaves (*jam i gewel*) 'are regarded in some ways as untouchables: they cannot be buried in the village graveyard, and members of other classes will not eat with them out of the same dish'. But, wrote David Ames, 'despite the pretence of laziness presented to the public for business purposes, most of the *gewel* are hardworking farmers and entertainers. They take pride in their artistic abilities, and virtuosos among them are recognized by the whole community and often have a reputation beyond it.' Drums are used by the Wolof; these, however, are not made by them but by Fulbe woodcarvers. Among string instruments the most frequently employed and one of the most favoured of all Wolof instruments is the five-stringed *halam*. A hollowed wood body has hide stretched over it to form a resonator and the strings are fixed by leather tuning thongs to the rounded neck and stretched over a bridge on the resonator. 'The strings are plucked by the fingernail of the thumb, forefinger and the middle finger of the right hand, and the *gewel* keep their fingernails long for this purpose. Occasionally all of the fingers are used to strike the resonator as in *flamenco* guitar-playing. The two longest strings are stopped with the fingers of the left hand without the aid of frets. The three shorter strings are not stopped but are left "open" and are plucked in constant pitch', Ames has explained, understandably hazarding the guess that the *halam* 'may have been the "grandfather" of the American banjo'. A similar African lute with a gourd bowl also employed in Senegal has, too, been considered to be the source of Jefferson's '*banjar*'. Known as the *bania*, as Curt Sachs has noted in *Reallexikon der Musikinstrumente*, not only its form but even its name may have been transported to North America. Certainly it is not hard to believe that

12 *Griots* playing a *halam* duet, Senegal

the tradition which shaped the music of the *halam* and the *bania* was the progenitor of the music of such teams as Frank Stokes and Dan Sane or the Georgia Browns, when listening to two professional *gewel* each playing the *halam* in a rapidly moving, cross-rhythmic performance.

In the Hausa regions of northern Nigeria, 1,500 miles to the east of the Senegambia, instruments of a similar kind are played for *bori* rituals and ceremonies and on the hunt. The *komo* is a two-stringed lute with a bowl made sometimes out of a calabash, sometimes out of a section of hollowed wood like the *halam*. A strip of metal with vibrating rings inserted around it is to be found on one *komo* in my possession; another has no vibrator. These instruments are played with a pick or plectrum of rhinoceros hide and are found deep in the Republic of Niger where groups of as many as six *griots* play extremely large instruments, some nearly two metres long, called *garaya*. Among the Hausa of Nigeria the *kukuma* fiddle is also used to accompany praise songs. Horsehair is laid in a band to provide a single 'string' and the instrument is played with a long horsehair bow. Groups of musicians also play a larger form, the *goge*, while in Niger the *goge* (or *gogué*) is played by both solo singers and bands of *griots*. Though the distribution map of these instruments is complex, and the variations of the lutes and fiddles may have differing numbers of strings, like the long-armed *gouroumi* of Niger with its three strings but marked proportional similarity to the banjo, their widespread use over many countries and thousands of miles of savannah territory is without question.

Across the savannah belt drum orchestras among the *griots*, using drums for weddings, funerals and other ceremonies, for the praise of the chiefs and to accompany particular forms of work, are common, even if they are not as prevalent as in the rain forest. Tension drums, large calabash drums and small drums of skins stretched across potsherds are all to be found. But trumpets and horns are also found in many *griot* orchestras and in the bands maintained by the chiefs, headmen and emirs. The long Hausa trumpet, the *kakaki*, the so-called single reed oboe known as the *algaïta* and many other kinds of horn with flat disc mouthpieces, slender reeds, bodies of wood or bamboo and bells of tin or other metal are widely distributed. Much has been written of the 'talking drums' of the Ashanti and the Yoruba with the assumption made that in some way the vocalising techniques have been transferred to wind instruments in the Americas. It would seem that the influence could have been far more direct with a clear retention of savannah practice. Tolia Nikiprowetzky has drawn attention to the virtuosity of the players of the Béri-Béri *algaïta* who are able with 'an ingenious system of phonetic equivalents to transmit virtual messages which the initiated can translate with ease'. The Béri-Béri of Niger use similar instruments to the Hausa who employ the use of 'talking' techniques widely. David Ames recorded a Fanfare for the Sultan of Sokoto who is 'senior to all the Emirs and appropriately his musicians are the most expert and proud of all the court musicians'. The court orchestra included three *kakaki* long trumpets, three *algaïta*, two double membrane drums with snares (*gangan na sarki*) and five medium-length horns of the *farai* type. 'Though there is no singing, all the instruments are "talking"', Ames emphasised. On wind instruments it is possible for imitations to approximate the sounds of speech and song, but this is only practicable on the drums with 'pitch and tone' languages like Twi (Ashanti) or Yoruba. As Wolof is not a tone language the members of the Wolof tribe do not use this technique, and neither do other language groups which do not share this characteristic, though some employ communicative rhythms much as a bugler may sound a 'reveille', or a drummer sound 'retreat'.

4 · SAVANNAH SONG

Far to the north-west of Ghana where the Black Volta divides the country from the southward dipping finger of Upper Volta, live the Lobi. They have moved from further north at some time and their houses are of a kind most suited to the arid regions of the Sudan. Settling along the Black Volta, where seasonal rains can damage mud-built compounds, they have devised means to adjust to the somewhat more variable climate of the savannah parkland. Their compounds are of rounded buildings, or rectangular huts with rounded corners, and the roofs, with low mud walls, become areas for drying crops and for communication across the compound. When a man builds a house he gets his companions to throw mud balls up to the level where he lays them on the wall. It is hot work in the sun and to make it easier and assist with the rhythms of throwing, catching and laying the balls of mud, a group of musicians plays nearby.

Their principal instrument is the African *balafon*, or xylophone, called a *gil* by the Lobi, and a group may have two, three or even more xylophones. The long strips of hardwood are laid on a sling suspended within a frame structure which stands on the ground before the player. Beneath the slats, which are bevelled until they are tuned correctly, are suspended gourds to amplify the sound. Most of the gourds have patches of white on their surfaces – membranes of a spider's egg which are used to seal holes made in the gourd. Some of the holes are made by termites, but many of them are deliberately made to achieve refinements of tuning, for the Lobi have a refined ear for the qualities of sound which they expect from the *gil*. On occasion two or even more musicians may play the same

13 Lobi musicians, Lawra, Ghana, playing the fourteen-key *gil*

xylophone, striking from opposite sides or playing a rhythm pattern on the end key. When the melodic–rhythmic patterns of several *gils* and musicians are flowing freely, a complex of rippling instrumental lines creates an enchanting sound. In support are two small drums – *dale* – made from the necks of broken pots over which snake-skins have been stretched. The drums are played with the fingers and gripped between the knees of the player; the sound is surprisingly crisp and loud. A *kor*, or stem based drum with a goatskin head, provides the bass rhythm and any number of bystanders may join in by clacking *pira*, or iron finger castanets. The musicians do not sing; in this they resemble the Ashanti *adowa* bands, though there is little similarity in other respects. Instead, the singing is carried by a leader whom the orchestra supports. When I recorded a group of Lobi musicians from Lawra, the singer was a powerfully built man with a string of plastic beads round his neck and a strong, strained voice. Most of his songs were *shebre*, a general term for a song type used for marriages, festivals, harvest ceremonies and other occasions of feasting and celebration. His words were uttered rapidly and he often broke into shrill ululations and shrieks.

What, I wondered, had happened to the *gil*? The Lobi, or those who had previously occupied their territory, would have been easily accessible to slave raiders from Ashanti; did any go to the United States and did they bring the *gil* with them? Of course the Lobi *gil* was only one of the many kinds of xylophone to be found right across Africa, spreading across West Africa as far as Guinea. If there is little evidence of Lobi tribesmen in the south, there is evidence enough of Bambara and Malinke (Mandingo), both of which have important traditions with the *balafon*. Was the marimba, the xylophone, ever brought to North America? And what happened to the unique gapped heptatonic scale of the marimba which Father A. M. Jones has shown is essential to the instrument and displays its Oceanic origins?

It may be, as Mack McCormick has suggested, that the lack of the appropriate hardwoods caused the disappearance of the instrument, whereas in mahogany-growing countries further south it has survived. But strips of bamboo and other woods could have been used; perhaps it was simply that the stringency of American slave ownership did not permit the slaves time to make the instrument; the time necessary to fashion a modest *bania* would have been far less. Again, it may have been simply that the piano was available for talented slaves who might perform on a keyboard instrument. It would certainly seem that the combination of repeated rhythm patterns and rhythmic–melodic patterns set against them, such as are characteristic of boogie-woogie and blues piano, is a fairly logical extension of the elements of *balafon* playing. But this does not explain the time-lag that apparently exists before such a pianistic equivalent emerged; perhaps no explanation can be reached.

Undoubtedly the *balafon* has a long history, and its music continually fascinated European travellers and traders to the savannah region. 'When the king had seated his visitors in state before his palace, one of the court musicians – a *griot* as they were called – gave a concert on the *ballafeu*. Of all the strange instruments that the Europeans heard resounding across the Gambia, the *ballafeu*, or xylophone, was the one which most impressed them, both its tones and its ingenious construction', Professor Douglas Grant has noted, instancing William Smith whose *A New Voyage to Guinea* was published in 1745: 'Smith was so struck by it that he sketched the musician squatting cross-legged before his instrument striking the wooden keyboard with his padded sticks.' But even if the traders were impressed, they seem to have suppressed the instrument in North America even though it became popular in Latin American countries. Suppression of the *balafon* may also have been caused through suspicion that, like the drums, it could be used as a means of communication and therefore as incitement to insurrection. Mungo Park had noted that the drum was applied at wrestling matches 'to keep order among the spectators, by imitating the sound of certain Mandingo sentences: for example, when the wrestling match is about to begin the drummer strikes what is understood to signify *ali boe see*, – sit all down; . . . and when the combatants are to begin, he strikes *amuta, amuta*, – take hold, take hold'. Conceivably it was recognised that what was transmittable on the Mandingo drum was also communicable on the Mandingo *balafon*. But it seems more likely that the instrument declined in North America because it was not encouraged and neither the making nor the use had the sanction of the slave-owners. Like the great traditions of African wood sculpture which were shared by innumerable tribes of the slave-producing regions, not excluding the savannah – the Bambara are among the most gifted of sculptors and smiths in West Africa – the *balafon* music withered away with scarcely a trace.

If instrumental skills were encouraged, as in the case of the playing of the fiddle and the banjo, or discouraged as in the instances of the drums and perhaps the xylophones and horns, the natural skills requiring no musical instrument were free to flourish and be developed. The hand-clapping which accompanied musical performances in all parts of West Africa persisted in the Negro church; it was noted as early as the eighteenth century and remained a familiar characteristic of the services of the 'Sanctified' and 'Pentecostal' churches. In the 1930s it was still far from uncommon for witnesses to report a 'ring-shout' – a shuffling dance in counter-clockwise direction performed by a circle of worshippers which gradually intensified in tempo and collective excitement. In form and character it appears to have been close to the circular dances performed throughout West Africa. Dr Lorenzo Turner even identified the term 'shout' as being identical with the Arabic *saut* used by West African Muslim peoples to mean walking round the *Kaaba*. However, neither hand-clapping nor the ring dance are particularly associated with the blues. On occasions blues singers and audiences will clap on the off-beat, and 'slow-dragging' couples may be seen to be shuffling in a manner reminiscent, perhaps, of the 'shout'. But neither could be said to be characteristic.

Common to most Negro folk music forms in the United States is the vocal. It is not a feature of ragtime, and it is a moot point whether ragtime, with its self-conscious composition, has more than the faintest echoes of African retentions anyway. The vocal is more important in New Orleans jazz, though the emphasis on the use of vocal intonation, in trumpet, cornet and trombone playing in particular, has possibly robbed the earliest jazz bands of singing of special quality, allowing certain exceptions. Any African retentions in the vocal blues would appear to have arisen from a different tradition from that of jazz.

Undoubtedly the strongest vocal tradition extending to the very roots of slavery lies in the work song. The distribution of work song patterns in West Africa has yet to be plotted, but it must be strongly affected by the nature of the crops and produce grown. Work songs by a group of workers engaged in the applications of identical labour are mainly to be found in agricultural and farming communities. In the rain forest regions where cocoa, coffee or bananas are grown, the work involved requires less collective labour than does the hoeing, digging or planting of fields. Work songs of a collective kind are therefore less characteristic of the forest regions of western Nigeria, Dahomey, Ashanti or Ivory Coast where cocoa, bananas and coffee are grown. In the tropical grassland or savannah regions, guinea corn, millet and peanuts are among the principal crops and in these regions collective work songs are heard, frequently sung to the accompaniment of small orchestras of strings, rattles and hand drums. They are often intermittent and have less of the organised structure of the North American work songs, with whistles, shouts and calls breaking up their sequence against the regularity of the work. David Sapir recorded examples of the work songs of the Diola-Fogny of the Basse Casamance, the south-western section of Senegal, and has written: 'A Diola usually works his peanut fields by himself or with the aid of a brother or son. But there are certain times when the men of a village quarter work in common cultivating the fields of an elder or earning, for the entire quarter, either money or cattle. Singing is always a part of such communal cultivation.' When a field has been cleared for digging the men line up in a row with as many as fifty preparing to dig: 'It is at this time that the men sing, all together and in rhythm to the digging, interjecting shouts of encouragement and blasts from European-made whistles.' The singing is extemporaneous, in a manner which the Diola have derived from the Mandingos. 'There is a tremendous amount of repetition in the words. However it is just this repetition that allows the singer to go on indefinitely.' In group singing, phrases are sung collectively in chorus and this feature is developed in the songs for rice cultivation: 'Instead of extemporaneous singing, the workers group into two antiphonal choruses to sing songs to set words. A song is repeated over and over again until someone breaks in with a new melody to be taken up by the two choruses.'

In communities where grain is cultivated, the women generally sing over the grinding stones. Their songs are often directed to other women grinding corn with them or in the vicinity. An example recorded by David Ames of a corn-grinding song by Hausa wives in Zaria is typical. 'The number of verses is determined by the quantity of corn to be ground and obviously many are improvised', Ames explained, his subject satirising or praising other women. 'She boasts that girls living in certain wards of Zaria city are the best dressed, the most competent sexually and are so "thorny" that it is a mistake to trifle with them.' Such work songs are to be found in all parts of Africa where co-ordinated labour is required or where the rhythm of the work itself gives the basis for song. All the same, the farming communities provide the most notable examples. Even in these the singing is not always contributed by the workers, however. Very often an orchestra, a small band of *griots* or a group of professional musicians may play for the work of farmers, grass-cutters, blacksmiths, butchers and so on. A lead singer may acclaim the skills or the efforts of individual workers, although these may not sing themselves. The custom of music-accompanied work is one of the many which died out in the slave plantation system.

Though examples of polyphony in African song are not as rare as they were once thought to be, they are rare enough in West Africa, where the polyphonic songs of the Pygmies of the Ituri Forest with their delicate nuances or the many forms of polyphonic music among the Ghimira, Gidole or Aderi in Ethiopia have no parallel. Generally speaking, West African collective song is antiphonal, following what has been frequently termed the 'leader-and-chorus' pattern. In this the vocal line of the leader is often improvised and changes with every verse sung, while the responses of the chorus vary little. A kind of harmony may result from the over-lapping of lead line and chorus, but it is usually accepted, though not by Richard A. Waterman, that harmony is either not present, or is rudi-mentary. Choral singing is generally in unison or in organum, employing parallel octaves, parallel fifths, parallel fourths, thirds, or even, in rare instances, parallel seconds. It has been pointed out by Father A. M. Jones that the tribes from Senegal to Nigeria – that is, in Negro rather than in Bantu Africa – sing in parallel thirds or in unison. Gunther Schuller has summarised that 'from this, one can assume that neither the unison nor the thirds group had much difficulty in integrating their melodies into Western harmony'. Unison singing was a practice in fundamentalist white churches while, as Schuller notes, 'the Western tradition between approximately 1700 and 1900 developed exclusively along the triadic prin-ciple of building harmonies in thirds'. Adaptation to western custom in the Southern United States may have presented little basic difficulty to the slaves.

Where the difficulty may have arisen, it has been frequently suggested, was in the accommodation of African 'scales' with the western diatonic. Ballanta Taylor posited an African scale of sixteen intervals in the octave; on the other hand many writers have assumed a pentatonic scale as being fundamental to African music. In jazz and blues the widespread use of 'blue notes', where the third and seventh degrees are flattened, has led to considerable speculation on the uncertainty of 'the African' in relating his concept of scale to the European diatonic. Though Father Jones has stated that he has 'never heard an African sing the third and seventh degrees of a major scale in tune' and has confirmed his impression that the so-called 'blue notes' are widespread among Africans, his observations were based on his knowledge of East and Central Africa – which probably contributed little to the slave trade. Other writers, including Alan P. Merriam and W. E. Ward, have concluded differently. 'In view of the evidence' wrote Merriam 'it seems safe to say that the "scale" of African music, if such exists, is diatonic in its major aspects, although exceptions occur and although there is certainly a considerable range of variation from area to area and even from tribe to tribe. The pentatonic is also widely used; the evidence for a sixteen-tone scale is scanty, indeed. Finally the question of the flattened third and seventh of the diatonic scale must be referred to future investigation.'

In his 'Cantometric' study of world *Folk Song Style and Culture* Alan Lomax has emphasised a 'remarkable homogeneity illustrated in the African map' and concludes that 'the Western Sudan clearly belongs with the Guinea Coast–Madagascar–Ethiopia–Northeast Bantu cluster. The Moslem Sudan lies between the two clusters.' His analysis of the regional profile in the Cantometric chart states that it is 'dominated by the style features of the Bantu-African hunter core. The major approach to song is choral and antiphonal, with the characteristic use of overlap, so that at least two parts are frequently active at the same time. A well-blended, rhythmically tight, often polyphonic choral performance is the norm in most areas. The major vocal style is clear and unconstructed but with playful and intermittent use of high register, yodel, nasality, rasp and forcefulness. The melodic line is almost entirely free of ornamentation. Rhythm is strictly maintained . . . Everything contributes to an open texture, inviting participation by a rock-steady beat, and by clear, liquid voices singing one note per syllable.' He concluded that 'the overall impact of the African style is multileveled, multiparted, highly integrated, multi-textured, gregarious, and playful-voiced'. This emphasis on choral song and relative disregard of the solo and duet forms invites argument. However, the 'Cantometric Cultural Samples' for West Africa are themselves arguably grouped, the Western Sudan being represented by Malinke, Dogon and Diola-Fogny; the Guinea Coast by Baule, Fon, Toma, Susu-Mende, Yoruba and, inexplicably, Bambara; while Muslim Sudan consists of Hausa, Wolof and Fulani. Of all these only the Malinke, Yoruba and Hausa were chosen for Select Samples and Test Samples, and the Dogon and Toma were chosen for Select Samples only. On a world comparative basis this was no doubt all that was possible, but it is not altogether surprising that 'United States Negro' (unspecified) as a part of 'Afro-America' is included in the generalisation that the latter 'shows close similarities with the Guinea Coast and the Equatorial Bantu, hence the majority of American slaves were carried off by the slavers'. *Folk Song Style and Culture* therefore throws little light on the relationship of American Negro blues singing to the vocal forms of West Africa.

Such investigation may have to be undertaken further from the coastal regions, where, in Ashanti, for instance, Ward was basing his conclusions. In broad terms it would seem that the practice of embellishment and therefore very often of fluctuations and 'bends' in the notes becomes steadily more marked as one moves through the savannah regions to the desert. Perhaps it is the Arabic influence that determines this; or perhaps it is an outcome of the greater use of bowed string instruments which may both rival and stimulate the use of the voice. Certainly the ornamentation of the Tuaregs reaches a degree of enrichment that exceeds any in the blues and comes very close to that of *cante hondo* and *flamenco*. In the singing of many of the parkland and semi-desert peoples the use of shadings and falling notes that approximate to those of the blues can be widely heard. Father Jones has spoken in general of 'the outline of an African tune' which he likens to 'a succession of the teeth of a rip-saw; a steep rise (not usually exceeding a fifth) followed by a gentle sloping down of the tune; then another sudden rise – then a gentle sloping down, and so on'. His description is broadly applicable to West African song and creates a picture of the falling sound of many vocal recordings. It does not, however, underline the calling character of much West African singing: the use of a high pitch, often an octave or two above the speaking voice of the singer, which is so marked a feature. I have continually had the impression in the singing of *griots* of the vocal line slipping back towards speech tones, to be hastily recalled to the high pitch with which the song started, before a slow downward drift begins once more.

To the element of pitch must be added that of attack. This seems to depend on whether the singer is directing his song to others, or whether he is singing mainly for himself. In the latter case the song is often soft

14 Tuareg woman playing the *inzad*

and introspective, with an attention to melody which is 'musical' in the Western sense. As African song is often functional; when not, and performed for the entertainment of others, it is frequently declamatory. The professional musician or entertainer who performs in the market-place

of a Hausa city, or who sings at feasts or at ceremonial functions in Mali
or Upper Volta or Senegal, depends on the response of his audience. He
may tell traditional stories in song, he may spread current news and
gossip, he may taunt the unmarried men and raise laughs with *double-entendre* verses – but in the market-place or beneath the shade tree he
needs to be heard. With the high, projecting pitch he couples a strident,
hard-edged vocal that cuts through the bustle and rumble of the market-place. Sometimes he will employ falsetto cries, sometimes he will sing a
whole song in falsetto; shrieks and ululations are part of his vocal equip-ment. Deep chest tones from 'heavy' voices are extremely rare and seem
to be reserved only for special rituals among certain tribes. In general,
low voices with rich timbre and full, rounded tones are seldom used, while
high, forced tones which drop to a speaking tenor are common.

How much of these elements in West African vocal tradition may be
found in the blues? Though group singing is fundamental to both Negro
church services and to the collective work songs that have persisted in
the penitentiaries and penal farms of the Deep South, it is unusual in
the blues. On occasion blues musicians will sing together, even to the
extent of sharing the same verses of a known and standard blues, but it
is by no means common in the idiom. When it is to be heard, as in the
recordings of some of the jug bands, it is almost invariably unison singing.
Singing in parallel thirds would seem to be exceptionally rare in the blues,
which is after all, as a vocal music, mainly performed solo. For this
reason the antiphonal 'leader-and-chorus' patterns which have persisted
so strongly in Negro religious song, and in the work songs, are unfamiliar
in the blues vocal as such. But there is a frequently expressed opinion
that the use of the 'answering' guitar in some blues traditions is a reten-tion from the custom of leader-and-chorus singing. This would suggest,
however, that the answering phrase should be standardised in each per-formance, as is customary in choral responses. It would seem more likely
that if a retention from African practice is present, it is rather in the use
of the stringed instruments by praise singers and others who use them
imitatively to augment the content of their songs.

In vocal quality it would appear that the employment of high voices
among certain blues singers – Sam Collins, Blind Lemon Jefferson, Barefoot

15 Stem and hollow-log drums of the West African rain forest, with pegged heads and angled drum-sticks

Bill, Little Brother Montgomery, Kokomo Arnold among them – are closer to vocal practices in West Africa than are those like Charley Patton, Tommy McClennan or Blind Willie Johnson, who employed deep and sonorous voices or cultivated a deliberately low pitch. Though the rasp in the voice of a Bukka White can be compared with the strained tones of many African singers, its 'heaviness' cannot. Some blues singers use falsetto calls or may pitch part of a word an octave higher than the rest of the line: Tommy Johnson carried this technique to a refined degree. Others, like Arnold, may have used it with perhaps more spontaneity, though only an occasional blues singer appears to use his voice with the attack of the *griots*. Texturally there seem to be many points of correspondence and the deliberate rejection of qualities of European purity in blues singing would suggest a direct persistence of West African practice. Similarly the 'saw-tooth' pattern of the vocal is reflected in the blues, to be heard in the singing of artists as varied as Hambone Willie Newbern, Texas Alexander or Roosevelt Sykes. Alexander's voice, however, approximates to that of the soft-voiced African singers and does not have the strained and constricted character of the higher, tenser singers heard throughout the Sudan and reflected most dramatically in the singing of a Robert Johnson, or less intensely but consistently in the singing of a Frank Stokes. This soft-toned, introspective singing, representative of a whole tradition of African solo vocals, is mirrored in the recordings of Mississippi John Hurt, Furry Lewis, Peetie Wheatstraw, even Otis Spann. Embellishment of the vocal line is characteristic of blues and the use of sliding and passing notes is found in almost every blues singer's recordings. A Carl Martin or a Big Bill Broonzy extemporised with a greater freedom of inflection than many blues singers, but the use of elaborations was somewhat surprisingly developed more by the classic blues singers, and in particular 'Ma' Rainey and Bessie Smith, than by the folk blues men.

The extent to which West African singers use expressive tone to extend the meaning of their words has not been ascertained, but it seems on aural evidence that vibrato, forced timbre and dropped notes are employed for dramatic effect. This is a blues characteristic, although such techniques are more strikingly developed in Negro religious sermons by the so-called 'straining' preachers. In blues, expressive tone often means the dropping of the voice and the employment of gutturals, as in the singing of Bukka White: sometimes the vocal becomes more of a snarl. But gospel preachers frequently pitch up the voice when using this technique, dropping an octave at the ends of lines with a rough drone. Recordings of Bussani tribesmen in Upper Volta singing praise songs for the chief of the village of Yarkatenga reveal uncanny resemblances to the singing of straining preachers like Reverend Nix or Reverend Burnett. They also use a device much employed by Negro preachers, of cupping the left hand to the ear while singing with intense vehemence. Though blues singers are frequently also instrumentalists, those who only sing often employ the same technique: St Louis Jimmy for example and, it has been reported, Texas Alexander. The use of a drone or continuous humming between sung phrases is also a vocal feature shared by Voltaic peoples and some blues singers such as Kokomo Arnold or Whistling Alex Moore.

Writing in 1899 on African survivals, Jeanette Robinson Murphy recalled that she had followed many 'old ex-slaves, who have passed away in their tasks, listened to their crooning in their cabins, in the fields, and especially in their meeting houses, and again and again they assured me the tunes they sang came from Africa'. Commenting on the inadequacies of transcriptions in the Jubilee and Hampton song books, she remarked that there was nothing to show the singer 'that he must make his voice exceedingly nasal and undulating, that around every prominent note he must place a variety of small notes, called "trimmings", and he must sing notes not found in our scale; that he must on no account leave one note until he has the next one well under control. He might be tempted . . . to take breath whenever he came to the end of a line or verse! But . . . he should carry over his breath from line to line and from verse to verse, even at the risk of bursting a blood vessel. He must often drop from a high note to a very low one, he must be very careful to divide many of his monosyllabic words in two syllables . . . He must intersperse his singing with peculiar humming sounds – "hum-m-m".' To those accustomed to both blues and Sudanic singing these observations made halfway between the arrival of the last Africans on American shores and the present suggest some continuum of vocal traditions in delivery and conception.

5 · THE SOURCE OF THE SLAVES

If the evidence of their music suggests that the savannah peoples were the most influential in shaping the course of Afro-American music in the United States, what is the evidence of their presence among the slaves? Before any examination of the provenance of the slaves is made, in the first place it is necessary to consider how many slaves could in fact have brought any direct survivals from Africa with them. Over 300 years it has been estimated that anything between 10 and 30 million African slaves were shipped from their homelands. J. C. Furnas estimates that between 15 and 20 million arrived in the New World and that some 3 to 4 million died on the passage: 'The yearly average is something like 60,000 – less than one per cent of the total population of West Africa at any time up to 1800.' With a population of Negro Americans which now exceeds 20 million, it is somewhat surprising that in 1790 the total black population of the United States was only three-quarters of a million. Henry C. Carey's careful compilations show that the actual annual number of Negroes imported into North America averaged around 3,000 until 1760, rose to 7,400 in the following decade, fell to less than 2,000 a year for the next twenty years and rose again to nearly 4,000 up till the end of legal slavery in 1808. The total number imported and accounted for was 333,500; Gunnar Myrdal considered that 'a figure of slightly below 400,000 slaves imported before 1808 seems reasonable'. Even allowing for extensive smuggling of slaves after the abolition of slave trading, Myrdal concluded that 'whatever historical research ultimately determines these figures to be, it is extremely likely that the total number of slaves imported before 1860 by whatever means, was less than a million'. This means that authentic African 'survivals' can have been handed down only by extensive processes of enculturation, and that an acceleration of slave importation in the latter phases, legal or illegal, may have kept some of the memories fresh.

Perhaps the most thorough research on slave sources has been made by Melville Herskovits, who has shown the proportion of slaves brought from various sources and to various centres. Tabulating the materials kept in Virginia for the period 1710–90, he noted that some 20,000 were given as 'Africa', 6,700 came from 'Guinea', 9,200 from Calabar (Nigeria), 3,800 from Angola and 3,600 from Gambia, including Senegal and Goree. His figures, quoting Miss Elizabeth Donnan for importations to South Carolina between 1733 and 1785, listed 18,000 from the Guinea Coast from Gold Coast to Calabar, some 22,000 from Angola and Congo and 16,500 from the Gambia to, and including, Sierra Leone. Though French ships going to the West Indies via Nantes showed a surprisingly low number of cargoes from Senegal, it is generally accepted that Senegal-Gambia, the Gold Coast and Calabar were the principal sources of African slaves for much of the trade, though Angola and Congo became sources of illegal trade through Portuguese trading. Arthur Ramos, in *The Negro in Brazil*, noted that 'at the beginning of the slave trade, the largest number of those imported into Brazil were from Angola, the Congo and Guinea. When more active communication began with Bahia, the leading source of supply was Guinea and the western Sudan. There began a remarkable influx of Yorubas, Minas from the Gold Coast, Dahomans and various Islamized tribes such as the Hausas, Tapahs, Mandingos and Fulahs.' Similarities between Negro music in the United States and that of Brazil have been noted and the possibility of common derivation demands more research.

For Herskovits the argument seemed proven that African survivals stemmed from what he termed the 'core area', the region of the Ashanti, Dahomey, Yoruba: the Akan-, Fon-, Ewe-, and Twi-speaking peoples of the Kwa group. All these fall within the greater, simpler subdivision of languages which distinguishes only the Sudanic, the Bantu and the Hamitic, and form a part of the Sudanic group: 'It is to be noted that the "typical" Sudanic forms of West Africa . . . Twi, Ewe, Fon, Yoruba

– are the principal linguistic stocks of our "focal" area. This means that the slaves who came from them outside this focus spoke tongues related to those found at the center of slaving operations. Among the more important of these found in regions to the west of the "core" are the languages of the Gambia and Senegal (Wolof or Jolof), Sierra Leone (Temne and Mende), and the Middle Sudan (Mandingo). To the east are Ibo, Nupe, and Efik. To the north of the forested coastal belt Sudanic dialects also are spoken – Mossi, Jukun, and Kanuri among others.' Accepting that the Sudanic languages and cultures have much in common he stated, rightly enough, that 'in contrast to European custom, the resemblance of these coastal cultures to those of Senegal and the prairie belt lying north of the forested region of the west coast, or in the interior of the Congo, is appreciable'. In his view the 'core area', whose survivals are unquestioned in the West Indies as has been seen, dominated the others. 'It might be hazarded', he said with respect to the United States, 'that, in the instance of early Senegalese arrivals, whatever was retained of aboriginal custom was overshadowed by the traditions of the more numerous Guinea Coast Negroes; while as for late-comers such as the Congo Negroes, the slaves they found were numerous enough, and well enough established, to have translated their modes of behaviour – always in so far as Africanisms are concerned, and without reference to the degree of acculturation to European habits – into community patterns.'

In view of Melville Herskovits' detailed knowledge of Dahomey–Yoruba–Ashanti cultures and his familiarity with Negro cultures in Latin-America, this argument may be accepted for much of Central and South America. It was a guess 'hazarded' as far as the USA was concerned and merits questioning. Dr Lorenzo Turner's detailed studies of *Africanisms in the Gullah Dialect* showed that nearly 6,000 African words survived in the Sea Islands, representing nearly thirty West African languages. Among them are many examples of Fulah, Hausa, Mende, Mandingo, Temne, Vai and other languages of the Senegal-Gambia, Sierra Leone and savannah peoples, as well as Twi, Yoruba and other survivals. Undoubtedly the high proportion of survivals from the coasts closest to the United States demands reconsideration of the problem. It has recently received attention from Professor David Dalby who notes that 'Senegambia, the nearest

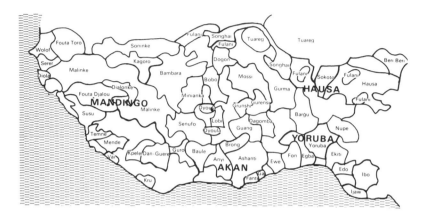

16 Tribes of West Africa (adapted from G. P. Murdock)

part of the Atlantic coast to North America, was a major source of slaves for the former English colonies, and many of these slaves were therefore conversant with the two main languages of Senegambia: Wolof and Mandingo.' The Wolof he notes 'were frequently employed as interpreters and mariners during early European voyages along the African coast. As a result the Wolof names of several African foodstuffs were taken into European languages, including "banana" and "yam". It therefore seems reasonable to look for a possible Wolof influence on the development of American English vocabulary and the initial results of this investigation have been most encouraging.' Dr Dalby's extensive researches have revealed a remarkable incidence of Wolof survivals in terms and usages including a significantly high number in jazz usage: too high for mere coincidence. While he does not claim that all can be proven with certainty he does state that 'the frequency of these resemblances is unlikely to be the result of chance and points to the contribution of at least one African language to American vocabulary'. Researches in comparative studies with other African languages may make significant new discoveries.

The importance of the Senegambian slave trade lies in the accessibility of these ports to the Sudan savannah interior. Herskovits has contempt for what he terms the 'thousand-mile' theory, which argued that slaves were brought from deep in the interior. A trip of 1,000 miles was reported to have been undertaken by slaves on a number of occasions. Captain Samuel

17 *Algaïta* players, from Denham, Clapperton and Oudney's *Narratives*

Gamble, for instance, was slaving off the coast of Sierra Leone in 1794 and reported that he saw about twelve vessels with a 'representation of a Lott of Fullows (i.e. Fulahs) bringing their slaves for a Sale to the Europeans which generally commences annually in December or early January, being prevented from coming down sooner by the river being overflow'd'. Gamble added that 'they sometimes come upwards of One Thousand Miles of the interior part of the country' and he noted that their 'Principal Places of trade are Gambia, Rio Nunez and the Mandingo country. Fifteen Hundred of them have been brought here in one Season. They are of [off] in May as the rains set in in June.' In exchange for the slaves he added 'their darling commodity that they get from the Whites is Salt'.

Only a year later Mungo Park arrived at Jillifree on the Gambia River and commenced his remarkable penetration of the Interior in search of the source of the Niger. His report of his exploration lends support to the argument that the music of the country was substantially the same in his day as it is now. He described the musical instruments of the Mandingoes, 'the principal of which are the *koonting*, a sort of guitar with three strings, the *korro*, a large harp with eighteen strings; the *simbing*, a small harp with seven strings; the *balafou*, an instrument composed of twenty pieces of hard wood of different lengths, with the shells of gourds hung underneath to increase the sound; the *tangtang*, a drum, open at the lower end; and lastly the *tabala*, a large drum commonly used to spread alarm throughout the country. Besides these, they make use of small flutes, bowstrings, elephants' teeth, and bells; and at all their dances and concerts, *clapping of hands* appears to constitute a necessary part of the chorus.'

Park's descriptions of the *korro* (kore) or *balafou* (balafon) among others are clearly recognisable today. He also described the *griots*, or 'the *singing men*, called *Jilli kea*' who 'sing extempore songs in honour of their chief men, or any other persons who are willing to give "solid pudding for empty praise". But a nobler part of their office is to recite the historical events of their country; hence in war they accompany the soldiers to the field, in order, by reciting the great actions of their ancestors, to awaken in them a spirit of glorious emulation.' On his return, Park joined up with a slave coffle which was journeying to the coast from Kamalia. They were all prisoners of war who had been taken by the 'Bambarran army in the kingdoms of Wassela and Kaarta, and carried to Sego, where some of them had remained three years in irons'. From his descriptions of their movements it is evident that some had travelled 600 or 700 miles in fetters. They were joined by other groups of captives and a number of free persons, 'so that the number of free persons and domestic slaves amounted to thirty-eight, and the whole amount of the coffle was seventy-three. Among the free men were six Jilli keas (singing men), whose musical efforts were frequently exerted either to divert our fatigue, or obtain us a welcome from strangers.' The singing men marched in front of the coffle as they got beyond the limits of the Manding territory and when they arrived at a town retold in detail through their song the entire story of the travels of the coffle. When they finally arrived at Goree the total number of slaves prepared for shipment was 130. Because of the 'mode of confining and securing Negroes in the American slave ships' many of the captives suffered greatly; 'besides the three who died on the Gambia, and six or eight while we remained at Goree, eleven perished at sea, and many of the survivors were reduced to a very weak and emaciated condition'.

Though the numbers were not large compared with the great quantities of slaves shipped from the southern coast of West Africa, the numbers of slaves shipped from the Gambia in the 1730s was reaching as much as 2,000 a year and the competition between the French traders on the Senegal and the British on the Gambia kept a steady flow of slaves moving from the hinterland to the slave ships of Goree and St Louis. The Muslim penetration from the North meant that a great many scholars and Muslim missionaries with their personal slaves, as well as African traders whose routes were often extended through vast tracts of country, were moving through the savannah regions. The unsettled nature of the country with the shifts of power occasioned by the wars of the Bambara, the Mandingos and the Fulani often meant that the travellers found themselves in hostile country subject to the attacks of raiding parties and ultimately themselves sold into slavery. This applied to Muslims from deep in the savannah and semi-desert regions who moved south, as well as to those who moved westwards. One who did was Abu Bakr.

Though he was born in Timbuktu in about 1790, Abu Bakr was raised in Jenne and completed his education in Bouna. Bouna is in the north-east of Ivory Coast and was then a centre for learned Muslims, their servants and slaves who had come from all over West Africa. The Ashanti warrior Adinkra attacked the town and after a severe battle, took it; 'On that very day they made me a captive. They tore off my clothes, bound me with ropes, gave me a heavy load to carry, and led me to the town of Bonduku, and from there to the town of Kumasi. From there through Akisuma and Ajumako in the land of the Fanti, to the town of Lago, near the salt sea (all the way on foot, and well loaded). There they sold me to the Christians, and I was bought by a certain captain of a ship at that time.' Abu Bakr was shipped to Jamaica, became the slave of a stonemason and there worked until he was freed, partially by public subscription in Kingston, in 1834. He was not a musician, he was not shipped to North America; his relevance here is only to demonstrate the routes and misfortunes that led a savannah Muslim into slavery and to being sold from the Guinea Coast, a sale made singular by his erudition, his scholarship and his letters.

Mohammedans from the savannah regions were certainly known on the plantations. Writing in *A Second Visit to the United States* in 1849, Sir Charles Lyell described life on the Hopeton plantation and the head driver, 'African Tom', a 'man of superior intelligence and higher cast of feature. He was the son of a prince of the Foulah tribe and was taken prisoner at the age of fourteen, near Timbuktou. The accounts he gave of what he remembered of the plants and geography of Africa . . . confirm many of the narratives of modern travellers. He has remained a strict Mahometan, but his numerous progeny of jet-black children and grand-children, all of them marked by countenances of a more European cast than that of ordinary negroes, have exchanged the Koran for the Bible.' In 1901, Georgia Bryan Conrad recalled Negroes she had known forty years before: 'On Sapelo Island, near Darien, I used to know a family of Negroes who worshipped Mahomet. They were all tall and well-informed, with good features. They conversed with us in English, but in talking among themselves they used a foreign tongue that no one else could understand. The head of the tribe was a very old man called Bi-la-li. He always wore a cap that resembled a Turkish fez. These Negroes held themselves aloof from the others as if they were conscious of their own superiority.'

Sālih Bilāli, whose descendants were interviewed and discussed at length by Lydia Parrish in her *Slave Songs of the Georgia Sea Islands*, was born about 1770 near Mopti, some 700 miles from the coast in a Muslim Fulbe (Fulah) community. When he was about twelve years of age he was captured by Bambara slave raiders and taken to Segu 'and was transferred from master to master, until he reached the coast, at Anomabu. After leaving Bambara, to use his own expression, the people had no religion, until he came to this country.' In addition to his recollections noted by James Hamilton Couper and published in 1844, Sālih Bilāli wrote in Arabic a religious paper, long thought to be his 'diary'. Such Muslims, devout, learned and given positions of responsibility on the plantations, undoubtedly stood out from the rest. There is no reason to consider that the presence of Fulahs, Bambaras, Wolofs, Diolas, Hausas, Béri-Béri and other tribes from the savannah regions was rare in the plantations of the South. In his *Survey of the Supply, Employment and Control of Negro Labor*, Ulrick Bonnell Phillips specifically noted that 'in South Carolina, Negroes from Gambia, chiefly the Mandingoes, were the preferred ones, but those from Angola were quite acceptable'. While, to quote Gilberto Freyre, 'we also meet with references to Senegalese Negroes with their drop of Arabaic blood as being favoured for housework, by reason of their "greater intelligence"'. The securing of slaves was done by the inhabitants of the mainland of Africa. 'The normal practice was for the Europeans to stay at the coast', noted Oliver and Fage. 'The earliest slaves to be exported were doubtless already slaves in their own communities, often criminals or debtors', they wrote of the Guinea Coast, where 'invariably the Europeans bought their slaves from African kings and merchants'. Later, when the 'demand increased, peoples living just inland from the coast began to use the firearms they had acquired through trade to venture further into the interior and deliberately capture slaves for export'.

Though the Yoruba, Ibo, Fon and other tribes undoubtedly sent large numbers of their own tribesmen into slavery, the Ibo priests operating the 'Aro' system whereby witchcraft had to be paid for in captives, the consolidation of the coastal kingdoms, such as the federation of the Ashanti, strengthened them in their fight for more captives from the interior. 'The heart of the trade was the Slave Coast and the Gold Coast, and behind this territory extending into the interior for 700 miles or more. From this territory Senegalese Negroes, Mandingoes, Ibos, Efikes, Ibonis, Karamantis, Wydas, Jolofs, Fulis, together with representatives of many of the interior Bantus were brought to America', recorded Weatherford and Johnson. This list includes many from the Guinea and Windward Coasts, but also those from far back into the savannah regions. Savannah tribes were in fact depopulated from both the west and the southern coast of the Guinea region: subjected to a pincer movement. Although on the coast the population may reach over 100 persons to the square mile, only a short way back it rapidly diminishes and most of the savannah region and much of the rain forest has a population of less than 25 persons to the square mile. Such low population is due to many causes, but the authors of *Africa and the Islands* note that 'the slave trade certainly contributed to the sparseness of the population. Estimates of the volume of this trade vary, but it is possible that 20 million Negroes were exported to the Americas between the sixteenth and nineteenth centuries, and that many millions more were massacred in the process.' They added, moreover, that 'the trade in Negro slaves to the Islamic countries has been estimated at 10 to 15 millions . . . The worst affected were the Sudanese Negroes and the Bantu.' Ignored by most writers on the subject were the interior wars caused by the spread of Islam, the rise of the Bornu states, the kingdoms of the Mande and the Bambara, and, at the very close of the legal slave trade, the rise of the Fulani empire which overthrew the Bornu and the Bambara states; these all provided captives and slaves for the markets of Timbuktu, Kano, or the traders from the coast. So it can be concluded that slaves were drawn not only from the 'true Negro' region of the Gold and Slave Coasts, Guinea and Calabar, but from deeper in the interior, and that those from the savannah regions, from the Senegambia and among the Wolof and Mandingo peoples, formed a not inconsiderable number of them. Their culture may have been transplanted to the United States in many forms, including that of music. It is even possible that they formed an unusually high proportion of the imported slaves. It has been established that slaves were sent often to the West Indies for acclimatisation before being distributed to various countries, including North America. It seems likely that those who coped best with the tropical heat and humidity and whose coastal rain forest environment was closest to that of the West Indies were kept in Latin America, while those who were accustomed to the Sudanese climate, with its somewhat more temperate but still extremely hot days, may have been chosen for shipment to the States. With them they may still have brought memories of their own traditions.

At this point it is instructive to return to the earliest reports of Congo Square (Congo Plains or Circus Square) in New Orleans. The architect Benjamin Henry Latrobe visited New Orleans in 1819 when the functions were at their height and there is little doubt as to the African survivals in the music and instruments described. Latrobe spoke of players of a cylindrical drum, of an open-staved drum and other drums of various kinds. He also described a 'most curious instrument' which was 'a stringed instrument which no doubt was imported from Africa. On the top of the fingerboard was the rude figure of a man in a sitting posture, and two pegs behind him to which strings were fastened. The body was a calabash.' Though there has been speculation on the origins of the instrument, Dr Curt Sachs suspecting a Congo origin, Lorenzo Turner pointed out that it could be found among the Hausa. The calabash bowl is of significance in a region of Louisiana where other materials were readily at hand, while the instrument has its parallels among some other savannah peoples. Writing in 1886, a lifetime later, George W. Cable described a scene of essentially similar character. Probably he was depicting events which he had seen earlier, for at one point he mentions slaves, and he had been in the city during and before the Civil War. Other estimates have suggested that he was depicting Congo Square in the 1880s, but this is implicitly denied by Herbert Asbury who records that, in October 1817, the square 'was designated by the Mayor as the only place to which slaves might resort, and thereafter all such gatherings were held under police supervision. The dancing was stopped at sunset and the slaves sent home. Under these and other regulations the custom of permitting slave dancing in Congo Square continued for more than twenty years when it was abolished for reasons which the old city records do not make clear. It was resumed in 1845 . . . (and) reached the height of its popularity during the fifteen years which preceded the Civil War.'

According to Asbury the custom was abandoned in the troubled period following the Union occupation of New Orleans and would therefore have been concluded by the time Cable was writing. However, at that period, in the 1880s, dances still continued in a vacant lot on Dumaine Street. Cable recalled the instruments he had seen with the accuracy of a close observer, at length and in great detail – drums, a gourd filled with pebbles, jews-harps, the jawbone of a mule or ox, empty casks and barrels. In his day, Negroes still played the 'Marimba brett, a union of reed and string principles. A single strand of wire ran lengthwise of a bit of wooden board, sometimes a shallow box of thin wood, some eight inches long by four or five in width, across which, under the wire, were several joints of reed about a quarter of an inch in diameter and of graduated lengths.' It was played by plucking the reeds with the thumbnails and was clearly the African *sansa* or thumb piano (and not, as the marimba name might suggest, a xylophone). 'But the grand instrument at last, the first violin, as one might say, was the banjo', he wrote; 'It had but four strings, not six: beware of the dictionary.'

An examination of his careful list of the tribes represented in Congo Plains is instructive. His principal descriptions were of those 'wilder than gypsies; wilder than the Moors and Arabs whose strong blood and features one sees at a glance in so many of them; gangs – as they were called – gangs and gangs of them, from this and that and yonder direction; tall, well-knit Senegalese from Cape Verde, black as ebony, with intelligent, kindly eyes and long, straight, shapely noses; Mandingoes, from the Gambia River, lighter of colour, of cruder form, and a cunning that shows in the countenance; whose enslavement seems specially a shame, their nation the merchants of Africa, dwelling in towns, industrious, thrifty, skilled in commerce and husbandry, and expert in the working of metals, even to silver and gold; and Foulahs, playful mis-called "*poulards*" – fat chickens – of goodly stature, and with perceptible rose tint in their cheeks; and Sosos, famous warriors, dextrous with the African targe: and in contrast to these, with small ears, thick eyebrows, bright eyes, flat upturned noses, shining skin, wide mouths and white teeth, the Negroes of Guinea, true and unmixed, from the Gold Coast, the Slave Coast and the Cape of Palms'. Later he described a dancer, a 'glistening black Hercules, who plants one foot forward, lifts his head and bare shining chest and rolls out the song from a mouth and throat like a cavern'. He had 'an African amulet that hangs about his neck – a *gree-gree*. He is of the Bambara, as you may know by his solemn visage and the long tattoo streaks running down from the temples to the neck, broadest in the middle, like knife gashes.' Even the name of the charm, a long established one in New Orleans rites, had similar ancestry, as Puckett noted: '*grigri* (noun signifies "charm" – verb means "to bewitch") seem to be of African origin, the term *gris-gris* being employed in the Senegal as a general name for amulets'. But of all Cable's comments, one of the most telling occurs in his description of the *bamboula*, the celebrated dance of Place Congo and perennial attraction for visitors: 'The quick contagion is caught by a few in the crowd, who take up with spirited smitings of the bare sole upon the ground, and of open hand upon the thighs. From a spot near the musicians a single male voice, heavy and sonorous, rises in improvisation – the Mandingoes brought that art from Africa – and in a moment many others have joined in refrain, male voices in rolling, bellowing resonance, female responding in high, piercing unison.' Cable's description of the Bambara Negro in New Orleans is entirely in accord with Lafcadio Hearn's description in 1885 of 'The Last of the Voudoos', Jean Montanet. 'In the death of Jean Montanet, at the age of nearly a hundred years, New Orleans lost, at the end of August, the most extraordinary African character that ever gained celebrity within her city limits', he wrote: 'He was a native of Senegal and claimed to have been a prince's son, in proof of which he was wont to call attention to a number of parallel scars on his cheek, extending in curves from the edge of either temple to the corners of his lips. This fact seems to me partly confirmatory of his statement, as Berengee Feraud dwells at some length on the fact that all Bambaras, who are probably the finest race in Senegal, all wear such configurations.'

Montanet was not the last of the Voodoos though he was among the last of his stature with a direct African background; Marie Leveau was born in New Orleans. With its flourishing cult of Voodoo, New Orleans was an exceptional American city, but it was exceptional, too, in permitting slaves such freedom of musical expression. Until the ordinance of 1817, slaves were permitted to congregate at weekends in many parts of the city for their dances and the dances in the confines of Congo Plains remained a major tourist attraction. Elsewhere, in the United States, slaves were not permitted to use drums. 'The slave-owners found to their cost that drums which beat for dances could also call to revolt, and thus it came about that in many parts of the New World, the African types of hollow-log drums were suppressed, being supplanted by other percussion devices less susceptible of carrying messages', wrote Herskovits. Though Courlander gives details of hollow log drums of comparatively recent date in the South, there was specific legislation in many states against the use of drums by Negroes, including the Black Codes of Georgia, where 'beating the drum and blowing the trumpet' were forbidden, and Mississippi. A drum dated 1728 is displayed in the British Museum, made by a Negro in Virginia; but the use of the drums as a means of communication common to Ashanti, Yoruba and a number of other tribes might have led to slave revolts, and generally they were suppressed. The heavy restrictions imposed in all states following the Nat Turner insurrection of 1831 included forbidding Negroes to learn to read or write and also severe repression of music making which could incite slaves to violence or rebellion.

In 1803 New Orleans, as part of the Louisiana Purchase, became American. French traditions persisted and to some extent persist still, and among these was a liberalism towards the Negroes of the city not to be found elsewhere. The confining of slave celebrations to Congo Square might be seen as a contraction of those liberties, but drumming, along with other forms of musical expression, nevertheless continued in the predominantly Catholic city to a degree that the Protestant state could not tolerate. In New Orleans Negro smiths were engaged on work in wrought iron and the skills of the African blacksmith – who was frequently, as among the Bambara and Dogon, also the wood sculptor – were given rein. But, except in isolated instances on the Sea Islands and in Georgia graveyards, little of the African skills in the plastic arts survived in North America. The great traditions of wood carving, the masks and the ancestral figures which typified the arts of Ibo, Yoruba, Baule, Bambara, Dogon, Dan, Guere, Bobo or Mossi alike – both forest and savannah tribes – dissipated in the strict observances of Protestant America. Suppressed partly through godliness and partly through fear, they disappeared more completely than did even the drumming traditions. In Mississippi the drum-and-fife bands of Lonnie Young and Napoleon Strickland exist today as a possible African survival – though this is open to dispute: there is no hint of African plastic arts to be seen. To a great extent this reflects a difference of attitudes among Catholic and Protestant communities and, in James A. Porter's words, their influence 'in respect to cultural trends and Expression in the two American continents. While Catholic policy and practice seem deliberately to have encouraged and tolerated the African deviations from conventional Christian forms and then to have made it possible for the African bias to rise to the surface, Protestant dogma and cultural restrictions in the North utterly discouraged African religious traditions, extirpated them when they could be reached or by other repressive means prevented or nullified their influence. Nevertheless the abiding power of the African essence in Negro life is especially suggested in the folk creations of the North American Negro.'

6 · AFRICA AND THE BLUES

'I made it out of a guitar neck and a tin pan my mama used to bake up biscuit-bread in . . . If any of them livin' can remember back to the day of yesterday – it was a bread pan . . . but the old guitar, I bored a hole in the neck and run it through this here pan'. So Gus Cannon, or 'Banjo Joe', as he called himself, described his first instrument. Big Bill Broonzy told a similar story: 'When I was about ten years old I made a fiddle out of a cigar box, a guitar out of goods boxes for my buddy Louis Carter, and we would play for the white people's picnics.' The home-made instrument is almost a cliché of blues history and the description that Dave Mangurian made of Big Joe Williams' first guitar could be echoed in a score of interviews: 'When he was about six or seven years old he made a one-string guitar for himself by stapling two thread spools to a small box and stretching baling wire between the spools. He played it with the neck off a half-pint whisky bottle.' Many of these primitive instruments were monochords it seems. When I drew an illustration of Big Bill Broonzy as a boy, the singer commented 'man, that's just like me, like I was 'cept for one thing – my fiddle didn't have but one string on it'.

Many blues singers apparently first learned to play music on one-string instruments of their own manufacture. Children are the guardians of old traditions and customs and in the lore, language and games of children may be found clues to the history of centuries, and folk beliefs that may date to pagan origins. It does not seem unlikely that the custom of making a fiddle, guitar or banjo from available materials – lard can, broomhandle,

18 Savannah instruments with one or more strings

fence picket, cigar box, or whatever may be at hand that meets the ingenuity of the maker – has a history that extends back to enslavement and beyond. Their counterparts in West Africa, meanwhile, make flutes out of bicycle pumps, sansas out of opened cans and monochords out of polish tins, such as I have collected for myself.

With the story of the first instrument runs another: the learning of the instrument from a relative, often the father or an uncle, even a grandfather. Sometimes a visitor or neighbour in the community would be the principal influence. Rubin Lacy's story, as recounted by Dave Evans, may be considered fairly typical: 'His mother, half-brother and eldest brother were all good harmonica players . . . his brother-in-law, Walter McCray, was a good guitarist and singer of old songs like *John Henry* and *Stagolee* and *Rabbit on a Log*. Lacy didn't learn much from these people, however – although he liked their music. His real idol was George "Crow Jane" Hendrix. This man was a professional musician and the finest Lacy ever heard. He was old enough to be Lacy's father.' And Lacy himself stated: 'He could play anything he sat down to or anything he picked up, organ, piano, violin, bass, violin, mandolin, ukelele.' Rubin Lacy was born in 1901; Mance Lipscomb's memories go back a few years longer and his family associations extend back into slavery. As Mack McCormick reported: 'Mance's father was born a slave in Alabama. When still a boy he and his brother were separated from their parents and shipped to the newly settled Brazos bottoms of Texas. Then he made a fiddle out of a cigar box, and after emancipation became a full-time professional fiddler playing for dances in the Scotch–Irish, Bohemian and Negro settlements of the valley . . . Mance was born on April 9, 1895 in Brazos County and when still a youngster he began travelling with his father, bassing for him on guitar.' He too had musicians he admired, like Hamp Walker: 'About the best guitar man and songster as I ever met.'

Many of the older blues singers and songsters recall playing for white functions, and many of the veteran white musicians were impressed by their playing, as Tony Russell recounts in a parallel study. 'Now the first fiddle I ever heard in my life was when I was a kid', recollected Hobart Smith, 'there was an old colored man who was raised up in slave times. His name was Jim Spenser . . . and he would come up to our house and he'd play one night for us, and he'd go on over to my uncle's house and play one night for them, and then go to my aunt's in the other hollow.' The techniques of playing their instruments were often picked up by the white musicians from the coloured ones. 'My younger brother Rosco brought a colored man home with him one evening who played with a brass band that used to be around Norton', said the banjo player Dock Boggs: 'I heard him play *Alabama Negro*. He played with his forefinger and next finger – two fingers and thumb.'

A full documentation of the chain of influence and education whereby blues singers learned their instruments and their music would reveal much concerning the passing on of tradition and technique, while an impartial study of the people and places for whom they played might be instructive on the meeting of black and white music. It is clear from present knowledge that the processes of acculturation and enculturation are both present in Negro music as we know it, with much of the blues containing elements that come essentially from the European dance and ballad traditions, and yet having a character that is distinct and special.

It seems possible that some of the distinctive elements have a history that extends far back into slavery and that they have within them, as this book has attempted to show, some features which may well be inherited from West Africa. But, it is my contention, not from the 'West Africa' that has been assumed in most writings on jazz and related subjects. To summarise, it seems to me that the whole conception of music in the rain forest regions, and especially in the drum orchestras, has little to do with the folk music of the American Negro, whatever it may have had to do with jazz. The evidence of the music of the Ashanti, Yoruba, Ewe and Baule is of music of great rhythmic complexity which seems not to have survived in any significant way in the United States. That it is to be heard in a remarkably pure form in Haiti and other parts of the West Indies serves to emphasise that, given the right hospitable circumstances, this powerful music can thrive on foreign soil after the passing of a century and much more. But, like other aspects of rain forest culture and the image-making of African sculpture, when it ran counter to the patterns of behaviour acceptable to the American slave-owners, it died.

In contrast to the music of the drum-dominated tribes of the coastal regions, the music of the savannah Sudanic regions appears to have been of a kind that would have accorded well with the Scots and English folk forms and been acceptable enough to have survived among the slaves. The banjo, as we have seen, survived and flourished, while the skills of the players of *kukuma* or *goge* would soon have been adapted to the European fiddle under active encouragement. And encouragement was certainly there, as 'A small Farmer' wrote in *De Bow's Review*, acknowledging that 'Negroes are gregarious; they dread solitariness, and to be deprived from their little weekly dances and chit-chat . . . I have a fiddle in my quarters, and though some of my good old brethren in the church would think hard of me, yet I allow dancing; ay, I buy the fiddle and encourage it, by giving the boys occasionally a big supper.' Another slave-holder, describing the management of his plantation in the same periodical, remarked that he 'must not omit to mention that I have a good fiddler, and keep him well supplied with catgut, and I make it his duty to play for the Negroes every Saturday night until 12 o'clock. They are exceedingly punctual in their attendance at the ball, while Charley's fiddle

19 Butch Cage, fiddle, Willie Thomas, guitar, and Mrs Thomas, patting, Zachary, LA

is always accompanied with Ihurod on the triangle, and Sam to "pat".'
As one old slave, Cato, who was born in 1836 near Pineapple in Alabama,
remarked: 'We used to have frolics, too. Some niggers had fiddles and
played the reels and niggers love to dance and sing and eat.'

Under these circumstances the musicians among the slaves from
Senegal, Gambia, Mali, Upper Volta, Niger, Northern Nigeria and other
savannah regions corresponding to the territories within these present
political boundaries, found opportunities to profit from their skills. Negro
musicians were encouraged to play for plantation dances and balls at the
'Big House' and exercising their abilities gave them a chance to escape
the drudgery of field work. The bands of fiddles, banjos, tambourines
and triangles accompanied by slaves 'patting Juba' on thighs and knees

meant that Bambara and Wolof, Mandingo and Hausa had the opportunity to play in groups of a kind to which they were accustomed, and
on instruments with which they were more or less familiar. It seems likely
that the guess which Melville Herskovits hazarded to the effect that
'in the instance of the early Senegalese arrivals, whatever was retained
of aboriginal custom was overshadowed by the traditions of the more
numerous Guinea Coast Negroes' may well have been very wide of the
mark. On the contrary, they may have found themselves considerably at
an advantage in a community where the playing of drums was largely
discouraged. Notwithstanding their numerical inferiority, they may have
established themselves very well as musicians. In fact the rider that
Herskovits made, that late-comers found the earlier Negroes 'well enough
established to have translated their modes of behaviour . . . into community
patterns' could well operate against his argument. The slaves from the
Senegambia were early on the scene and by this token had the longest
opportunity to establish their role within the community pattern.

Though there is considerable evidence to support this hypothesis, it
is readily acknowledged that there is too little available data for conclusive
argument. To a large extent the documentary and other source material
could well be examined again without the conditioning and limiting
assumption that the majority of the slaves came from the rain forest tribes.
Careful scrutiny of the surviving records of plantations might reveal clues
as to the provenance of many of the slaves, which a thorough knowledge
of the distribution of tribes throughout West Africa and not merely in
the coastal regions may make more significant. The logs of slavers' ships
and the books of the slave-traders may merit re-examination, while the
records of the import of slaves to the West Indies and subsequent export
to the United States could be informative. Slaves who were most able
to cope with malarial infection, with tropical heat and high humidity may
have been kept back for work in the West Indies plantations, while those
who came from the regions beyond the rain forest and who were accustomed to conditions somewhat closer to those of North America may have
been shipped there later.

It seems possible then, that work along the lines of Elizabeth Donnan's
monumental *Documents Illustrative of the Slave Trade to America* and other

sources, with a more careful consideration of the map of West Africa, may reveal patterns of importation. Records of the export of slaves from the coastal ports might also be revealing; it seems inadequate to assume, because slaves were shipped from the Gold and Slave Coast forts, that they were therefore members of the rain forest tribes. As has been seen, there is evidence to suggest that a great many came from the interior, deep in the Sudan, having been passed from trader to town on a south-bound route that would culminate at the shipping ports. Bearing in mind, however, that few of the shippers and traders were greatly concerned with the origin of their slaves, except perhaps for meeting the special prefer-ences of buyers, a large resource of information cannot be anticipated. But we might turn with profit to the developing sciences in the study of race.

Mention has already been made of sickle cell distribution in West Africa. Sickle cell distribution is closely related to the prevalence of malaria-bearing mosquitos, but, as Frank B. Livingstone has shown in a detailed analysis of the implications of the sickle cell gene distribution in West Africa, it has been greatly conditioned by patterns of subsistence economy and the movement of peoples and tribes. The results can be confusing for 'in many cases there are significant differences in the frequency of the trait even within the same tribe. For example, the Fulani have frequencies ranging from 8 to 25 per cent, and the Mandingo in the Gambia vary from 6 to 28 per cent. Although this great variability impedes analysis about the distribution, some significant generalizations can nevertheless be made. Broadly speaking, the higher frequencies tend to be toward the south, and despite many exceptions, there is some indication of a north–south gradient in the frequency of the sickle cell trait.' Perhaps this is too little to go on, but the distribution map shows a wide Sudanic belt where the distribution is less than 8 per cent, while the Kwa-speaking peoples – Ewe, Fanti, Twi, Ashanti, Yoruba among them – have read-ings higher than 20 per cent. It is interesting to note that the inhabitants of Liberia, which was largely settled by repatriated slaves, offers read-ings from nil to only 2 per cent. This might imply that the genetic decline had resulted from the importation of slaves with relatively low counts to North America, where malarial infestation was too low to promote

further distribution of the sickle cell gene. Though such genetic analyses among Negroes, and blues singers in particular, would be of great
interest, it is highly unlikely that the research will ever be undertaken.

Nevertheless, analyses of gene flow from the white population to the
Negro population in America have been made. Dr Bentley Glass and
Dr C. C. Li used samples from South African Bantu, East Africans and
Egyptian Sudanese for their studies and these have been questioned by
D. F. Roberts who noted that 'the extensive researches of Herskovits
showed that the provenance of the Negro slaves in the USA was of more
limited area than had been earlier thought. A few were derived from
Madagascar and east coast localities, but the large majority originated from
the western regions of Africa.' In his re-analysis Roberts unfortunately
took Herskovits' writings literally and without the re-examination of
these assumptions, which he applied to his own field. Thus his African
samples were drawn from the Ewe, Ashanti, Yoruba, S. E. Nigeria
(presumably Ibo) and the only examples from savannah regions were in
northern Nigeria and the Jos Plateau. This meant that Mande-speaking
peoples were entirely omitted from his samples. The American Negro
samples from which the calculations of gene flow were deduced were
drawn almost entirely from Baltimore, Washington and New York with
an isolated 'Southern' instance (Ohio). Again, gene-flow analyses which
drew samples through other regions of West Africa and from Negroes
in the Deep South might be revealing in their results.

Such studies reflect Herskovits' own analyses of 'racial crossing', first
published in *The American Negro* in 1928. In his anthropometric comparisons of Africans he used the available data on samples taken among
the Ekoi (south-east Nigeria), but also from among the Vai from the Ivory
Coast and the Kagoro, a scattered tribe living among the Bambara and
Soninke. The small samples – ranging from a score from one tribe to 70
in another – were commented on at the time, and raised some doubt as
to the validity of the comparisons with nearly 1,000 'mixed American
Negroes'. Of his American samples nearly 500 were from Howard University, more than 200 from Harlem and less than 100 from 'West Virginia
rural'. Again, the African samples were probably not widely enough distributed to be significant, while the predominance of northern Negroes

and those from the social upper class, against virtually no representation of statistics from the Deep South, probably strongly affected his
conclusions as to the emergence of an American Negro type. To the
observer without the benefit of statistical analysis the physical types
represented among blues singers are by no means always typically West
African rain forest, and neither are they consistent within the group. There
is little relationship to one type, American Negro or otherwise in say,
Leroy Carr, Roosevelt Sykes, Big Joe Williams or Clifton Chenier. On
the other hand, some singers, like Big Bill Broonzy, Little Son Jackson,
John Lee Hooker or Sunnyland Slim, have features which could merge
easily enough among the Ashanti or the Yoruba. Most striking to me,
however, is the predominance of certain physical characteristics among
a large number of blues singers which relate closely to those of savannah
peoples. The high cheek-bones, long features, narrow jaw-lines and, frequently, straight noses, of a surprisingly large number of blues singers
have been previously unremarked, although applicable to many of them.
In such singers as Fred McDowell, Scott Dunbar, Carl Martin, Bumble
Bee Slim, Sleepy John Estes, Honeyboy Edwards, Tommy and Mager
Johnson among many others, these characteristics are markedly present.
In some cases the straight nose becomes even hooked, as in the case of
Yank Rachell; in others the long features are particularly pronounced,
as with Doctor Ross; in still others lean features are deeply outlined from
the sides of the nose to the chin as in the cases of T-Bone Walker or
Elmore James. 'The typical Mandingo', wrote C. G. Seligman, 'are
described as tall and slender in build, with finer features, fuller beard,
and lighter skin than the neighbouring populations.' Of the Songhai he
wrote that physically they 'are moderately tall, with a stature of about
68 inches. They are long-headed, with a cephalic index of 75.5, their
northern blood being especially obvious in their relatively well-formed
noses . . . Other evidence is to be found in their skin colour, which is
described as coppery-brown, never of the dark, almost black colour of
the Negroes of Dahomey and Ghana. Their hair, however, is always
spiralled.' Such descriptions could well apply to a large number of blues
singers, whose presence in the regions stretching east from Senegal for
1,500 miles would not be physically out of place. It may be noted that

many of the peoples who come within this belt *are* very dark, the Wolof being among the blackest of all African peoples, although refined and well-made in feature and build.

Of course, such comparisons are subjective and unscientific, but they are striking enough nevertheless. It could be argued that the influence of inter-breeding with North American Indians – several blues singers claiming such ancestry – might account for the physical features mentioned above. While recognising that such claims are made by many Negroes and a high proportion of Herskovits' and Meier's subjects, Dr Bentley Glass, in a paper 'on the Unlikelihood of Significant Admixture of Genes from the North American Indians in the Present Composition of the Negroes of the United States', has brought careful evidence to refute this argument in general, if not in the case of blues singers in particular. In cases where miscegenation has clearly accounted for marked Caucasian features, as in the instances of Charley Patton, or the Chatman family, it is not suggested that any inherited physical characteristics might be savannah in origin.

Another area which might merit further study is that of linguistic analysis. If the music of the 'shout' (from, as noted above, the Bambara *saut*) has traceable savannah associations, what of the music of the jukes? Dr Lorenzo Turner has traced the very word *juke* to the Gullah *joog*, meaning, in the Georgia Sea Islands, 'disorderly'. This in turn he has traced to the original Bambara *dzugu* meaning 'wicked'. Dr David Dalby has drawn some remarkable comparisons between Wolof words and currently surviving American Negro usage, relating 'jive' talk to the Wolof *jev*, meaning 'to talk disparagingly'; 'hip' to the Wolof *hipi*, meaning 'to open one's eyes'; and the jazz term to 'jam' to the Wolof word *jaam* for slave. Does the name of one of the more primitive savannah tribes – the Bobo – remain in the title and words of the dance-song *Georgia Bobo*, or *Louisiana Bobo* and the line from the *Dozens*: 'if you ain't doin' the bobo, what's your head doing down there?' Perhaps the frequent use of a number of words in the blues which appear in no American lexicon may eventually be traced back to such origins.

Whatever the outcome of anthropological research might be, whether in the analysis of genetic flow or anthropometric statistics (and one must admit that the chances of any such analysis being made among blues singers is, to say the least, slim); whatever historical or linguistic research may uncover, ultimately the most important area of examination must be that of musical analysis. This may well mean the upsetting of old theories concerning the relation of jazz and blues. As Charles Duvelle, writing on the music of Upper Volta, has observed: 'The usual hypothesis is that Negroes of African origin used to sing on a pentatonic scale and that when they attempted to sing Lutheran hymns, based on a heptatonic scale, they had to deform the 3rds and 7ths, which were unknown to them, these alterations leading to the "blue notes" characteristic of jazz music. But this theory is ill-founded in assuming that the pentatonic scale was the only one used by the Negroes, while in fact there is sufficient evidence that other scales were used in Africa, including the heptatonic. Moreover, the "blue notes" themselves are found in Africa. Many other features of jazz music (its formal rhythmic and polyphonic characteristics) are also found in Africa.' Tolia Nikiprowetzky in fact has noted that in Senegal 'nearly all pieces are based on heptatonic scales, which could be compared to a nontempered variety of modal scales'.

Musicological analyses of the blues have scarcely been undertaken to date and John Fahey's study of the structure of Charley Patton's repertoire, which it is hoped will be published in this series, is singular. Future studies which examine the scales and structures in the blues would make a basis for comparison with those employed in the savannah regions of West Africa. Similarly the melodic lines employed by the *griots* could be examined against those of the blues singers, and with appropriate equipment (such as Metfessel's phonophotography), the employment of ornamentation might be compared. The responsorial techniques of savannah playing and singing might profitably be compared with those of the blues, while the important use of rhythmic patterns on the instruments against which vocal lines modally structured around one note are heard in these regions may again have echoes in the singing and playing of, say, a Robert Pete Williams.

Another line of enquiry might be made in the examination of tunings in the blues and the tuning of strings in West African instruments – whether, for instance, the 'cross-note' tunings of blues guitarists have their

20 Fingering positions of *griot* Amadou Coly Sall are similar to those of many blues
instrumentalists

savannah parallels. In this connection the instrumental approach of the respective musicians might be instructive, chordal playing being exceptionally rare among African cultures, but no less so in the guitar playing of a John Lee Hooker. The use of drone strings may also be studied and the degree to which the slackening of a string to render it 'out of tune' – a blues instance is in the work of Sam Collins – relates to savannah practice. As the long metal vibrators on the chordophones, the spider's egg mirlitons on the calabashes of the *balafon*, or the chains on the *sansas* all demonstrate, West African instrumentalists have a dislike of 'pure' notes and tones; to what extent is this reflected in the approach of bluesmen to their instruments – the pianists for instance, with the opened fronts of upright pianos or the newspaper slipped behind the piano strings? A comparison might also be made of the methods of fingering; of the picking and brushing of the strings by the *khalam* players, the sliding of the fingers along the strings; even the manner in which the *griots* bring the thumb over the arm of the *goroumi* to stop a string; or the manner in which the player of the monochord fiddle, the *gnagnour*, places the shell of the resonator against his chest, 'alley-fiddle' style.

Listing the functions of Hausa music played by the professional musician who may be found in the emirates, David Ames identified a number of major categories. They included recreational music that was not bound by ritual or related to major social institutions; ceremonial performances for rites, which include songs of praise and ridicule; educational songs which 'affirm important social values', transmit oral history and record current events; affirmatory forms of song which stress position, rank, title and ancestry; songs of regulation and social control in which desirable values are stressed and undesirable ones criticised; songs of work and commerce used to accompany labour or to attract custom; and music for modern political activity. Not all of these have their counterparts in the blues, or even in the forms of music which directly preceded the blues, but some at any rate seem functionally close to the idiom. Blues has, of course, an important part to play as an entertainment music, recreational without any formal structure within the institutions of Negro society. If the blues is not employed for rites either, it is nevertheless true, as Charles Keil has shown in his study of the responses of black audiences to such singers as B. B. King or Bobby Blue Bland, that the atmosphere is one of a kind of ceremonial in many blues clubs, and the performance of the singer a kind of ritual. There is evidence to show that this is by no means a new phenomenon in the blues; the triggered responses that B. B. King may invoke with the first few notes of his guitar seem to be of a similar kind to those produced by Tommy Johnson as he swung into his particular rhythm pattern. Again, if songs of praise are not now a strong feature of the blues, the blues singer's predecessors sang of traditional heroes in *John Henry*, the *Boll Weevil* and other ballad subjects which clearly emphasised values. Songs of ridicule, on the other hand, persist still, with the *Dirty Dozen* having a long history. Until a couple of decades ago the blues still commented liberally on current events with disasters and participation in the Second World War being recorded fairly frequently. At a subtle level the blues also operated as a vehicle for social control, with the attitudes of the black society fairly represented within the songs. Admired characteristics, especially physical ones, have also been prominent in the blues and attitudes of mind and aspects of personal behaviour are frequently criticised. With the demise of the work song, the blues became the song vehicle to accompany labour and, in earlier years, for the medicine show or the barber shop; and, most obviously and persistently, for restaurants and bars, the blues has been used to attract custom. Mass media have made this role effective on a larger scale, for blues still drums custom for baking flour or a multitude of consumer goods on radio. Only in the field of political activity does the blues seem to have remained neutral in comparison with the functions Ames describes.

There seem to be many interesting parallels between the attitudes of the savannah communities to the *griot* and those of the black community to the blues singer which also bear comparison. Blues singers are not necessarily socially acceptable in the black community, but they are certainly known to most members of it. They, too, are the source of humour and entertainment, of gossip and comment, and a singer like Lightnin' Hopkins is very much a *griot* in personality, with a similar flair for spontaneous and devastating comment on the passing scene. But if blues singers appeal because of these talents as well as their musicianship, they are, like the *griots*, frequently considered as lazy, lacking in industry and job application. In similar fashion many blues singers hire themselves to a single employer or are closely affiliated for long periods with one patron, club or bar; but there are likewise blues singers who are free agents and who, like Big Joe Williams, say, are continually on the move, obtaining employment where and for as long as they wish. Not a few blues singers make – and sometimes lose – considerable sums of money through their work, especially those like Muddy Waters or Howling Wolf who have a record company as patron. These singers work with groups today, rather than as solo singers. Like the *griot*, there are individual performers, duos and small groups, similarly depending on stringed instruments, the occasional horn, and rhythmic accompaniment. Those qualities of light rhythm, swing and subtle syncopation which characterise the music of many blues singers, those aptitudes for improvisation in music and in verse, those repertoires of traditional songs, stock-in-trade lines and phrases and sudden original words and verses – all these are no less recognisably the hallmarks of the *griots*.

Further examination might uncover in detail close correspondences in content and approach: there is in blues a sizeable body of fairly obscene song, little recorded in unexpurgated form, but familiar in euphemism and *double-entendre*; this too is familiar among the *griots*, but recordings and text analyses are still woefully few. To what extent any similarities are coincidental and arising from parallel situations would also have to be examined, and a detailed study of the growth of Negro singers and groups in the slave period in North America might be revealing on this aspect also. For all this is largely speculative, even if the speculations are based on a considerable body of material which has been little related in the past. As this study is concerned with the possibility of African retentions in the blues, and a consideration of where, in 'Africa', these traditions may have originated, little has been said of jazz. As blues is sung and played mainly on string instruments and the piano, with harmonicas, kazoos and occasional rhythm and wind instruments augmenting, the prevalence of the counterparts of some of these instruments in the savannah regions has been emphasised. Jazz, however, is a music of wind instruments against rhythm sections. Hardly any mention has been made here of the *griot* orchestras of drums and horns, or of drums alone, which may also be found in the savannah. But it has been shown that the techniques of complex rhythms, of 'speaking' instruments and vocalisation are not peculiar to the drum orchestras of the rain forest, but are shared by the musicians and groups of the savannah belt. It may be found necessary in the future to write a new chapter in the history of the blues, which examines the extent and the source of African retentions in the music. But it may also be necessary to re-write the first chapter in every history of jazz.

BIBLIOGRAPHICAL NOTES

2. AFRICA AND THE JAZZ HISTORIAN

Melville Herskovits published *The Anthropometry of the American Negro* in 1930 (Columbia University Press). His quoted conclusions appear on p. 177. In *An American Dilemma* (Harper and Row edition, 1962) Gunnar Myrdal's team analyse this and other data in Chapter v. Professor von Hornbostel's propositions were questioned by Herskovits in 'The Negro in the New World', an article in *American Anthropologist*, 32:1 (1930), 146–7. Herskovits also discussed in *Cultural Anthropology* (Alfred A. Knopf, 1955) the subjects of acculturation, pp. 471–9, and enculturation, pp. 327–32 and 453–4.

    Shining Trumpets by Rudi Blesh (Cassell, 1949) examines African music and its relation to jazz on pp. 25–46. So does Marshall Stearns in *The Story of Jazz* (Sidgwick and Jackson, 1957), pp. 3–64. Similar space is devoted to the subject in Gunther Schuller's *Early Jazz* (Oxford University Press, 1968), pp. 3–62. Other views are expressed in Winthrop Sargeant, *Jazz Hot and Hybrid* (Dutton, 1946), pp. 149–57, 220; Robert Goffin's *Jazz – From the Congo to the Metropolitan* (Doubleday, 1946), pp. 7–30; Leonard Feather's *The Book of Jazz* (Arthur Barker, 1957), pp. 10–12; and Francis Newton's *The Jazz Scene* (MacGibbon and Kee, 1959), pp. 39–40. The quotation from André Hodeir comes from his *Jazz: Its Evolution and Essence* (Grove Press, 1956), p. 42.

    The references to Ernest Borneman's writings include his articles 'Creole Echoes' in *Jazz Review* for September and November 1959 and 'The Roots of Jazz' in *Jazz, New Perspectives*, ed. Hentoff and McCarthy

(Rinehart, 1959). His booklet *An Anthropologist Looks at Jazz* was published by Jazz Music Books, 1946, and the quotations appeared on pages 9 and 10. Harold Courlander's *Negro Folk Music USA* (Columbia University Press, 1963) discusses 'Blues' in Chapter VI and lays great emphasis on African survivals in American Negro music. Richard Alan Waterman's important paper on 'African Influence on the Music of the Americas' appeared in *Acculturation in the Americas*, ed. Sol Tax (University of Chicago Press, 1952), pp. 207–18.

Herskovits's 'Scale of Intensity of New World Africanisms' illustrated his paper 'Problem, Method and Theory in Afroamerican Studies' in *Afroamerica*, 1 (1945), pp. 5–24, and the quotation from *New Republic*, 84:1083, published in 1935, comes from an article on 'What Has Africa Given America?' pp. 92–4. Herskovits published his extensive findings on African survivals in the Americas in his invaluable if controversial *The Myth of the Negro Past* (Beacon reprint, 1958); see particularly for West Indian survivals, pp. 246–7.

William Russell's comments appear in a letter to the author for July 1968 and the extensive study of early fiddles and fifes appears in Henry A. Kmen's *Music in New Orleans – The Formative Years 1791–1841*, from Chapter XII of which, 'Negro Music', come most of the references here, except the quotation from George Washington Cable's celebrated article 'The Dance in the Place Congo', originally published in *Century* magazine for February 1886 and reprinted in *Creoles and Cajuns*, ed. Arlin Turner (Doubleday Anchor, 1959). Thomas Jefferson's oft-quoted note on the *banjar* appears on p. 19 of his *Notes on Virginia*, and early minstrelsy is discussed in *Gentlemen, Be Seated* by Sigmund Spaeth and Dailey Paskman (Doubleday Doran, 1928), pp. 11–19. The quotation from Fanny Kemble comes from her *Journal of a Residence on a Georgia Plantation 1838–1839* (Alfred A. Knopf, 1961), p. 131. In *The Peculiar Institution* (Random House, 1946), pp. 367–70, Kenneth Stampp gives references on Negro music. *The Bluesmen* by Samuel B. Charters is published by Oak Publications (1967), and the references to African influence on blues are on pp. 16–20. *The Musical Instruments of the Native Races of South Africa*, by Percival R. Kirby (Witwatersrand, 1934), discusses and illustrates the ramkie and associated instruments. See also *Musical Instruments. A Comprehensive Dictionary*, by Sibyl Marcuse (Doubleday and Company, 1964).

3. MUSIC IN WEST AFRICA

The fullest discussion of the roles of music in Ashanti society appears in the descriptions of ritual in *Religion and Art in Ashanti*, by R. S. Rattray (Oxford University Press, 1927), while the roles and kinds of drums are detailed in *Drumming in Akan Communities of Ghana*, by J. H. Kwabena Nketia (University of Ghana, 1963). Alan P. Merriam's classification of musical regions in Africa appears in his study 'African Music' in *Continuity and Change in African Cultures*, ed. William R. Bascom and Melville Herskovits (University of Chicago Press), pp. 76–80. See 'African Influence' above for Waterman's concept of 'hot' rhythm.

Olaudah Equiano's autobiography, published as *The Interesting Narrative of Olaudah Equiano, or Gustavus Vasa, the African*, was first published in London in 1789; the quotation comes from Chapter 1. The discussion of Yoruba drums appears in Anthony King's *Yoruba Sacred Music* (University of Ibadan Press, 1961), in the Introduction. A. M. Jones' *Studies in African Music* is published by Oxford University Press, 1959, and his paper on 'African Rhythm' was published in *Africa*, vol. 24, no. 1, January 1954; the quotation comes from p. 39. J. H. Kwabena Nketia's paper on the 'History and the Organisation of Music in West Africa' is published by the University of Ghana, *c.* 1959. Other references are from his *Drumming in Akan Communities* (above) p. 166 and pp. 22–3, and his paper 'Historical Evidence in Ga Religious Music' [Institute of African Studies (Ghana), 1962]. Harold Courlander's comments on the African drum in North America appear in his notes to *African and Afro-American Drums* (Folkways Record Album no. FE4502 C/D). Other references to Waterman and A. M. Jones come from sources already cited.

Joseph H. Greenberg's *Studies in African Linguistic Classification* (Compass Publishing Co., New Haven, 1955) is the standard work on this subject, but he also contributes an article on 'Africa as a Linguistic Area' in Bascom and Herskovits' *Continuity and Change* (above). For African climate and topography see, for instance, *Africa and the Islands* by R. J. Harrison Church, John I. Clarke, P. J. H. Clarke, and H. J. R. Henderson (Longmans, 1964) and P. H. Ady, *Africa: Regional Economic Atlas* (Oxford: Clarendon Press, 1965). For tribal distribution see G. P. Murdock, *Africa: Its Peoples and their Culture History* (McGraw-Hill, 1959).

For details of the *griots* the notes to *Niger, la Musique des Griots* (Disques Ocora OCR20), and *La Musique des Griots* (Disques Ocora OCR15) by

Tolia Nikiprowetsky, who made the recordings, are exemplary. Other comments come from Curt Sachs, *The Wellsprings of Music*, ed. Jaap Kunst (McGraw-Hill, 1965), p. 205, and William Seabrook in *Jungle Ways* (Harrap, 1931) pp. 35–8. The notes on the *griots* among the Dan are by Hugo Zemp for *The Music of the Dan* (UNESCO Collection BM30L2301) and *The Music of the Senufo* (UNESCO BM30L2308). The *gewel* are described by David Ames in the notes to *Wolof Music of the Senegal and the Gambia* on Folkways FE4462, where he compares the *halam* to the banjo. David Ames also made the recordings and wrote the notes for *Nigeria-Hausa Music*, Volumes 1 and 2 (UNESCO BML2306 and 2307). All these recordings are recommended to those who wish to study musical examples of the *griots* and professional savannah musicians.

4. SAVANNAH SONG

William Smith's *A New Voyage to Guinea* (1745) is quoted in Douglas Grant's *The Fortunate Slave: An Illustration of Slavery in the Early Eighteenth Century* (Oxford University Press, 1968) p. 10, and Mungo Park's *Travels in Africa* (1798) has been reprinted by Dent's Everyman's Library, 1969. See p. 30.

For a mid-'thirties description of a 'ring-shout' see Chapter III of Carl Carmer's *Stars Fell on Alabama* (Lovat Dickson, 1935). Lydia Parrish discusses ring-shouts at length in Chapter III of *Slave Songs of the Georgia Sea Islands* (1942) (Folklore Associates, 1965) and quotes Dr Lorenzo Turner on the subject. Work songs of the Senegal Casamance are discussed by J. David Sapir in the notes to his recordings of *The Music of the Diola-Fogny of the Casamance, Senegal* (Folkways FE4323). African song is discussed (pp. 91–5) in *Folk Song Style and Culture*, by Alan Lomax (American Association for the Advancement of Science, 1968). The list of tribes selected for the cultural sample is on pp. 32–3.

Quotations and references to the writings of Father Jones, Gunther Schuller and Alan P. Merriam are as given in the notes to Chapters 2 and 3 above. The singing styles of the Boussani and tribes from Upper Volta are discussed in the notes to his recordings, by Charles Duvelle, in *Haute Volta* (Disques Ocora SOR10). Jeanette Robinson Murphy's article from *Popular Science Monthly*, 1899, of 'The Survival of African Music in America' is reprinted in *The Negro and His Folk-Lore*, ed. Bruce Jackson (University of Texas Press, 1967), pp. 331–2.

5. THE SOURCE OF THE SLAVES

For J. C. Furnas' analysis of the numbers of slaves imported to North America see his *The Road to Harper's Ferry* (Faber and Faber, 1961), pp. 111–12. Henry C. Carey's figures appear in Gunnar Myrdal's *An American Dilemma* (as above) p. 118. The sources of the slaves as published by Melville Herskovits appear in *Myth of the Negro Past*, pp. 46–53, and his arguments as to the linguistic stocks and the 'core area' appear on pp. 79 and 295. Arthur Ramos' *The Negro in Brazil*, translated by Richard Pattee (Washington, 1939), gives details of the sources of slaves to South America. See also, for comparison, Gilberto Freyre, *The Masters and the Slaves* (Alfred A. Knopf, 1946).

Dr Lorenzo Turner's *Africanisms in the Gullah Dialect* (University of Chicago Press, 1949) gives extensive African survivals in speech and Dr David Dalby's comparison with Wolof words was published in *The Times* for 19 July 1969. Herskovits discusses and dismisses the 'thousand-mile theory' in *Myth*, pp. 35–6, and Captain Samuel Gamble is quoted in *A History of Sierra Leone 1400–1787*, by Peter Kup (Cambridge University Press, 1961) p. 90.

In his *Travels* (above) Mungo Park describes the instruments of the Mandingoes and the '*Jilli kea*' on p. 213, and the journey with the slow slave coffle on pp. 248–77. The story of Abu Bakr is told in *Africa Remembered – Narratives by West Africans from the Era of the Slave*, ed. Philip D. Curtin (University of Wisconsin, 1967), where extracts from Olaudah Equiano also appear. For Abu Bakr, see pp. 161–2. In *Slave Songs* Lydia Parrish quotes Sir Charles Lyell on African Tom on p. 24, and on p. 26 discusses Sālih Bilāli whose *Recollections of Massina* appear in *Africa Remembered*. The quotation comes from p. 151. Ulrich B. Phillips' *American Negro Slavery; a Survey of the Supply, Employment and Control of Negro Labour as determined by the Plantation Regime* was published by D. Appleton and Company in 1918, while Elizabeth Donnan's *Documents Illustrative of the Slave Trade to America* (Carnegie Institution, 1930–5) remains an indispensable source-work. The quotation from Roland Oliver and R. D. Fage comes from pp. 120–1 of their *A Short History of Africa* (Penguin Books, 1962), and that from Church, Clarke, Clarke and Henderson's *Africa and the Islands* (as above) is on p. 67. Note that the apparently conflicting figures for the slave trade as given by these authors refers to the *total* of slaves exported to *all* the Americas.

The reminiscences of New Orleans by Benjamin Henry Latrobe are quoted by Kmen in *Music in New Orleans*, pp. 227–8, and Stearns in *The Story of Jazz*, p. 51. Herbert Asbury's *The French Quarter* (Alfred A. Knopf, 1936), pp. 240–4, gives full descriptions of the reports of Congo Square. Cable's 'The Dance in the Place Congo' has been noted above – the descriptions of slaves come from pp. 372–80 in *Creoles and Cajuns*. Note, incidentally, that the Fulah were probably *not* mis-called 'poulards' – the tribe is known as Peul in the previous French colonies. Niles Newbell Puckett, in *Folk Beliefs of the Southern Negro* (Chapel Hill, 1926), notes other African words in addition to *gris-gris* on p. 16. The description of Jean Montanet by Lafcadio Hearn comes from the article 'The Last of the Voudoos' in *Harper's Weekly*, for 7 November 1885, and the suppression of drums is noted by Herskovits in *Myth* on p. 138. Finally, the concluding quotation from James A. Porter comes from his article on 'The Trans-Cultural Affinities of African Art' which appeared with Waterman's 'Influence' in Sol Tax's *Acculturation in the Americas*, p. 125.

6. AFRICA AND THE BLUES

Gus Cannon's description of his first banjo is quoted from a recorded interview on the album *American Skiffle Bands* (Folkways FA2610); Big Bill Broonzy's guitar is described on p. 8 of *Big Bill Blues* (Cassell, 1955) and the note on Big Joe Williams' instrument was published in Dave Mangurian's article on him in *Jazz Journal* for December 1963. Dave Evans published his article on 'Reverend Rubin Lacy' in *Blues Unlimited* for January 1967 and Mack McCormick's notes on Mance Lipscomb accompany the album *Mance Lipscomb, Texas Sharecropper and Songster* (Arnoclie F1001). The quotation from Hobart Smith comes from an article 'I Just got the Music in my Head' in *Sing Out!* for January 1964, and from Dock Boggs in an article 'I Always Loved the Lonesome Songs' in *Sing Out!* for July 1964. Tony Russell's study *Blacks, Whites and Blues* (Studio Vista, 1970) studies the Negro–White interchange of song and blues traditions in detail.

The 'small Farmers' who described music on their plantations are quoted in full in *The Negro and His Folk-Lore* (see above) pp. 345–6 and 350–1, and the quotation from the slave Cato appears in *Lay My Burden Down*, ed. B. A. Botkin (University of Chicago Press, 1945), p. 86.

On the possible use of anthropological techniques of analysis the article on 'Anthropological Implications of Sickle Cell Gene Distribution in West Africa', by Frank B. Livingstone, which was published in *American Anthropologist*, 60:3 (1958), 533–62, was of great interest. Derek F. Roberts' study of 'The Dynamics of Racial Intermixture in the American Negro – Some Anthropological Considerations' was published in the *American Journal of Human Genetics*, 7:4, 361–7, in answer to a previous study on 'The Dynamics of Racial Intermixture – An Analysis based on the American Negro' by Bentley Glass and C. C. Li published in the same journal for volume 5:1 (1953). Herskovits' *The American Negro – A Study In Racial Crossing* (1928) has been reprinted by the Indiana University Press (1964), while similarly C. G. Seligman's *Races of Africa* (1930) has been reprinted by the Oxford University Press (1966), the quotation coming from pp. 35–7. Dr Bentley Glass published the paper 'On the Unlikelihood of Significant Admixture of Genes from the North American Indians in the Present Composition of the Negroes of the United States' in the *American Journal for Human Genetics* in the same issue as Derek F. Roberts' paper above, pp. 368–85.

Lorenzo Turner's linguistic studies have already been noted; mention should also be made of his paper 'African Survivals in the New World with Special Emphasis on the Arts' in *Africa From the Point of View of American Scholars* (Présence Africaine, 1958), pp. 101–6. Dr David Dalby's article in *The Times* for 19 July 1969, from whence these examples come, has also been noted above. The comments on blue notes by Charles Duvelle appear in his notes to *Haute Volta* (Disques Ocora SOR10) and John Fahey's 'Textual and Musicological Analysis of the Recordings of Charley Patton' was a Master's thesis for the Department of Mythology and Folklore at University College of Los Angeles, 1965. The list of categories of Hausa music was published by David Ames in the notes to *Nigeria-Hausa Music 11* (UNESCO BM30L2307). In his *Urban Blues* (University of Chicago Press, 1966), Charles Keil shows 'Big Bobby Blue Bland on Stage' in chapter v and discusses 'Role and Response' in chapter vi.

ACKNOWLEDGEMENTS

I am grateful to a number of people for their help in drawing my attention to books, other publications and recordings while I was engaged in collecting material for this study; my thanks to them all.

My special thanks, however, must go to Professor J. H. Kwabena Nketia for inviting me to lecture at the Institute of African Studies, University of Ghana, and for giving me every facility to record tribal music while there. Sincere thanks, too, to John Lloyd, then Dean of the Faculty of Architecture at Kumasi University of Science and Technology, for bringing me to Ghana, and for accompanying myself and my wife on the field trip to Nangodi, and for much advice and help with recording. Dr Colin Painter, who was lecturing in linguistics in 1964 at the University of Ghana and who is now in the Department of Linguistics at the University of Indianapolis, has continually advised and opened up new lines of enquiry for which I am very grateful. I am particularly indebted to M. Charles Duvelle, General Editor of the Collection Radiodiffusion Outre-Mer (Disques Ocora), for help in many ways, including the loan of photographs and access to recordings; and to Folkways Scholastic Records for much help with recorded material – my warm appreciation to them both; also to Colin Fournier, whose help with translations was most valuable. Finally I must express my sincere appreciation to my partner in the study of the Texas Blues, Mack McCormick, whose insistence that the problem of African retentions in the blues be re-examined caused this introductory study to be written.

PAUL OLIVER

7 · AFTERWORD

In the seventh issue of *Ethnomusicology* published in 1963, Richard A. Waterman, author of the much-cited chapter 'African Influence on the Music of the Americas' of eleven years before, published his later reflections on the subject. 'On Flogging a Dead Horse: Lessons Learned from the Africanisms Controversy' was more instructive of his disenchantment with the debate. It is not surprising therefore that he was less than happy to discover that, a decade later, there was much life still in the equine cadaver. In an interview, Lynn Summers briefly presented some of my findings in *Savannah Syncopators* to Waterman. Unwilling to accept the arguments of (in Summers' term) an 'iconoclast', he replied that I 'was probably talking about the griots, and the Wolof bunch, because they are the ones who have the plunkety-plunk balafon playing'.

Richard Waterman adhered to his long-held belief that any influences on the music of the Americas stemmed from the West African coastal peoples. 'I think you probably find more of the materials that went into the blues on the coast. Although superficially the fact that you do have something plunking like a guitar makes it sound a bit like it', he said, dismissing both savannah music and my argument: 'I think his hunch is wrong.' In fact, Waterman who had not even mentioned blues in his 'African Influence' paper, had not read the book and it was not in his possession when he died shortly after, before my reply was published. As my response has been reprinted in Steven C. Tracy's *Blues Reader*, together with the discussion, also in *Living Blues*, between David Evans and myself, I shall not repeat them here. Nevertheless, I feel that it is important to summarise and comment upon some of the other research and writings which bear upon the subject of African retentions in the blues.

Before going further I should explain my use of the term 'retentions' which has inspired some criticism. 'Influence(s)' (as used by Waterman, among others) seemed to communicate a sense of immediate contact, or contiguity of traditions, which was not applicable to African music and American blues. 'Survivals', on the other hand, implied a struggle for continued existence which had largely been lost. I favoured the *Shorter Oxford Dictionary* (1972) definition of 'retention', a term in use since the fifteenth century, meaning 'the fact of retaining things in the mind; memory' or, from 1540, 'the action or fact of keeping to oneself, or . . . under one's power or authority', and later, 'of maintaining, keeping up, or continuing to use'. These meanings and associations, dating from the earliest contact of Europeans with Africa and still applicable, seemed to me to be most appropriate for the sustaining of certain elements of African culture in twentieth-century America – and especially in this context, in the blues.

Broadly, and not necessarily in the order in which these themes are discussed in *Savannah Syncopators*, related research since its publication has concentrated on the following: (1) the origins of the slaves in Africa and their importation into the Americas; (2) the linguistic evidence of African retentions in speech and, hence, in certain behaviours, including their origins and recent use; (3) African and African American musical instruments, their distribution, popularity and use; and (4) speculations on the relation of African musical traditions to the blues and associated forms. In some papers two or more of these themes are addressed or commented upon, as is the case with the writings of Joseph E. Holloway (1990). Drawing upon the researches of Winifred K. Vass among the Luba of Angola, he suggests that a higher proportion than hitherto stated came from the Bantu regions, principally from Congo-Angola. Citing analyses by William S. Pollitzer and Peter H. Wood of the slaves imported into South Carolina between 1733 and 1807, who conclude that Angolans made up about 32 per cent of the total, Holloway comments that 'other data' (unspecified) indicate that 'the percentage actually was closer to 40'. When the Senegambia, Sierra Leone and Windward Coast, from which were drawn the Wolof, Sudanic and Mandingo-Mende peoples, are taken together they represent over 36 per cent of the total (the balance coming from 'West Africa').

The crux of Holloway's argument is that 'unlike the Senegambians, the Bantus brought to South Carolina a homogeneous culture identifiable as Bantu' indicated by a common language which 'no doubt influenced West African groups of larger size'. Data published by Phillips and Littlefield 'shows that North Americans preferred Senegambians (Mandingos, Fulani, Bambaras and Malinkes) as house servants . . . they wanted slaves from the West African region (Fons, Fantees, Yorubas and Asantes) to work as domestic servants and artisans'. While Senegambians 'were considered the most intelligent Africans and were to be trained especially for domestic service and as handicraft workers' Holloway noted that 'the majority of Angolans were used as field slaves because they were large and robust'. Quoting McGowan, however, he also observed that 'familiarity with the cultivation of rice, corn, yams, and millet in the Senegambian hinterlands prepared them for the kind of labour that was required in the Mississippi Valley'. It was a point he seems to have forgotten when drawing his conclusions.

West Africans and Senegambians, being employed as servants and artisans, were 'forced to give up their cultural identities to reflect their masters' control and capacity to "civilize" the Africans'. Central African Bantus, employed as field hands, Holloway argued, were relatively removed from the ' "civilizing" influence' and by bringing a homogeneous culture 'indicated by a common language', were able to retain much of their cultural identity, which was shared with various African ethnic groups among the slaves to produce cultural expressions such as 'music (jazz, blues, spirituals, gospels)'. Unfortunately he adduced no evidence to support this sweeping assertion.

In another work, jointly written with Winifred K. Vass, *The African Heritage of American English*, Holloway again makes this claim, laying even greater emphasis on the proportion of Bantus imported as slaves through Charleston, South Carolina: 70 per cent of the incoming 11,500 in the five years 1735–40, a rate which dropped to 40 per cent thereafter. 'But even with this 30 per cent drop, the Bantus still remained the largest cohesive group on the American plantations', he extrapolated, inferring that the proportion, which may apply to the Gullah population of the Sea Islands, is applicable to all the plantation culture.

Apparently drawing his list from Courlander and Evans, Holloway claims in the Introduction that 'Bantu musical contributions' to South Carolina and Louisiana 'include drums, diddley bow, mouth bow, quills, washtub bass, jug, gongs, bells, rattles, ideophones, and the loikoimbi, a five-stringed harp'. In the section on 'Musical Instruments' he is rather more cautious in ascribing their origins to the Bantu of Angola. Professor Holloway's work is the most concerted opposition to the emphasis on the West African origins of the slaves and their influence in North America to be published. There seems little doubt that the Gullah spoken in the Sea Islands retains much Bantu vocabulary, but it remains unproven that this extended through much of the South. On the contrary, the persistence of Gullah among the Sea Island groups must surely have emphasised their isolation rather than facilitated contacts with other black communities. The Luba, to whom many of the words and cultural features are ascribed, live in the south-east of the Congo, and though the Luba kings were slave-owning, slavery historian Paul E. Lovejoy states that 'there is no direct evidence of a firm link with slave exporting'. In the first issue of *The Black Perspective in Music* Professor Kwabena Nketia agrees with my recognition of the 'striking resemblances between the musical techniques and usages of the savannah cultures of West Africa and those of African–American music', advising anyone 'searching for the origins of the musical resonances in the blues to pay some attention to these'. It had been my intention to do this in the field, but other commitments prevented me from doing so. However, in 1972 the great Manding Conference, organised by the School of Oriental and African Studies of London University, was held, which I attended along with some 200 participants from Europe, North America and Africa. Some 30 musicians from Gambia, Senegal and Mali performed, including *balafon*, *khalam* and drum players, though the more arresting 19- and 21-string *kora* lute-harp players were the most prominent. I interviewed several, and invited one of the *kora* players, Jali Nyama Suso, to perform at the Architectural Association where I was able to pursue and verify many aspects of the musical traditions of the region.

Nyama Suso was a *jali*, who performed 'the role of the *griot* (praise singer)' which 'is a vital one in some societies', as Nketia commented in 1974. To another African author and musician, Francis Bebey, the *griot* was a 'troubadour, the counterpart of the mediaeval European minstrel' whose 'art is essentially contemplative (hence static), individualistic, and pre-eminently self-interested'. Sidia Jatta, a linguist in Banjul, Gambia, emphasised that *jalis* inherit their profession and in spite of their artisan status enjoy certain freedoms, being able 'to break taboos and ignore social restraints without fear of reprisal'. A *jali* may have several patrons, host important visitors, act as intermediary in marriage arrangements and perform many other functions besides those of praise singer, historian or musician.

In 1982, Samuel Charters published an autobiographical account of his research in Gambia (and, briefly, in Bamako, Mali), where he met and recorded Jali Nyama Suso and other *kora* players. 'At first I was surprised at how little the music sounded like the blues', he observed, though 'the vocal timbres, the shaping of the melody, the rhythmic openness of the singing all seemed to be directly related to the blues'. Apparently he was unaware of previous writing on the possible relationship of the music of the *griots* and the blues. Among other musicians that he encountered was the balanjie (*balafon*) player, Alhaji Fabala Kanuteh, a Mandingo *griot* who recorded a remarkable narrative of the origins of the Gambian slave trade. Charters also heard the players of the *khalam*, the *riti* and the *konting*, even though he was 'surprised to hear how much Arabic influence there was in the music'.

Concentrated research on the instruments and musicians of the Senegambia was being undertaken at this time by ethnomusicologist Michael T. Coolen. His articles in specialist journals included an examination of the five-stringed *xalam (halam/khalam)* tradition among the Wolof, tracing it to the fourteenth century and comparing it with other plucked lutes played by the Mandinka, Jola, Soninke, Fulbe and other peoples of an extended region that includes Mauritania and Mali. Wolof *xalamkat* (players) employ the *fodet*, or basic rhythmic–melodic pattern appropriate to a song with primary and secondary tonal centres, and the *tukull* or instrumental 'improvisatory interlude between several statements of the fodet'. While a master musician can play the *fodet* in any tuning, tunings special to particular melodies are preferred, an approach 'analogous to that of the American folk fiddle tradition'. The one-string bowed lute *riti* was frequently played with the plucked lute, and with a tapped calabash, 'paralleled strikingly by the fiddle, banjo, and tambourine ensembles so popular in the United States in the 19th century'.

That there were dominant stringed traditions in the Senegambia and the Mande-speaking regions there is no doubt, but the question of the numbers of Africans exported from the region has to be addressed. An authority on such statistics, Philip Curtin, concluded that in the early centuries of the slave trade Senegambia was 'the largest single contributor to the repopulation of the New World'. His figures have been criticised for being too low, and recent research on the trade, including French involvement, has led to extensive revisions. His estimate of some 260,000 slaves exported in the century between 1711 and 1810 has been questioned, as Boubacar Barry states, 'for 1775 and 1786, the years for which data on all slave shipment ports are available, figures for Senegambia as a whole were 6300 slaves for the first year, 8000 for the second'. He concludes that 'on average, Senegambia exported 6000 slaves annually throughout the century'. To these figures must be added the extensive trans-Saharan trade, and the running of large British plantations in Gambia, which were farmed by thousands of slaves, prior to their being exported, as described by Lovejoy.

Summarising extensive evidence Darold D. Wax cites a number of planters and traders in North America who expressed a strong preference for slaves from the Gambia. These included planters in Georgia, though the state did not condone slavery until the mid eighteenth century, when traders commenced importing direct from Africa, with over half being from Gambia and Senegal in the period 1765–75. Holloway's Bantu figures were based on importations through Savannah, but the trade in Maryland and Virginia was as important, 52 per cent of slaves shipped to Maryland in 1750–72 also coming from Senegambia. Most authorities agree that slaves from the Senegambia and Windward Coast were believed to be quicker to learn, and suited to work as house servants and artisans, as well as to work as field hands.

Slaves were not in bondage to their owners for their musicianship, but those that displayed musical skills were soon given opportunities to use their talents, gaining privileges in the process. Owens noted, however, that other 'slave musicians regularly entertained in the quarters spontaneously, and some of the better ones practiced diligently for weeks, preparing themselves for an anticipated slave outing'. Some planters did not appreciate the music, one confiscating twenty fiddles within a year on his plantation. Yet many encouraged them, even hiring out their musicians, like the celebrated fiddler George Walker who was 'admitted, by common consent, to be the best leader of a band in all eastern and middle Virginia', as one agent cited by Bancroft advertised in 1853. 'Some of the earliest known black musicians were the fiddlers who entertained and provided popular dance music. By the 1770s as the letters of Judge James Iredell of North Carolina reveal, dancing was almost a daily activity in communities around the state' wrote Nancy R. Ping, who documented black music in Wilmington, NC, before the Civil War.

Many accounts of slaves playing music in the quarters and at the planters' houses are to be found in the great collections of 'Slave Narratives' of the Federal Writers Project and Fisk University. These have been analysed by Robert B. Winans who records that the fiddle was cited 205 times, the banjo 106 times, quills 30, patting 22, bones 15 and the guitar 15. The drum was cited only 8 times, though other forms of percussion were noted on 75 occasions. While the fiddle played solo rated 122 mentions, and the solo banjo 37, jointly they were noted 28 times and with other instruments a further 22. 'We'd go to these dances. Every gal with her beau and such music!' recalled ex-slave Betty Jones in Virginia, quoted by Julius Lester. They 'had two fiddles, two tangerines, two banjos and two sets of bones. Was a boy named Joe that used to whistle too' – Jones' exuberant memories giving meaning to the statistics.

In playing for both white and black dances, parties and functions the musicians' abilities were much sought after. The inheritors of the talents of the *griots* were also recognised for their capacity to improvise, praise, amuse or comment, as Meltzer noted. Composer Olly Wilson has observed that 'in most accounts Blacks were sought out for their peculiar ways of performing, especially for performing music for the dance. What this suggests is that the slave dance musicians performed differently from their white counterparts, that they approached the instruments with a certain stylistic bias.' The elements of such stylistic character remain the subject of much analysis, whether it is of rhythm, syncopation, form or vocal and instrumental tonality.

William Tallmadge, writing on the question of 'blue' tonality, queried, if my argument in *Savannah Syncopators* is accepted, 'how was the Muslim proclivity for pitch play and inflected pitches, maintained in North America?' Noting that inflected 'blue' tonality occurred in North America but not in Latin America, he found the solution in Appalachia and in folk music collections of Cecil Sharp and others: 'When savannah slaves arrived in this country they found a musical culture, which, instead of suppressing their own inflected practice, actually sustained and reinforced it. Later arrivals unable to dominate adopted the Muslim and white folk singers' inflected system.' In his remarkable study of the antecedents of twentieth-century popular music, entitled *Origins of the Popular Style*, Peter van der Merwe made a detailed discussion of the blues in relation to African and British traditions. With reference to African music he commented that 'the only distinction we can make with any confidence is that between the Arab-influenced savannah culture and the rest of West or Central Africa'.

Since *Savannah Syncopators*, 'it has become orthodox to take note of the Afro-Arab element in North American music. But even here we must tread carefully', Van der Merwe cautioned. Nevertheless, he acknowledged that 'before we can fully account for the blues . . . we must look further north, to the Arab-influenced savannah. The famous hollers, those rhapsodic forerunners of the early blues, seem to have derived as much from the savannah as from the coastal style.' Not surprisingly, as the savannah supported a plantation culture which, in Barry's documentation, was of immense proportions, some plantations working as many as 5,000 slaves each, their crops produced for export and for victualling the slave ships and the 'factories' where traders held the captives. Such work songs and holler traditions persisted in the Senegambia at least until the 1960s.

Hollers, though they may be significant forerunners, are not the whole of the blues; their free form does not correspond with blues structures. Harriet Ottenheimer suggested that hollers may have developed from street cries, which were rarely noted by Europeans by whom 'they would have been considered as such an ordinary, everyday, functional occurrence that they would not have been written about'. Her observation was based on speculation and not research: hardly any form of popular vocal apart from the ballads was more extensively documented than the street cries of London, Paris, Basle, Prague and throughout Europe, the earliest collections dating from the sixteenth century, as has been copiously demonstrated by Massin, for instance. The music of the cries was noted by Thomas Morley and others, and inspired the compositions of, for example, William Byrd. As called vocals they may be compared, but direct links with black American hollers are not evident, any more than they are in her example of a song from the Comoro Islands (near Madagascar). It is Ottenheimer's contention that the blues derives from the 'East African bardic style'.

Coolen has stated (1982) that examples of the Senegambian *fodet* (noted above), like the blues, are cyclic and usually contain at least one phrase that has a secondary tonal centre: 'A repeated musical structure of a variable number of beats, the fodet displays remarkable similarities to blues structure.' In his view its similarity 'is so close that it would have been predisposed to combine syncretically with whatever elements helped shape the blues'. Van der Merwe goes even further, claiming that the 'music of the banjo-like West African lutes . . . uses a shifting-level harmonic technique which may well lie behind the boogie-woogie piano style'. He argues, however, that the transformation of African idioms in the blues was one of limitation, the modes simplified to the bare tonic triad, and cadences to the dropping third. In effect, he was agreeing with Tallmadge, believing that much of this reduction was largely due to the catalytic influence of British folk styles.

Quite the most exhaustive analysis of the music of Africa and of the blues both in its forms as a distinct idiom, and as played by early jazz musicians, has been made by Gerhard Kubik. For forty years Kubik has done extensive field-work and recording in countries throughout

Sub-Saharan Africa, and has written frequently of the relationship of some African traditions to Afro-Brazilian music. He draws upon his researches in Malawi, Namibia, Uganda, Zambia, Congo/Zaire and elsewhere in Central and Southern Africa to examine aspects of African rhythm, instrumental and vocal tonality, and more recent developments in guitar playing. Long associated with studies in Angola and Congo, Kubik might be expected to bring strong evidence to support Holloway's arguments for African elements in blues origins from that region. Indeed, he does identify part of the area as an 'intensity zone of monochord zithers' comparing them, with David Evans' help, with the diddley-bow, and, creeping into Namibia, identifies the 'areas with mouth bows'.

Substantially, however, Kubik's conclusions are very different. His field recordings in the Cameroon, in the Hausa region of Nigeria and among the migrant Fulbe (Fulani) have led him to conclude that the 'more central Sudanic region as one core area of some of the rural blues' has the most characteristic traits: the region from 'Mali across northern Ghana and northern Nigeria into northern and central Cameroon' which he acknowledges corresponds with, but extends 'Oliver's own savanna hinterland'. Referring to *Savannah Syncopators* as 'the first attempt to paint an interconnected profile for the west central Sudanic region' he cites such observations as the importance of chordophones, of simpler rhythmic frameworks of the region, and the declamatory song style which I considered may have related to the hollers.

Kubik's book, the most exhaustive study of the relationship of African traditions to the blues, is too musicologically detailed to be summarised now. Nevertheless, it brings unparalleled field-work and erudition to the subject, supporting some of the essential arguments of the book reprinted here. This is not to say that there are no points of disagreement or contention. Kubik quotes, apparently without question, Ottenheimer's erroneous belief that the street cries were unrecognised. He contends that blues began in the 1890s, and suggests that it may have been initiated by a single charismatic performer. While this is not impossible, the fact that the identity, real or mythic, of such an innovator did not persist in the folk memory for even a couple of decades after brings such a contention into doubt. Yet I agree with him that blackface minstrelsy 'prepared the ground psychologically for the later ascendancy of ragtime and blues'.

Much has been published since the early 1970s on minstrelsy, its first exponents, its repertoire, and the performance of 'Blacks in blackface'. Dale Cockrell has traced the use of blackface in the legitimate theatre and in popular street entertainment including mummers' plays and morris dancing. Relating to these British folk traditions, blackface was popular in the United States before the advent of Dan Emmett and the Virginia Minstrels. Performed to the music of the fiddle, they may represent a form of convergence phenomenon comparable to that discussed by William Mahar. He considers with respect to minstrelsy that there was 'a greater interdependence between African-American culture and American ethnic humour than previously believed' and that the 'vigorous denials of those relationships' by many writers 'can no longer be considered valid'.

Makeshift instruments from domestic objects were used by both white and black entertainers – including the 'charivari' at Italian weddings which became the 'shivaree' of African American functions. To an extent their extempore nature may have been promoted as percussion substitutes, Marian H. Winter suggests, as an outcome of the laws of 1740 that 'stringently prohibited any Negro from "beating drums, blowing horns or the like which might on occasion be used to arouse slaves to insurrectionary activity"'. That the banjo and the fiddle were the instruments of the plantations seems undeniable, though Jackson's collection indicates that there was some disagreement between Joel Chandler Harris and George Washington Cable as to the extent of the use of the banjo, Harris contending that he had 'never seen a banjo, a tambourine, or a pair of bones, in the hands of a plantation-negro'. Cable agreed that the banjo was not very common, but maintained that it was an authentic plantation instrument, nevertheless. It seems possible that the banjo achieved greater use and attention through the minstrel show. Cable's celebrated article on 'The Dance in the Place Congo' in New Orleans was quoted from and summarised in *Savannah Syncopators*. His use of the 'ethnographic present' (the depiction of past events as if they were current) was misleading, resulting in a number of jazz writers drawing a connection with early New Orleans jazz, which Henry Kmen dismissed as erroneous. Even so, this did not invalidate the details of Cable's account, written in 1886, which was compiled from the recollections of more than a dozen contemporaries. His sources were fully acknowledged, including H. E. Krehbiel and the 'natural adept in research, Mr Lafcadio Hearn'.

It was not my thesis in *Savannah Syncopators* that African retentions constituted all of blues, nor that blues singers were the *griots* of black America. Rather, it was my contention that the blues was a product of acculturation, of the meeting of African (notably Senegambian) musical traditions with Euro-American (notably British) ones: a process, as Evans prefers to term it, of syncretism. For syncretism to take place it was essential for certain African musical practices to be retained, instrumentally, vocally and functionally, and it was to these that I wished to draw attention. Moreover, it was only possible for the genre to survive as a distinctive form if these retentions continued to be fundamental to blues vocal and instrumental expression. But acculturation implies the meeting of at least two cultural traditions, and it was to the other major constituent in the process, the survival, sharing and adaptation of the British-American folk traditions, that Tony Russell addressed his study of *Blacks, Whites and Blues*.

BIBLIOGRAPHY

Anon. 1884. 'Banjo and Bones', *Saturday Review* (London), 57 (7 June), 739–40, in Jackson (1969), 181–8.
  1972. 'Report of the International Conference on Manding Studies'. London: School of Oriental and African Studies, for the Centre for African Studies.
Bancroft, Frederic. (1931) 1959. *Slave Trading in the Old South*. New York: Frederick Ungar Publishing Co.
Barrow, David C. (1882) 1969. 'A Georgia Corn-Shucking', *Century Magazine*, 24, 873–8, in Jackson (1969), 168–76.
Barry, Boubacar. *Senegambia and the Atlantic Slave Trade*. Cambridge University Press, 1998.
Bean, Annemarie, Hatch, James V. and McNamara, Brooks (eds.). 1996. *Inside the Minstrel Mask: Readings in Nineteenth Century Blackface Minstrelsy*. Hanover NH: Wesleyan University Press.

Bebey, Francis. 1975. *African Music. A People's Art*. London: George G. Harrap and Co.

Charters, Samuel. 1982. *The Roots of the Blues*. Boston, London: Marion Byars.

Cockrell, Dale. 1997. *Demons of Disorder: Early Blackface Minstrels and their World*. Cambridge University Press.

Coolen, Michael Theodore. 1982. 'The Fodet: A Senegambian Origin for the Blues?' *Black Perspective in Music* (*BPM*), 10:1, 69–84.

— 1984. 'Senegambian Archetypes for the American Folk Banjo', *Western Folklore*, 43: 2, 117–32.

— 1991. 'Senegambian Influences on Afro-American Musical Culture', *Black Music Research Journal* (*BMRJ*).

Curtin, Philip. 1975. *Economic Change in Pre-Colonial Africa: Senegambia in the Era of the Slave Trade*. Madison: University of Wisconsin Press.

Dalby, David. 1972. 'The African Element in Black American English', in Kochman, Thomas (ed.) *Rappin' and Stylin' Out*. Urbana: University of Illinois Press, 170–86.

Evans, David. 1972. 'Africa and the Blues', *Living Blues*, 10, 27–9. Reprinted in Tracy (1999), 63–8.

— 1978. 'African Elements in Twentieth-century United States Black Folk Music', *Jazz Forschung*, 10, 85–110.

— 1990. 'African Contributions to America's Musical Heritage', *World and I*, 5:1 (January), 628–39.

Harris, Joel Chandler. 1969. 'Plantation Music', *Critic*, 3:95 (15 December 1883), 505–6, in Jackson (1969), 177–80.

Holloway, Joseph E. 1990. 'The Origins of African-American Culture', in Holloway, Joseph E. (ed.) *Africanisms in American Culture*. Bloomington: Indiana University Press, 1–18.

Holloway, Joseph E. and Vass, Winifred K. 1993. *The African Heritage of American English*. Bloomington: Indiana University Press.

Jackson, Bruce (ed.). 1969. *The Negro and His Music in Nineteenth-Century Periodicals*. Austin: University of Texas Press.

Jatta, Sidia. 1985. 'Born Musicians: Traditional music from the Gambia', in Haydon, Geoffrey and Marks, Dennis (eds.) *Repercussions. A Celebration of African-American Music*. London: Century Publishing.

Kmen, Henry A. 1972. 'The Roots of Jazz and the Dance in Place Congo: A Re-Appraisal', *Yearbook for Inter-American Musical Research*, 5–16.

Kubik, Gerhard. 1999. *Africa and the Blues*. Jackson: University Press of Mississippi.

Lester, Julius. 1968. *To Be a Slave*. London: Longman.

Lovejoy, Paul E. 1983. *Transformations in Slavery: A History of Slavery in America*. Cambridge University Press.

Mahar, William J. 1991. 'Ethiopian Skits and Sketches: Contents of Blackface Minstrelsy, 1840–1890', in Bean *et al.* (1996), 179–222.

Massin. 1978. *Les cris de la ville. Commerces ambulants et petits métiers de la rue*. Paris: Editions Gallimard.

Meltzer, Milton (ed.). 1964. *In Their Own Words: A History of the American Negro*. Vol. I. New York: n.p.

Nketia, J. H. Kwabena. 1976. *The Music of Africa*. London: Victor Gollancz.
    1973. 'African and African-American Music', *BPM*, 1:1, 9.

Olbrechts, Frans M. 1959. *Les arts plastiques de Congo Belge*. Brussels: Erasme.

Oliver, Paul. 1972. 'Some Comments: African Influence and the Blues', *Living Blues*, 8, 13–17. Reprinted in Tracy (1999), 57–62.
    1973. 'Echoes of the Jungle?' *Living Blues*, 13, 29–32. Reprinted in Tracy (1999), 69–75.

Ottenheimer, Harriet Joseph. 1987. 'The Bardic Origins of the Blues', *World and I*, 2:11 (November), 492–503.

Owens, Leslie Howard. 1976. *This Species of Property: Slave Life and Culture in the Old South*. New York: Oxford University Press.

Ping, Nancy R. 1980. 'Black Music Activities in Antebellum Wilmington, N. Carolina', *BPM*, 8:2, 139–56.

Southern, Eileen (ed.). 1971. *Readings in Black American Music*. New York: W. W. Norton and Company.

Summers, Lynn S. 1971. 'African Influence and the Blues: An Interview with Richard A. Waterman', *Living Blues*, 1:6, 30–6.

Tallmadge, William. 1984. 'Blue Notes and Blue Tonality', *BPM*, 1:6, 161–2.

Tracy, Steven C. (ed.). 1999. *Write Me a Few of Your Lines: A Blues Reader*. Amherst: University of Massachusetts Press.

Van der Merwe, Peter. 1984. *Origins of the Popular Style. The Antecedents of Twentieth-century Popular Music*. Oxford: Clarendon Press.

Vass, Winfred Kellersberger. 1979. *The Bantu-Speaking Heritage of the United States*. Los Angeles: UCLA Center for Afro-American Studies.

Waterman, Richard A. 1952. 'African Influence on the Music of the Americas', in Tax, Sol (ed.) *Acculturation in the Americas*. University of Chicago Press, 207–18. Reprinted in Tracy (1999).
    1963. 'On Flogging a Dead Horse: Lessons Learned from the Africanisms Controversy', *Ethnomusicology*, 7, 1–83.

Wax, Darold D. 1973. 'Preference for Slaves in Colonial America', *Journal of Negro History*, 43:4, 371–401.

1978. 'Black Immigrants: The Slave Trade in Colonial Maryland', *Maryland Historical Magazine*, 73:1, 30–45.

1984. 'New Negroes are Always in Demand; The Slave Trade in Eighteenth Century Georgia', *Georgia Historical Quarterly*, 48:2, 193–220.

Winans, Robert B. 1990. 'Instrumental Music in the Ex-Slave Narratives', *BMRJ*, 10:1, 44–53.

Winter, Marian Hannah. 1997. 'Juba and American Minstrelsy', in Bean *et al.* (1996), 223–41.

Wood, Peter H. 1974. *Black Majority*. New York: Alfred K. Knopf.

GLOSSARY OF AFRICAN INSTRUMENTS

Apart from the instruments mentioned in the text, a number of instruments used by West African peoples have been added to this glossary, which, however, is representative only and in no way complete. Most of the West African instruments listed may be heard on recordings issued in Europe and the United States. The names of the instruments vary from tribe to tribe and their spelling has not been standardised.

abeng, collective term for horn instruments among Akan peoples

abitin, Timne term for drum, Sierra Leone

adabatram, Ewe war drum, Ghana and Togoland

adedemma, Akan vertical pegged drum with wedged feet

adewu, Ewe drum for hunting ceremonial, Ghana

agonga, cylindrical drum of the Tuareg, Mali and Niger

akalumbe, harp of the Timne, Sierra Leone

akonde, Susu fiddle, Sierra Leone

akoroma, drum of Ashanti warrior societies

akrima, egg-cup shaped drum, hand beaten, Dahomey

akukuadwo, semi-cylindrical, slightly tapered Ashanti (Asante) drum

algaïta, shawm of the Hausa and Tuareg, but widely used in Savannah regions

anuman, whistle of the Baule, Ivory Coast

apentemma, large bottle-shaped stem Ashanti drum used in Akan orchestras

asiko, frame drum of the Yoruba, Western Nigeria and Dahomey

asokoben, Ashanti elephant tusk horn

assakhalabo, water drum made from floating calabash, Tuareg atsimevu, five-foot-long master drum of Ewe drum orchestras, Ghana and Togo

atukpani, pair of drums, male and female, of Ewe drum orchestra

atumpan, pair of stem drums, male and female; principal talking drums of Ashanti

bala, correct term for West African xylophone in Guinea, Senegal, Mali: see *balafon*

balafon (also *balafou, balafeu*), European term for the **bala**. *Fo* or *fon* means, literally, 'to speak'

bania, Senegal lute with three or four strings, which probably gave its name to the banjo

banjar (also **banger**), early name for the banjo in North America

banjo, plucked chordophone of West African origin, developed in North America, originally with four strings, the fifth being added in the early nineteenth century

baradundu, calabash drum of the Dyoula

baratyu, Mandingo calabash drum similar to the baradundu

bàtá, drum family used for the worship of Sàngó. Yoruba, Western Nigeria; also conical drum with laced heads of the Yoruba

batá, drum of the Nago of Dahomey

batta, spherical calabash drum of the Hausa, Northern Nigeria

belly harp, European term for West African harp with half-gourd resonator held against the stomach

bennde, large drum of the Dyoula

beta, musical bow of the Ewe, Togo

bolange, Susu xylophone with twenty wooden bars on frame structure

bolo, three-stringed harp-lute of the Fulah, Sierra Leone

bolon, three-stringed harp of the Malinke and Senufo, Mali and Ivory Coast

bondofo, Mandingo side-blown antelope horn

bones, animal bones, shaped and carved to present flat surfaces which clack when vibrated between the fingers, North America

boumpa, length of cane, slit and side-blown, with calabash resonators at each end, Upper Volta

b'ru, trumpet of the Dyoula

bulu, side-blown horn, Mende, Sierra Leone

bulumbata, large arched harp of Senegambia, with gourd resonator, ten strings, and metal vibrator

buru, Mandingo side-blown horn, made of wood or ivory

buru, Bambara horn, Upper Volta

dale, Lobi drum made from neck of a broken pot

dawuro, Ashanti slit gong or conical gong

donno, hour-glass tension drum of the Ashanti, Ghana

dundu, widespread term for a drum among Mandingo- and Mende-speaking peoples

dundufa, two-headed drum played to stimulate trade for butchers among Hausa

dundun, large hour-glass tension drum, Yoruba of Western Nigeria and Dahomey

dyegele, Senufo xylophone with twelve bars on wood frame

earth bow, presumed origin of the North American washtub bass, made from hide membrane stretched over depression in the ground. String attached to one side of the depression, and to a length of wood. Generally found in Congo and Central Africa

ekpe, friction drum of Efik in South-East Nigeria

elong, xylophone of fourteen bars, Lobi of Upper Volta: cf. **gil**

etwie, friction drum of the Baoule, used to imitate a leopard

farai, medium-length horn, Northern Nigeria

furi, three-hole end-blown flute, Niger

gah-gah, percussion gourd widely used by Savannah *griots*

ganga, Hausa drum. Generic term for drum in Upper Volta, Niger, Northern Nigeria

gangalan, Tuareg cylindrical drum

gangana, Dogon percussion bell

gangano, drum of the Mossi, Upper Volta

gankogui, clapperless bell of the Ewe, Ghana

garaya, two-stringed lute, over five feet long including resonator, Niger

gil, xylophone of the Ghana and Ivory Coast Lobi

gimbeh, bottle-shaped drum with metal vibrators attached, Fulah, Sierra Leone

gingiru, Dogon harp-lute, Mali

gnaghour, bowed monochord

goge, **gogué**, calabash fiddle with single string of hair, played with arched bow, widely used among savannah peoples

gogeru, Fulbe fiddle with two or three strings, Cameroun

goly, Baoule monochord, Ivory Coast

gong-gong, European/pidgin term for the Ashanti clapperless bell or gong

gorong, Wolof upright log drum, Senegal and Gambia

gouroumi, three-string lute, over a metre in length, Niger

gudu-gudu, Yoruba kettledrum, Western Nigeria and Dahomey

gui dounou, Malinke water drum of similar kind to the Tuareg type. Guinea

halam, five-stringed lute of the Wolof and other Senegambian tribes, with three open strings

harp lute, chordophone indigenous to West Africa with the strings in a plane rising vertically from the belly of the instrument

igbin, drum-family for the worship of Obàtálá, Yoruba

ikoro, Ibo ritual long drum, Nigerian Eastern region

inzad, imzhad, Tuareg bowed monochord, generally played by the women

isanzi, West African sansa, or 'thumb piano'

iyá ilù, Yoruba tension drum in dun-dun and bàtá orchestras

jawbone, jawbone of a mule, ass, cow or other domestic animal used as a rattle. A North American plantation instrument. The jawbone was also struck or played with a nail or length of iron

jojo, drum of the Fulbe, Senegal

kakaki, long trumpet of Nigerian emirates, six feet or more in length

kalangual, Fulbe hour-glass drum, Cameroun

kalungu, Hausa hour-glass drum, Nigeria

kambreh, plectrum lute played widely in the savannah regions – Niger, Sierra Leone and Senegal

kanango, Yoruba hour-glass tension drum

kani, triangular frame zither with seven strings, Kru, Sierra Leone

karaning, Mandingo monochord spike fiddle

kasso, harp lute of the Gambia with twenty-two strings, cf. *seron, kora*

kazoo, submarine-shaped tube mirliton, played in blues bands

kele, drum of the Nago, Dahomey

kele, side-blown flute of the Dogon, Mali

kele, Mende slit-drum with three slits along its length, Sierra Leone

kete, four-hole notched flute, Ghana: also Ashanti drum orchestra for chiefs

khalam, alternative spelling for the Wolof **halam** lute

kidi, Ewe vertical barrel drum, Ghana and Togoland

ko, hunter's harp of the Dan, Ivory Coast, with six strings in two parallel rows

komo, two-stringed lute with long bowl of calabash and with metal vibrator, Nigeria, Hausa

kone, sansa of Upper Volta

koni, six-stringed harp-lute played for hunting by the Malinke and borrowed by the Senufo, Guinea and Ivory Coast

kontigui, plucked monochord of the Songhai, Niger

koonting, three-stringed Mandingo lute, as noted by Mungo Park

kor, stem-based drum, Lobi

kora, massive twenty-one-stringed harp-lute of the Senegal *griots*

kori, six-stringed harp-lute of the Senufo, Ivory Coast

korro, Mungo Park's term for the *kora*

kukuma, horsehair-strung monochord bowed fiddle, Hausa, Nigeria

kundye, Soso monochord bowed fiddle, Guinea

kunting, three-stringed Mandingo lute

kusukurum, master drum used in *apirede* orchestras of Ashanti paramount chiefs, Ghana

kyirem, drum orchestra for Ashanti warrior associations

lamba, large drum of the Wolof, Senegambia

lontoré, flute of Upper Volta tribes

lunga, large drum of the Mossi, Upper Volta

lunga, Dyoula hour-glass drum

marimba, African xylophone with slats of wood on a frame, each slat having a gourd resonator. The marimba was brought to Central and South America

marimba brett, African sansa as noted by Cable in New Orleans

musical bow, hunting bow used as a musical instrument, or musical arc patterned on the hunting bow, tapped or plucked, with sometimes a gourd resonator, or with the mouth used as a resonator. In the latter instance known as a *mouth bow*. Widely found in hunting cultures not only in Africa

mvet, four-string lyre with calabash resonator, Cameroun

ngenge, Fula monochord spike fiddle with movable bridge, Sierra Leone

ngùne, Mandingo monochord fiddle, Guinea

nsambi, home-made fiddle, of European influence, Congo

ntumpan, alternative spelling for **atumpan**

odurugya, Ashanti end-blown cane flute, Ghana

ogidàn drums, drum orchestra used for the worship of *Ogun*, Yoruba, Nigeria

pampane, long wooden trumpet, Fulbe

papo, side-blown split reed wind instrument with calabash resonators, Dahomey

para, arched harp, Niger

petia, drum used in Ashanti *adowa* bands for social dancing

pira, iron castanets to accompany Lobi orchestras, Ghana and Ivory Coast

pomsa, two-string lute, Niger

raft zither, **raft harp**, zither made of several lengths of cane bound together in a raft-like form. Each cane has a split length which forms the 'string', the lengths being raised over cane bridges

ramkie, **remkie**, three- or four-stringed guitar related to the Portuguese *rabequinha* brought from Malabar to South Africa and developed by the Cape Hottentots. Also *rábekin, ramakienjo, raamakie, ramki*

rasp, notched wood, gourd or metal instrument against which a rod is moved rhythmically. The **washboard** may be a North American equivalent

rattle, African rattles are frequently made of gourds with beans inside or strung on the outside of the instrument. Other rattles may be woven of basketwork

riti, Gambian monochord spike fiddle

riti, four-string spike fiddle, Guinea

sabar, long Wolof hour-glass drum

sangu, Ewe sansa

sanku, harp-lute with two rows of strings, Guinea

sansa, sanza, African 'thumb piano', or linguaphone, with a number of metal or cane tongues raised over a bridge. Sansas may be built over gourds or small containers and are played with thumbs or with fingers of both hands

seke, calabash rattle, Ghana

sérendou, side-blown flute played by herders in Upper Volta

seron, Malinke variant of the *kora* with fifteen to twenty strings

shekere, gourd rattle of the Yoruba

simbing, seven-stringed lute-harp, Mandingo

slit drums, log or bamboo drums with longitudinal slits opening to a hollowed interior

sogo, Ewe barrel-shaped drum, Ghana

soku, Mandingo bowed chordophone

stickado, Ibo instrument probably in xylophone form, though a slapstick has also been suggested

tabala, large sacred drum of the Wolof. Also a Mandingo warning drum

tabl, generic term for drum in Arab countries

tama, Senegalese tension drum, held under armpit

tamande, Mandingo drum, generic term: also **tomba**

tamatama, Tuareg term for drum

tangtang, Mandingo drum with one end open

tension drum, drum of hour-glass shape with skin membranes at both ends. These are tightened by thongs which extend between both heads and are compressed by the elbow or upper arm

tinde, Tuareg drum played by the women. It consists of a length of hide hand-held in tension over a mortar or gourd vessel

tomba, Mandingo hour-glass drum

washboard, washwoman's rubbing board, used as a rhythm instrument by rubbing its surface with spoons, nails, or with the fingers clad in thimbles. Rhythm instrument in blues bands in the United States

washtub bass, inverted washtub with string attached to one side and affixed to the end of a broom-handle held against the rim. When tautened it can be used as a one-string bass. May be derived from the **earth bow** (q.v.)

water drum, water gourd, an upturned calabash floating in a larger vessel half filled with water. The inner calabash is played with sticks

West African harp, indigenous harp made from a number of separately strung arcs joined at a common stem or resonator

xylophone, Melanesian in origin and brought via Madagascar to Africa. The African xylophone in its simplest form consists of a number of logs placed across the legs of the player. More advanced xylophones are fixed to a frame or slung over a trough frame. Under the slats of the latter, gourds are placed as resonators

zanze, alternative spelling for sansa

Further details on musical instruments of West Africa may be found in the books and other references cited in the notes to chapters; in the liner notes to issued recordings; in 'Terms for Musical Instruments in the Sudanic Languages', by Helen E. Hause, in *Supplement to the Journal of the American Oriental Society*, 68 (1948); and in *Musical Instruments, A Comprehensive Dictionary*, which has a detailed bibliography, by Sibyl Marcuse, published by Doubleday and Co., USA, 1964, and *Country Life*, UK, 1966.

GLOSSARY OF TRIBES AND PEOPLE

Tribes and peoples of Africa mentioned in the text are listed. Their location in relation to national political boundaries is given, but such boundaries have little relation to the distribution of tribes. For the territorial areas where the peoples are centred see the map in fig. 16. The spelling of African tribal names is not standardised but English and French alternatives are given where relevant.

Akan. Peoples of Ashanti and related regions, Ghana and Ivory Coast
Ashanti (Asante). Dominant people of a federation of tribes in the old Gold Coast (Ghana)

Bambara, Bamana. Extensive savannah people in south-west Mali
Baule, Baoule. Kwa-speaking people, one of the Akan tribes, of Ivory Coast
Beriberi, Béri-béri. Kanuric people situated north of the Hausa in Bornu province
Bobo. Tribe of Upper Volta (Burkina Faso)
Busanni, Boussani. Tribe of Nigritic stock, Burkina Faso

Dahomeans (Fon). Correctly termed Fon, but frequently identified with Dahomey (now Benin), where they live
Dan. Tribe in Ivory Coast to north-west of region close to Guinea Malinke
Diola, Diola-Fogny. Small coastal tribe of the Basse Casamance of Senegal
Dioula, Dyoula. Scattered people of Soninke stock, mainly in Upper Volta (Burkina Faso). Not related to Diola, Diola-Fogny (q.v.)
Dogon. Cliff-dwelling people of Mali

Efik. Bantoid-speaking people of southern Nigeria

Ekoi. South-west Nigerian people of Cross River region

Ewe. Twi-speaking people of Togoland and eastern Ghana, related to Fon of Dahomey (Benin)

Fanti. Small coastal tribe, Ghana

Fon. Dahomey people related to Ewe – *see* **Dahomeans**

Fra-Fra. Sub-tribe of Grusi (Gurunsi) complex, Northern Ghana

Fula, Foulah, Fulani, Fulbe, Peul. Nomadic, or semi-nomadic, pastoral people, widely scattered across West Africa. Other spellings include the early Feloop. Some Fulani are relatively settled, notably those of the Fouta Toro region of Senegal

Ga. Small coastal tribe in Ghana in whose territory stood a number of slave castles

Ghimira, Gidole. Peoples of Ethiopia

Grusi, Grunshi, Gurunsi. Complex of small tribes in border region of Ghana and Upper Volta – see also **Fra-Fra**

Guere, Guere-Wobe, Ngere. Tribe related to the Dan, Ivory Coast

Hausa, Haoussa. Extensive Muslim people in northern Nigeria, and Niger

Ibo. Large tribe of eastern region of Nigeria (Biafra)

Ila. Tribe in the Middle Zambesi region

Jolof, Jaloff. *See* **Wolof**

Kagoro. Scattered people part Bambara, Soninke and Fulani

Kru. Coastal tribal complex, Liberia

Lobi. People inhabiting region at intersection of Burkina Faso, Ivory Coast and Ghana

Malinke. Extensively distributed people occupying large areas of Senegal, Guinea and western Ivory Coast

Mande, Manding, Mandingo. Mande-speaking peoples of which the Malinke are the largest. Many references to 'Mandingo' are really to Malinke, but also applied loosely to Bambara, Soninke and others

Mandingo. *See* **Mande**
Mende. Sierra Leone tribe situated near the coast
Mina. Small tribe related to Ewe, Ghana and Togo
Mossi. Widely distributed people of Mali and Upper Volta

Nupe. Southern Nigerian complex of tribes
Nzima. Small coastal tribe, Ghana

Peul. *See* **Fulani**
Pygmies. Diminutive forest-dwelling people of the Congo

Senufo. Extensively distributed people of the Ivory Coast
Songhai. Ancient people of northern savannah region of Niger and Mali and
    of distinct linguistic stock
Soninke. Muslim people related to Malinke, inhabiting north-western Mali and
    northern Senegal
Susu. Moslem coastal tribe, Guinea

Temne. Coastal tribe, Sierra Leone
Toma. Tribe related to the Dan, Sierra Leone and Liberia interior
Tonga. People of the Middle Zambesi
Tuareg. Nomadic people of Berber stock but independent culture, extensively
    distributed, including Niger, Mali
Twi. Complex of tribes speaking Twi languages. *See* **Ashanti, Ewe**

Vai. Small coastal tribe, Sierra Leone, Ivory Coast and Liberia

Wolof, Jaloff, Jolof. Large indigenous tribe in the Senegambia
Wyda, Whydah. Coastal tribe of Dahomey engaged in the slave trade

Yoruba. Widely distributed people of western Nigeria and Dahomey (Benin)

RECORD LIST

The recordings listed here were issued on long-playing vinyl discs. Few items have been reissued on CD, but Folkways records may be obtained on cassette from the Smithsonian Institution, Washington, DC.

COMPARATIVE RECORDINGS

NEGRO FOLK MUSIC OF AFRICA AND AMERICA
Edited by Harold Courlander   Ethnic Folkways FE4500 (two records)
Twenty-four examples from Africa and the Americas. West Africa represented by Ibo and Yoruba recordings only. United States – examples of unaccompanied songs only. Items of interest include a Juba dance from Haiti and Shango cult song from Trinidad recorded by Herskovits.

AFRICAN AND AFRO-AMERICAN DRUMS
Edited by Harold Courlander   Ethnic Folkways FE4502 (two records)
Similar collection with West African examples from the Yoruba only. North American items confined to jazz drumming by Baby Dodds, and a remarkable children's street band recorded in New York.

AFRICAN COLLECTIONS

AFRIQUE NOIRE: Panorama de la Musique Instrumentale
                                                    Bam (France) LD409A
A broad selection edited by Charles Duvelle of Ocora recordings, including Lobi and Malinke xylophones, lute and bowed monochords from Niger and drum orchestras in Dahomey.

SOUNDS OF AFRICA, edited by Andrew Tracey

Verve Forecast (A) FVS9510

Stereo collection of fragmentary recordings. Unequal, but includes Mali lutes, Senegal *kora*.

MUSIC FROM WEST AFRICA, recorded by Gilbert Rouget

Vogue (F) LVLX193

Recordings of Baoulé in Ivory Coast with drum orchestras, flutes, xylophone, contrasted with Malinké recordings from Guinea including outstanding xylophone orchestras, *kora*, water-drum, harp and harp-lute. Valuable contrast of forest and savannah cultures.

PONDO KAKOU, recorded by Gilbert Rouget

Vogue (F) MC20.141

Baoulé ritual contrasted with Yoruba drums from Dahomey and recordings of harps and harp-lutes of the Malinké in Guinea.

WEST AFRICAN RAIN FOREST PEOPLES

DRUMS OF THE YORUBA OF NIGERIA   Ethnic Folkways (A) FE4441
Recorded by William Bascom, examples of *igbin* drums, *dundun* drums and *bàtá* drums. Also recordings of Sàngó cult drumming.

MUSIQUES DAHOMÉENNES, recorded by Charles Duvelle

Ocora OCR17

Drum orchestras accompanying dances, and ritual drumming. Also popular orchestra with drums, *sansa* and monochord. Side-blown flutes and musical bow.

MUSIQUE KABRÉ (North Togoland)   Ocora (F) OCR16
Instrumentally primitive bamboo flutes and log xylophone, but including remarkable 'lithophone' rhythms on basalt stones. Recorded by Raymond Verdier.

THE BAOULÉ OF THE IVORY COAST, recorded by Donald Thurow

Ethnic Folkways FE4476

MUSIQUE BAOULÉ KODÈ, recorded by Charles Duvelle

Ocora (F) OCR34

Mainly drum orchestras with both featuring Goli festival and extended 'Congassa' ritual of Baoulé Kodè. Former record has horns, flute and rare Baoulé harp.

THE MUSIC OF THE DAN, recorded by Hugo Zemp

Baren Reiter (UNESCO) BM30L2301

Drums for various rites and accompanying work. Also mirlitons, and hunter's harp borrowed from Malinké. Includes Malinké musicians from north.

FOLK MUSIC OF LIBERIA, recorded by Packard Okie

Ethnic Folkways (A) FE4465

Various tribes and descendants of repatriated slaves. Recordings of work songs, slit drums, belly harp and Mandingo *balafon* played by Mandingo settlers from north.

WEST AFRICAN SAVANNAH PEOPLES

DANSES ET CHANTS BAMOUN, recorded by Michel Houdry

Ocora (F) SOR3

Sansa, Cameroon lyre *mvet*, drums and horns for Sultans of Bamoun.

ANTHOLOGIE DE LA MUSIQUE DU TCHAD
Recorded by Charles Duvelle and Michel Vuylstèke

Ocora (F) OCR36/37/38 (three records)

Extensive survey of music of the Sara, the peoples of west Mayo-Kebbi and professional Islamic musicians. Drums, xylophones, horns, lutes, arc-harps, *algaïta* and long trumpets of considerable diversity of styles.

NIGERIA – HAUSA MUSIC, Volumes One and Two
Recorded by David Wason Ames

Baren Reiter (UNESCO) BM30L2306 and BM30L2307

Twenty-four items showing wide range of Hausa music illustrating Ames' classification of functions of music in this society. Drums, lutes, fiddles, orchestras for *bori* cult, for accompanying trades and work. Music of professional entertainers.

NIGER – LA MUSIQUE DES GRIOTS   Ocora (F) OCR20
Recorded by Tolia Nikiprowetzky; gives excellent picture of the music of *griots*, solo, duet and in orchestras, including *goge, godjié, garaya*.

NOMADES DU NIGER (Tuareg and Bororo), recorded by Tolia Nikiprowetzky   Ocora (F) OCR29

TUAREG MUSIC OF THE SOUTHERN SAHARA
Recorded by Finola and Geoffrey Holiday

Ethnic Folkways FE4470

The former includes virtuoso performances on the *inzad* one-string fiddle. Also water drums and flute. The Folkways issue mainly features songs with water drum and a striking Tazenkharet dance shared with Arabs and Negro Africans.

MUSIC OF MALI, recorded by Betty and W. Gurnce Dyer

Ethnic Folkways FE4338

LES DOGON, recorded by François Di Dio   Ocora (F) OCR33
Both records emphasise the drum music of the Dogon on calabash drums. The former also has recordings from Timbuktu and Tuareg lute players.

HAUTE VOLTA, recorded by Charles Duvelle   Ocora (F) SOR10
A striking collection of Bambara xylophone, *kondé* lute, musical bow, *sansa*, calabash drum orchestra from various parts of Upper Volta (Burkina Faso).

WOLOF MUSIC OF SENEGAL AND THE GAMBIA, recorded by David Ames

Ethnic Folkways FE4462

Professional entertainers and story tellers (*gewel*), accompanied by *halam*. Also drum rhythms for dances among the Wolof.

THE MUSIC OF THE DIOLA-FOGNY OF THE CASAMANCE, SENEGAL
Recorded by J. David Sapir   Ethnic Folkways (A) FE4323
Important recordings of Diola work-songs with extensive notes and translations. Also extempore song, and fetish dances.

LA MUSIQUE DES GRIOTS – SENEGAL, recorded by Tolia Nikiprowetzky

Ocora (F) OCR15

Outstanding collection of the music of the *griots* with exceptional examples of *kora*, monochords, solo, duet and group performances, from tribes represented in Senegal.

2 BLACKS, WHITES AND BLUES

Tony Russell

FOREWORD

This book attempts to draw together two lines of discussion that have up to now been almost completely separate. There are numerous books and articles on Afro-American folk music, and some on white American folk music, but this is the first essay which looks at both traditions and tries to describe their interaction. I hope it will be, if nothing else, a stimulus to new arguments and research topics, and a lead to new listening experiences.

I have not been stringent with terminology. White traditions are described indiscriminately as 'country', 'hillbilly' and 'old time'; 'blues' sometimes stands for 'black blues' and sometimes does not. I have not always stated the colour of a musician; in such cases it should be obvious from the context. Nor is there much biography, but gaps can be filled by consulting the standard works listed in the Bibliography. I have assumed an acquaintance with American folk music in my reader, but I have certainly not written for expert collectors or ethnomusicologists.

The evidence for musical exchange is enormous, and starts piling up as far back as the 1820s. I could not cover a century and a half in this book, so I brought my account to a ragged halt in the late 1930s. The subsequent thirty-odd years will be the subject of a second volume.

In writing this essay I plundered the published and unpublished work of many researchers, to whom I apologise – for space prevented me from acknowledging them very often in the text – and give hearty thanks. Information on black matters came from Bruce Bastin, John Houlston

Cowley, Bob Dixon, David Evans, John Godrich, Bob Groom of *Blues World*, Karl Gert zur Heide, Don Kent, and Mike Leadbitter and Simon Napier of *Blues Unlimited*; on white, from Joe E. Bussard, Jr, John Cohen, Norm Cohen of the John Edwards Memorial Foundation, Dave Freeman of County Records, Archie Green, John B. Larsen and Bill C. Malone. Albert McCarthy of *Jazz Monthly* lent magazines, George Tye photographs, Bert Whyatt recording-files; Dave Crosbie, David Pritchard, Francis Smith, Jim Vyse and David West assembled invaluable tapes. I owe much to Chris Comber, who supplied photographs, tapes and information without stint, and introduced me to some great music; much, too, to my friend and fellow enthusiast Bob Yates, who gave me access to many a quaint and curious volume of forgotten lore.

To the Series Editor, Paul Oliver, I owe a tremendous debt. Not content with giving me the opportunity to write this book, he provided records, photographic material, information and encouragement. For all these, but especially for the constant and friendly encouragement, my deepest thanks.

I built this book on a conviction: that, whether or not my own views meant anything to them, the musicians I was talking about had something worthwhile to say. Yet many of them, including some of the greatest artists, are almost forgotten. I shall be very happy if *Blacks, Whites and Blues* helps to give them the recognition they deserve.

8 · MINSTRELSY

'It's not very much of song that Negro got from white, because Negro people always was a kind of a singing group of people. You see, we was kind of a little different; we were a segregated bunch from down among the white people. The white man could get education and he could learn proper things like read a note, and the Negro couldn't. All he had to get from his music what God give him in his heart. And that's the only thing he got. And he didn't get that from the white man; God give it to him.'

The speaker was Willie Thomas, factory janitor and guitarist of Scotlandville, LA, talking to Paul Oliver in 1960. He is a preacher, which explains his notion of the divine inspiration of black song; surprisingly, he is also a blues singer. (Surprisingly, because to the religious man blues are devil music; 'A man who's singing the blues', said Lil' Son Jackson in retirement, 'I think it's a sin because it cause other people to sin.' But Thomas takes a broad and kindly view: 'It ain't nothin' to do with bein' against God . . . if it comes nach'al, *church* people sing the blues.') It is not evident from his remarks that Thomas was equating black song with the blues; but he was born in 1912, and by the time he was listening at all closely to music the blues had risen to great heights of popularity. The first generation of blues singers was born twenty or thirty years earlier.

What he did not say was whether Whites got very much of song from black people. There were many thousands of poor Whites who couldn't get education, nor learn to read a note; and most rural communities could fairly claim to have been 'singing groups of people' for as long as anyone could remember. It would be possible to make a case for an equally independent tradition of white song. In fact, neither tradition developed independently of the other; the races lived too close together, and each relied upon the other's support too much for any real cultural separation. 'Negro entered into White man', wrote W. J. Cash, 'as profoundly as White man entered into Negro – subtly influencing every gesture, every word, every emotion and idea, every attitude.' Though the Blacks were 'a segregated bunch', they received and passed out countless musical ideas from surrounding peoples – not merely southern, Anglo-Saxon Whites, but French-speaking cajuns, Mexicans, and perhaps even the German-, Italian- and Swedish-speaking immigrants. Their influence upon the folk music of other ethnic groups has perhaps been greater than the sum of influences from those peoples upon themselves, but in this book I hope to look at a few examples of both black-on-white and white-on-black impressions. The black man's contribution to the body of world folk music is nowadays widely recognised, but too often it is thought to stop at the blues, jazz and spirituals: the black people's most personal creations. It is nearly as important to see that white country music in America would not have its present form if it were not for black workmanship. Indeed, the only way to understand fully the various folk musics of America is to see them as units in a whole; as traditions with, to be sure, a certain degree of independence, but possessing an overall unity.

Consider the landscape. A musician would be open to sounds from every direction: from family and friends, from field and railroad yard, lumber camp and mine; from street singers and travelling show musicians; from phonograph records and radio; from dances and suppers and camp-meetings and carnivals; from fellow prisoners in jails, from fellow workmen everywhere. A white youngster could learn a song or a tune not only in the bosom of his family but from their black employees – mammy, Uncle Remus or anyone else. Racial antipathy, of course, hampered the free exchange of musical ideas, and it will become clear, in this book, that interaction was more fertile in areas where Blacks were scattered and thus less fearful. Nevertheless, in all but the most tightly enclosed communities, there was some degree of interaction, and, as the twentieth century grew older, and group isolation rarer, the threads of the two traditions were more and more often entangled. Moreover, there were always musicians to whom musical values were more important than racist ones, men who would not care a jot if they, as Whites, happened to like black pieces, or vice versa. Again, there were certain forms of musical expression to which it seems absurd to attach any racial origin or ownership; who, for instance, can say whether harmonica solos imitating trains or hunting scenes were first played by Blacks or by Whites? And lastly, while it is possible to pick out strains that are peculiarly black or peculiarly white, what can we say about the music of those who were neither? What 'ought' to be the song of the mulatto?

The answer to most of the questions about song origins is simply that there can be no answer. We can only trace country music back into the latter part of the nineteenth century, and as far as that only with difficulty; blues are an enigma until the 'teens of the twentieth century. We can begin the story only where our information begins; and we cannot ever be sure that we are not misrepresenting history. Recordings, which are much used in this book, can tell a deceptive tale; interviews are hard to get and often hard to believe. A folk tradition has no starting point, and most folk songs are like most jokes; everybody knows them, but nobody knows who invented them.

Nevertheless, we can go back several generations and find something about the work of the Blacks and Whites as a 'singing group of people'. We can go into the churches for hymns, into the mountain villages and little-visited flatlands for Celtic ballads; but let us go rather into the theatres of the cities, for the minstrel song. Let us consider vaudeville's grandfather.

'In the eighteen-forties,' wrote Newman Ivey White, 'Negro music, for the first time, spread beyond the plantation.' Through songs like *Zip Coon* and *Jim Crow* a vogue for slave music was created which took the entertainment world by storm. A gentleman writing in *Putnam's Monthly* in 1855, and speaking as a slave-owning planter, pronounced the 'coon' songs truly representative of black music-making. Not that, on stage, they were to be heard much from Blacks; the minstrelsy of the plantation was presented by white actors in blackface. Among the most famous bands of minstrels were the Christy and Moore & Burgess troupes, both of which toured extensively in America and Europe. The performers wore evening dress, and, in the words of a Christy advertisement of about 1871, 'anything appertaining to vulgarity' was 'strictly excluded'. 'Fun', Moore & Burgess chimed in, 'Without Vulgarity'. In a Moore & Burgess songbook of the period can be seen attempts to give authenticity to the whole minstrel genre; 'undoubtedly many of the negro melodies we hear today were, roughly, songs as were sung by the slaves hundreds of years ago – music that was never put upon paper, but handed down from one band to another'. There is much virtue in that 'roughly'. This was an age, remember, when folksongs were relentlessly 'improved', even by quite reputable field collectors. The author goes on to tell a story about Eugene Stratton, the white Alsatian-American 'Whistling Coon'. Questioned about a 'peculiar and exceeding pretty song' in his repertoire, Stratton explained, 'You see that young man over there? . . . He was a slave, and the song you have just heard was one they used to sing upon their plantation. He hummed it over to me and I have set it to music. But it's a very difficult thing to set coon songs to music.' To ease the difficulty Stratton employed compositions by professional writers like Leslie Stuart, who provided him with *Little Dolly Daydream* and the immortal *Lily Of Laguna*, a 'coon' love-ditty expressed in words very far removed from plantation speech. Of course, songs like these have no folk status – though *Laguna*, as a public-house 'standard', is taking on some of the characteristics of a folk song – but they have been popular, at times, with the folk; and the minstrel show did not die in its home country, but went out on the road, bringing to the rural audiences some of the sentimental coonery and a lot of corny comic routines. (Minstrels in the South probably observed less strict canons of taste than did the original dinner-jacketed ones.)

After the blackface shows came the music-hall. It is difficult to determine which characteristics of music-hall were purely American and which English (and which shared), but each country sent popular ideas to the other, and, if Stratton and his disciple G. H. Elliott, 'The Chocolate-Coloured Coon', made one kind of Americana appealing in England, there was certainly an enthusiastic response in the States to such gems of the music-hall era as *Champagne Charlie Is My Name, If You Were The Only*

21 Charlie Poole

Girl In The World and *She Was Poor But She Was Honest*. America's own contributions were numerous and in many cases enduring; Paul Dresser's *The Letter That Never Came* (1886), Harry von Tilzer's *Good-Bye, Eliza Jane* (1903) and *A Bird In A Gilded Cage* (1900) and Charles K. Harris' *There'll Come A Time* (1895) were all recorded several times by rural singers and issued in the 'hillbilly series' of the major recording companies. Other favourites that moved from stage or drawing-room to country shack were *The Fatal Wedding* (1893) and *In The Baggage Coach Ahead* (1896), a pair of tragic songs written by Gussie L. Davis and thereafter much recorded. Ernest V. Stoneman and Charlie Poole's North Carolina Ramblers, for instance, between them recorded versions of five of the last six titles. Unlike some of the artists whose records appeared in the hillbilly listings, Stoneman and Poole were authentic countrymen, and so they sounded; but these music-hall songs had a place in their repertoire just as much as the ballads and dance-tunes. The interesting thing about Davis' compositions is that they were the work of a black man. Davis once swept the halls of the Cincinnati Conservatory of Music – 'incidentally picking up some of the elements of composition', as Spaeth remarks – and at another time was a railroad porter, which experience inspired *Baggage Coach*. He provides a copiously documentable example of a black figure passing material into white tradition (mainly white, for very few Blacks sang his ballads), but of course this is all some way beyond folk areas – at this point in tradition, at least – and it is clear from the songs themselves that Davis, like the many other black vaudevillians, was working in a style basically white in the first place. However, the acceptance of his compositions, and others like them by both black and white musicians, was so considerable in the country communities that a mention of these vaudeville days is essential in any study of early twentieth-century folksong. Rural musicians were very frequently no more than frustrated vaudevillians; and the urban parlour ballads or musical stage hits were by no means always thought too classy for reproduction in country society. For instance, there is a twenties poster advertising a visit by the Carolina Tar Heels (Doc. Walsh and Garley Foster), which, though offering 'Honest-To-Goodness String Music Of The Hills', does inform the passer-by that Doc. will 'entertain (him) with . . . old time

Southern Songs mingled with the latest Broadway Hits'. This 'unusual program of high class entertainment' was no doubt being duplicated all over the countryside. For example, by the Carter Family, whose advertisements claimed 'The Program Is Morally Good'; by McFarland and Gardner, 'The Brunswick Recording Artist (*sic*) . . . hear them in person, old songs, new songs and any thing you like to hear, on most any instrument . . . A good Time for young and old'; by the 'Rip Roarin', Snortin', Burn 'Em Up String Band', Gid Tanner's Georgia Skillet-Lickers. Tanner's men used to perform *It's A Long Way To Tipperary* and *The Dark Town Strutters' Ball*, which, published in 1912 and 1915 respectively, would scarcely have been the *latest* Broadway hits, but personal appearances by the group would no doubt have featured solo spots by their blind guitarist Riley Puckett, whose immense repertoire included many popular songs of the twenties, some of which were issued not very long after the 'straight' dance bands' and crooners' renditions as, so to speak, countrymen's versions.

The black debt to stage music, however, took a different form. One of Riley Puckett's recordings was *On The Other Side Of Jordan*, also put on disc by Uncle Dave Macon. The tune, and possibly the words, of this merry piece were by Dan Emmett, and were published in 1853 as *Jordan Am A Hard Road To Travel*. The 'am' betrays the origin: it was a 'nigger minstrel' piece, and not surprisingly, for Emmett was the doyen of minstreldom, strengthening the foundations laid by Thomas 'Daddy' Rice (composer of *Jim Crow*) and laying a way for the Christys and the other troupes. While *Jordan* did not survive, in black circles, into the recording era, there were minstrel tunes that lived on; *Zip Coon* became *Turkey In The Straw*, while the jig *Buffalo Gals* was recorded under that name and as *Round Town Gals* or *Alabama Gal, Won't You Come Out Tonight?* It was possible to hear it in Nashville only a few years ago, played by Blind James Campbell and his street band. Chris Strachwitz, who recorded this black group for his Arhoolie label, commented in his notes, 'on this record the blues dominate since the group knew that my interests were mainly in that direction. Their work on the street and at social functions includes many more sentimental and pop numbers'. Campbell and his fiddle player Beauford Clay were both born in the first decade of the twentieth century, so could well have known those latter-day minstrel pieces which seem to have been popular among Blacks and Whites then; pieces like *I Got Mine* and *Chicken, You Can't Roost Too High For Me*, also known as *Chicken, You Can Roost Behind The Moon*, under which title it was recorded by the black Memphis singer Frank Stokes in 1927. *I Got Mine* was much collected by White's informants (from Blacks), and he refers to it, writing in 1928, as a 'popular vaudeville song about twenty years ago'; records are very numerous, and among them is a version by, again, Frank Stokes, who also performed *You Shall (Be Free)*, a sardonic song very extensively popular among Blacks in these years and found all over the place in White's and Scarborough's collections. *Chicken* is probably the piece published in 1899 under the names of Cole, Johnson and Accooe, and it is thus distinctive in that the composers were black; Bob Cole and J. Rosamond Johnson were perhaps the best-known of all black vaudeville writers and singers in the turn-of-the-century years. (J. Rosamond's brother, James Weldon Johnson, who worked with the team, became a distinguished poet and secretary of the NAACP.) *Chicken* embodied the belief that all Blacks were chicken stealers, and it is a little strange that Stokes, Pink Anderson and other black artists were willing to propagate it, or the similar sentiments of *I Got Mine*, which tells the story of a man who 'went down to a little crap game' and lost every penny that he had in his pocket, except for that folk-singer's standby, a green-back dollar bill. The police raid the joint, and in the furore the singer 'gets his', so ever since he's 'been livin' high on chicken and wine', a 'member of the knockdown society'. Of course this sort of thing would go down well at white dances, and it is not surprising that Whites, like the talking bluesman Chris Bouchillon of South Carolina, found it appealing; and the popular chorus of *You Shall Be Free*,

> Oh, well, you see that preacher laid behind the log,
>   A hand on the trigger, got his eye on the hog;
> The hog said 'Hmm!', the gun said 'Biff!';
>   Jumped on the hog with all the dripping.

was taken up by the Georgian fiddler Earl Johnson and the Virginian guitarist Frank Hutchison, and by many black singers as an element of

CHRIS BOUCHILLON
"The Talking Comedian of the South"

WHEN Chris Bouchillon says anything he does it in such a dry, humorous sort of way that you can't help but laugh.

Chris isn't averse to a bit of playing and singing, now and then, either. When he tunes up his voice and guitar, folks come from miles around to hear the melodies of this popular South Carolina minstrel.

In addition to being one of the foremost wits and singers of the South, Chris can tinker with an auto just as effectively as with a tune.

CHRIS BOUCHILLON

22 Chris Bouchillon, the instigator of the 'talking blues'

the common anti-clerical theme. On race records the anti-black sentiments of these early songs are generally redirected against sections of the black public – preachers, wife-stealers, fast-life women, and so forth – whereas the originals obviously poked fun, sometimes goodnatured and sometimes not, at black people in general. As White remarks, 'the Negro minstrel song, like many of the novels of ante-bellum southern life, was commonly used as an instrument of propaganda against the interests of the Negro himself'. This is obviously true, so, faced with the records of Blacks singing 'coon' songs, one may choose to believe either that the singers were Uncle Tomming, or that they were mocking the originals. The latter is, I think, closer to the truth. With what intent white singers used the material it is difficult to say, unless one knows the individual singer's views on colour, but, granted that some hillbilly artists would have shrunk from the faintest suspicion of nigger-loving, it is probable that their coon songs preserved, and indeed intensified, the racist flavour which they initially possessed.

COMIC AND COON SONGS

By ARTHUR COLLINS

V 409 Cindy, I Dreams About You
1635 Down Where the Wurzburger Flows
V 538 Every Race Has a Flag But the Coon
2408 Every Morn I Bring Her Chicken
        A Burlesque on "Violets"
1632 Helen Gonne
V 157 I Ain't Seen No Messenger Boy
1629 I Just Can't Help From Loving That Man
1965 I Wonder Why Bill Bailey Don't
        Come Home
160 I'd Leave My Happy Home for You
1631 If Money Talks, It Aint on Speakin'
        Terms With Me
647 If You Love Your Baby, Make
        Goo Goo Eyes
2051 I'll Be Busy All Next Week   A colored lady's
        excuses to an unwelcome suitor
2052 I'm a Jonah Man   Bert Williams' tremendous
        hit with Williams & Walker
2411 I'm Thinkin' of You All o'de While
650 I've Got a White Man Workin' for Me
651 Just Because She Made dem Goo Goo Eyes
V 163 Mandy Lee   Chattaway
1634 My Maid From Hindostan
162 Old Bill Jones   Rube Song

2153 Oh! My!   A Harrowing Tale of a Colored Belle
        a Pig and an Apple Dumpling
1630 Please Let Me Sleep   Wail of a Weary Coon
158 Pliny, Come Kiss Your Baby
V 539 Strike Up the Band
1964 The Pooh Bah of Blackville Town
2425 The Gambling Man
1633 Under the Bamboo Tree   Cole
V 170 Vaudeville Specialty
2407 You Can't Fool All de People All de Time

By BERT. A WILLIAMS

994 All Going Out and Nothing Coming In
991 My Castle on the Nile
993 Where Was Moses when the Light
        Went Out

VICTOR, Seven-Inch, 50c. Each, $5.00 Per Dozen
MONARCH, Ten-Inch, $1.00 Each, $10.00 Per Dozen

COON SONGS WITH BANJO

By SPENCER and OSSMAN

817 Coon, Coon, Coon
820 Hot Times on the Levee
1711 My Girl from Dixie
1710 On Emancipation Day
818 That Minstrel Man of Mine
816 The Colored Major
819 The Little Old Log Cabin in the Lane

ORIGINAL NEGRO SONGS AND SHOUTS

By BILLY GOLDEN

68 Bye Bye, Ma Honey
617 Crap Shooting
622 Rabbit Hash   Just Coon Nonsense
616 Roll on de Ground
V 618 The Mocking Bird   Whistling Solo
619 The Wedding O'er the Hill
65 Turkey in de Straw
621 Uncle Jefferson
620 Yaller Gal   Laughing Song

By GEORGE W. JOHNSON, the Whistling Coon

584 The Laughing Coon
583 The Laughing Song
582 The Whistling Coon
581 The Whistling Girl

DUETS

By DUDLEY and MACDONOUGH

1329 Bye and Bye You Will Forget Me
1076 In the Shadow of the Pines

23 'Comic and Coon Songs'. A page from the Victor catalogue, *c.* 1903

Coon songs were not always comic; there were also the sentimental 'darky' effusions, the great line that stretched each side of *Old Black Joe*. Judging black life by these – as European audiences very probably did in watching the 'nigger minstrel' shows, having nothing else to go on – one summons up a peaceful picture of woolly-headed slaves strumming their banjos, fishing in the sun and courting little octoroons with improbable names. When they were young they used to wait, on massa's table lay de plate, and so on, but in these songs they are generally old and venerable. They raise their voices in lamentation when *Massa's In De Cold Cold Ground*, but not, one feels sure, in exultation to *Shout, Mourner,*

You Shall Be Free – except perhaps in the safe metaphors of a hymn. Of chain-gangs and beatings and slave-drivers we hear not a whisper; nor of massa's hot intentions towards the estate's little octoroons, though that particular abuse was sometimes romanticised into such songs as *My Pretty Quadroon*.

> Massa had gardens and bowers,
>   And flowers that were always in bloom;
> He begrudged me my pretty wild flower,
>   Cora, my pretty quadroon.

And the separation of lovers was commemorated by pieces like *Lorena*, a mid-nineteenth-century weepie which was sung, movingly enough in its way, by the Blue Sky Boys and others. On the 'peculiar institution' itself songs were somewhat taciturn, and Fields Ward's *Those Cruel Slavery Days* is exceptional:

> On the day old master died, all the darkies stood and cried,
>   In those agonising cruel slavery days;
> For we knew we must be sold for the silver and the gold,
>   In those agonising cruel slavery days.

> Well, they sold my brother Sam to a man from Alabam',
>   My sister went to Georgia far away;
> Then they broke my heart for life when they sold my loving wife,
>   In those agonising cruel slavery days.

The singer goes on to reminisce about 'days of long ago', when 'the darkies all would sing and the banjo it would ring'; and he looks forward to the time when 'there never will be cruel slavery days'. Unless the song is repulsively satirical, it has a liberality rare in Southern expression; the language may be minstrel-flavoured, but the verdict on slavery days – 'agonising, cruel' – is unequivocal. For various comprehensible reasons, songs explicitly about slavery were recorded only by Whites; Blacks may have sung them in private, but no one would have encouraged them to perform them when white men were around. And when Whites did make records about Blacks they tended rather to be comfortably commercial couplings like the Skillet-Lickers' *Run, Nigger Run* and *Dixie*, which, with its affirmation of the Southern values of home pride and nigger-hating, would ensure for the band a warm welcome in any port-of-call.

The Fields Ward song just spoken of was made for Gennett Records, an Indiana firm which put out blues, country music and jazz, along with conventional popular material, in a multitude of series, and also pressed discs for private concerns. Some of these have survived, among them a few with a 'KKK' label, showing a fiery cross in gold on scarlet; the featured group is the '100% Americans', and one title is *Why I Am A Klansman*. The band's name was taken from the Klan periodical *The One Hundred Percent American*; their song, like most Klan pronouncements of those days, is vague about the organization's aims and nowhere mentions Blacks; the keywords are 'God', 'my country' and 'honour'. There is a story that the local Klavern in Birmingham, AL, for a time managed the black harmonica player Jaybird Coleman, which is odd, for Coleman, on the recorded evidence at least, had no truck with white music. Probably the Klan's interest was purely financial. It was an Alabamian, incidentally, who revived the KKK in the early twentieth century, one Colonel William Joseph Simmons, of whom Randel relates 'his Negro "mammy" had often regaled him with exciting Klan stories'. Stone Mountain, where he rekindled the Klan torch, is an unmissable landmark outside Atlanta. The organisation's work in that city throve with the help of country music; Fiddlin' John Carson regularly played for Klan functions. Fifty years later an identical mood can be observed on the 'Reb Rebel' records that issue from a Crowley, LA, store. *NAACP Flight 105* is reputed to have sold a million, and may even be heard – it is said – on black jukeboxes; its jokes, for all their racism, are much less offensive than the grotesque sophistries of *Looking For A Handout*, which urges Blacks to quit the breadlines and get decent jobs, or the vile *Kajun Klu Klux Klan* (*sic*). These underground discs use all the resources of country music to back their message; indeed, a rumour is circulating that 'Johnny Rebel' hides one of Nashville's most famous personalities. Students of American politics will also remember that the George Wallace bandwagon has its wheels greased by hillbilly bands; W. Lee 'Pappy' O'Daniel rode to the Texas state governorship on the same mixture of populism, old-time religion and country music.

The relationship between the Klan and Jaybird Coleman may be apocryphal. There are, however, plenty of instances of white interest in black musicians; many of the latter, for example, received their first instrument from white men – like Fred McDowell, who had reason to thank 'Mr Taylor, a white man from Texas'. Then, race records are turned up in white homes, though exactly *what* records, in *what* homes, no one has been concerned to find out. Whether Blacks bought hillbilly records to any extent is less certain, but we have a clear account of a broadminded black family from John Jackson of Fairfax, VA. John's sister played the piano, and her mail-ordered discs were mainly classical; his father bought blues records; he himself listened to a variety of material, from Jim Jackson to Jimmie Rodgers, Brownie McGhee to the Delmore Brothers.

Furthermore, there were dozens of hillbilly records on the market before the black singers of the South ever got on disc; a rural black in search of traditional music before about 1926 would have had to be satisfied with white artists. When Bill Helms, the Georgia-born fiddler, first heard the early (*circa* 1924) discs of Gid Tanner and Riley Puckett, it was on a phonograph owned by 'an old darkey out in the country'.

9 · OLD FAMILIAR TUNES

It has been said that the advent of phonograph recording in rural areas spelled the death of folk traditions, because the record ironed out regional characteristics and killed off all the forms which did not have widespread popularity. It is true enough that blues played a less dominant role than recordings suggest. But formal and stylistic qualities peculiar to a single region or school could be observed for some years, as one may see from the dozens of reissue collections which have been compiled on purely regional lines. Moreover, much recording activity was directed quite deliberately at regional markets.

The concept of the record as trend-setter is recent; in the twenties and thirties rural music was generally put on disc in order to meet an already established demand. Certain forms were undeniably ill served; Columbia's talent scout Frank Walker has testified that company policy did not permit much coverage of old ballads, or banjo or autoharp tunes. And mountain dulcimer music appears on a disproportionately tiny number of discs. Black stringbands were poorly documented, too; the Wright family, for instance, who had an importance and repute in Texas at least as great as the Chatmans in Mississippi, never made a record. Perhaps a high-level decision was passed that the neat categories of the 'race' and 'old time' catalogues should be maintained as far as possible; if so, it was only partly successful. The Mississippi Sheiks, that is the Chatmans, appeared more than once in the old-time listings, while the white Allen Brothers turned up in the Columbia race series. (For this

24 'Old Familiar Tunes'. Cover of the Columbia Records catalogue, *c.* 1927

they sued the company for $250,000, but they lost the case and the record remained where it was.) Then the Carver Brothers, a black group including the young Josh White, were marketed largely through Paramount's hillbilly listing. On the whole, of course, the old-time catalogue purveyed white, and the race catalogue black, material; but each list suffered musical infiltration from, and occasionally echoed distinctive sounds in, the other. And by the thirties the dichotomy had disappeared, black and white country material now being issued in common series. (Decca was the one exception.) The disc labels preserved the pigeon-holes with phrases like 'race blues' or 'old time singing', but not exclusively; many of the Memphis Jug Band's last recordings, for example, were described as 'novelty hot dance'.

During the thirties, too, the accusations of 'detraditionalisation' and 'deregionalisation' do become appropriate; but in this, again, the industry was often reflecting migration-patterns and other changes in the social behaviour of the South and ex-Southerners. Back in the twenties the recorded music of country folk really was representative of most of the stronger traditions. This is a point worth stressing, for there are scholars who would dismiss all this talk of phonograph recordings as matter irrelevant to the study of folk music. To side with these stern guardians is to misunderstand the folk process; the bearers of tradition are not purists, but eclectics. They will devour ditties from records with the same enthusiasm as they imbibe songs learned at mother's knee or other unimpeachably oral sources. Indeed, the whole business of 'oral tradition' is being reshaped by new media; to scorn the record is to ignore one of the most potent diffusers of folk-usable material. There is the radio, too; the shaping role of those old-time music hours, and guitar and mandolin clubs, could well be investigated. Had it not been for Fiddlin' John Carson's popularity over WSB, Atlanta, there would have been no impetus behind the OKeh field-trip of June 1923, and the great recording journeys of the decade might never have taken place. No, the enthusiastic response with which the early phonograph discs were greeted, even among the poorest country people, proves that their advertisement as 'old time tunes' was fair. What Southerners wanted to hear on record were, as an OKeh catalogue put it, 'melodies (which) will quicken the memory of the tunes of yesterday'; melodies, that is, sung and played in traditional mode by musicians steeped in tradition. There is every reason to believe that that was exactly what they got.

These records do something else; they confirm a suspicion which must come to everyone who reads through the text collections and reminiscences of the early twentieth century. The traditional music of the countryman was a repertoire shared by black and white; a common stock. Some tunes or songs might be associated by some of their users with one race rather than the other, but most would have no racial connotations. This sharing both stemmed from and resulted in an extraordinary variety of musical approaches. Pieces from the common stock could be performed equally comfortably by the solo singer with any kind of instrument or none; by duet, trio or quartet, or a combination of any size; by the brass band, the string band and the jazz band. And this adaptability is itself linked with the function of the music: group entertainment, particularly at dances. The old-time musician of either colour will, as often as not, describe a tune according to the kind of dance it accompanies; waltz or quickstep, slow drag or buck-dance, breakdown, shimmy or grind. (A lot of confusion arises from the fact that a popular dance of the twenties, and possibly earlier, was called the Blues. Many blues (songs) are Blues, but not all Blues are blues.) Further, since dance functions have subtle social differences, the music could not become absolutely standardised; what was played, and the manner in which it was played, would depend on the social standing of the guests, their age, their colour, their mood and their degree of musical appreciation.

What was this common stock? First, there were the ballads of hero or antihero: *Casey Jones, John Henry, Stack O'Lee, Railroad Bill, Delia, Frankie And Johnny, Joe Turner Blues*; one might add *He's In The Jailhouse Now, Bully Of The Town* and, in a sense, *Boll Weevil*. There were songs of gamblers: *Don't Let The Deal Go Down* and *Jack O' Diamonds* (and *Stack O'Lee* again); of low life generally: *Ain't Nobody's Business* and *Mama Don't Allow, Salty Dog* and *Easy Rider, Drunken Spree* and *All Night Long; Raise A Rucus Tonight, Chicken, I Got Mine*, even the aged adultery-song *Our Goodman* (known generally as *Three – Four, Five, Six, Seven – Nights Experience*). The powerful appeal of the locomotive, and the associated themes of separation, loneliness and homesickness, are expressed in *Poor*

Boy, Long Way From Home and *A Hundred Miles* (or *Five Hundred Miles*, or *Old Reuben*); in *Lonesome Road Blues* ('Going down that road feeling bad . . .'), *Red River Blues* and *Look Up, Look Down*; and, evocatively, in the melancholy tune which is best known, perhaps, through the Memphis Jug Band's version, *K. C. Moan*. There is the tender *Corrine Corrina*, with which we may group *Careless Love* and *Make Me A Pallet On The Floor*. Then the pieces with instrumental rather than thematic similarities; the fiddle and the banjo tunes which draw on a huge collection of couplets and quatrains that are nearly all interchangeable from piece to piece. Such are *Sourwood Mountain* and *Old Hen Cackle, Bile Dem Cabbage Down, Turkey In The Straw, Big Ball In Town, Leather Britches, Buffalo Gals* and the *Rabbit In The Log/Pay Day/Keep My Skillet Good And Greasy* group. From the jazz-composers came *Wang Wang Blues, St Louis Blues* and *Beale Street Blues*, as well as *Hot Time In The Old Town Tonight* and *At The Dark Town Strutters' Ball*. From earlier times: *Redwing, Little Brown Jug, It Ain't Gonna Rain No More; Arkansas Traveler* and *Travelin' Man; Old Dan Tucker* and *Old Black Joe*. Equally old were the hymns *Mary Don't You Weep, Give Me That Old Time Religion, No Hiding Place Down There*, and many others which were firmly common-stock by the turn of the twentieth century if not earlier.

One could group these songs and tunes in a dozen ways; they are arranged above only for a sort of conciseness. Some, admittedly, are better covered on records by Whites than by Blacks, or vice versa, but documentary work by ethnomusicologists, together with musicians' reminiscences, substantially corrects this imbalance in most cases. For every piece cited one could no doubt find two or three more which appear in both black and white tradition; but I think the selection gives a fairly comprehensive idea of common-stock material.

Why this shared repertoire should have existed is clear enough. In the first place, it is not in the nature of such songs and tunes to be segregatable, and, firm and ubiquitous though racial divisions may have been, they could not prevent – and probably few would have wished them to prevent – the use by Blacks of white, or by Whites of black, material. And increasingly the concepts of 'this is a nigra song' and 'this is one o' them hillbilly pieces' would become unreal when applied to *John Henry*, say, or *Ain't Nobody's Business*. No doubt white musicians

25 Black and white versions of *Salty Dog*, 1924 and 1930

used to perform blues with a certain consciousness that they were 'nigger picking', and expressed this consciousness to their audience; the phenomenon is observable even today. But, as the reader will see, I have put no blues in the common-stock list, except a handful which differ significantly from the run of blues; they are basically unimprovised, and retain, through all their manifestations, tunes and at least a few verses which are peculiar to themselves. In some cases they even keep charac-teristics of performance, like *Poor Boy, Long Way From Home*, which is scarcely ever played without bottleneck or knife-style guitar accompani-ment. (This is almost as true of *John Henry*.) Some later blues have the same 'fixed' structure, for instance *Key To The Highway* and *Milk Cow Blues*, but it would not be reasonable to call them common-stock pieces, for they are common only *within* the black tradition, not outside it, and when used in extratraditional circumstances have a perceptible quality of conscious adaptation. White versions of *Milk Cow Blues*, for example, sound not like independent expressions of a traditional song, but like 'covers' of Kokomo Arnold's hit.

Then, as indicated earlier, almost every opportunity of building his repertoire came to the rural musician through omni-racial media. Tent shows may not have played to integrated audiences, but broadcasts and records could not be subjected to racist controls, except in so far as many Blacks could not afford a radio or phonograph. And in the crowd at a carnival, or before a medicine show platform, though the black man might have to stand at the back, he was still in earshot of the music.

Again, it is easy to be swayed by the huge mass of blues and to suppose that they were always the dominant strain in the black tradition. But it is quite clear that the blues are a twentieth-century music, even though their roots may be found in the 1880s and 1890s. If the black man had any form of leisure-time music in the nineteenth century, it probably belonged to this common stock. Which is not to say that black music was merely derivative; one can point to countless verses and tunes which bear a strong black stamp. The great quality of the common stock was adaptability; its great power, assimilation; it was neither black nor white, but a hundred shades of grey. And the evidence from twentieth-century sources which suggests otherwise, which emphasises the divergent paths of the traditions, speaks to us not of the past but of the new century and its new mood. As the black man sought rights and equality, the tidily stratified society of the South was disrupted and the races drew apart. As if expressing this conflict of interests and of aims, the black and white musical traditions took different roads as well. The first decade of the twentieth century saw du Bois' *The Souls Of Black Folk* and the foundation of the National Association for the Advancement of Colored People (NAACP); it also witnessed the earliest burgeonings of the blues.

But time is a tortoise in the South, and as late as the thirties we can find musicians who drew as much from the common stock as from the newer blues. Many of them were located round east Tennessee, Kentucky and the Virginias – one of the most fertile areas in which country music grew. A musician from those parts could reach, without much travel, into North Carolina, northern Georgia and Alabama; the south-east was his oyster. A Black could be one week in the mountains of east Tennessee, where his people were outnumbered twelve to one; next in Memphis or Atlanta or Birmingham, in ghettos which reversed the ratio. There are some artists, however, whose strong allegiance to older, shared forms suggests that they were most at home in the areas where Blacks were scattered: such as Joe Evans and Arthur McClain, 'The Two Poor Boys'. Their extraordinary group of 1931 recordings includes a *Sitting On Top Of The World* based closely upon the Mississippi Sheiks' hit of the previous year, and a batch of blues; but also, as mandolin–guitar duets, *Sourwood Mountain, Old Hen Cackle* and *John Henry*; the 1927 'pop' *What Do I Care What Somebody Said?*, put over as *Take A Look At That Baby* with immense gusto and two kazoos; and, in *New Huntsville Jail*, a lugubriously paced parody of another recent hit, the white Darby and Tarlton's *Birmingham Jail*. The choice of Huntsville, and the Birmingham location of their earlier recordings, suggests that the Two Poor Boys were from north Alabama or east Tennessee; one may also find some-what abstruse similarities with Billy Bird (probably from Alabama) and Carl Martin, who moved from Virginia as a young boy to grow up in Knoxville. Brownie McGhee was born in that city, and his uncle – named John Evans, as it happens – was, according to Paul Oliver's gleanings, 'a fiddler who played in the hill country style which was characteristic of both Negro and white dance functions'.

Someone else who played for dances both sides of the colour line was the mandolinist Yank Rachell, who worked in the twenties in the Brownsville area of Heywood County, in west Tennessee. His book included *Bugle Call Rag* and *Turkey In The Straw*; and he also recalls *The Waltz You Saved For Me* and *You Are My Sunshine*, which is informat-ive, for these were written in 1930 and 1940 respectively, so Rachell must have continued his white dance engagements as late as the Second World War; at which time he was very well established, as a blues singer and blues writer, on the black market.

While Rachell's mandolin work is strongly blues flavoured, the pres-ence of that instrument in a black group generally brings a taste of white music. Coley Jones' Dallas String Band found much of its employment 'serenading' with *Shine, Hokum Blues* and the sparkling *Dallas Rag*. This last is of interest as one of the few rural ragtime recordings; a couple of others were *Easy Winner* and *Somethin' Doin'*, by Nap Hayes and Matthew Prater, who, like Evans and McClain, used the mandolin–guitar duet form widely popular among white musicians, such as the Callahan, Shelton and Monroe Brothers. Hayes was probably exposed to ragtime when working with the pianist Cooney Vaughn, and he ably supported Prater's fluent mandolin runs. Both *The Easy Winners* and *Something Doing* (to give them their exact names) are by Scott Joplin; and this version of the latter composition was the only one to appear on record between the piano-roll era and the Second World War. The same would be true of *Easy Winner*, were it not that Hayes and Prater do not play this tune at all, but assemble under its name two strains from Joplin's *The Entertainer* and one from J. Bodewalt Lampe's *Creole Belles*. As it happens, this is the only record of *The Entertainer* from the cited period, too. *Creole Belles* was recorded by Mississippi John Hurt, soon after his reappearance in the musical world in 1963; his guitar treatment may be compared with a 1902 version, by banjoist Vess L. Ossman.

The rest of the Hayes–Prater recordings had their surprises, for the pair was joined by Lonnie Johnson, singing and playing violin, and the trio rendered *I'm Drifting Back To Dreamland* and *Let Me Call You Sweetheart*, which one suspects Johnson sang; he readily produces numbers like these to this day. Neither performance, however, was issued, and the rags, with blues couplings, appeared only in the OKeh old-time series, about the same time as the Mississippi Sheiks were being similarly marketed with *The Sheik Waltz* and *The Jazz Fiddler*. *Let Me Call You Sweetheart*, incidentally, has struck a responsive chord in other black breasts; Furry Lewis of Memphis still sings it. It was written in 1910, the birth-year of *Dill Pickles*; this rag too is much favoured by rural mandolinists and fiddlers.

If Lonnie Johnson's dulcet and musicianly fiddling reflects his years of work with lady blues singers in St Louis clubs, the coarse tone of Eddie Anthony suggests the rough and noisy working life of a street busker. Anthony was a member of Peg Leg Howell's Gang, a cheery Atlanta-based combination whose work has some affinities with the white music of north Georgia, as played by Fiddlin' John Carson, Earl Johnson and Gid Tanner's Skillet-Lickers. Everyone here drew on common stock; the Gang performed *Turkey In The Straw* – masked, on record, as *Turkey Buzzard Blues* – and *Tickle Britches* and *Tantalizing Bootblack*, while in the work of the leading white musicians there repeatedly occur tunes like *Ain't Nobody's Business*, *The Arkansas Traveler*, *Bully Of The Town* and *I Got Mine*.

Some of these are also to be found in the repertoire of Stovepipe No. 1, whose real name was the prosaic one of Sam Jones. He probably came from Cincinnati; he certainly took his nickname from the length of stovepiping which he blew in jug fashion. Playing guitar, and soloing alternately on the pipe and a harmonica, he recorded *Cripple Creek, Sourwood Mountain, Turkey In The Straw, Arkansas Traveler, Dixie Barn Dance, Dan Tucker* and several blues and religious numbers. His music was strikingly similar to that purveyed by the white harmonica-and-guitar 'one man bands' – Walter Peterson, for instance, or Ernest Thompson, who played twenty-odd instruments, or George Reneau, 'The Blind Musician Of The Smoky Mountains'. Though an interesting figure, both for his material and for his early (1924) recording date, Jones played in a somewhat pedestrian fashion, less excitingly than, say, Daddy Stovepipe (Johnny Watson), who derived *his* name – it has been said – from the tall hat he wore; or, more plausibly, from his dark colouring. He claimed he was born in 1870, which made him an exact contemporary of Uncle Dave Macon; and he too made some records in 1924, playing guitar and harmonica, but he did not then show much white influence. When found in Chicago in 1960 by Paul Oliver, he had learned *Tennessee Waltz* and *South Of The Border*; no doubt he used the latter a good deal when he 'went down to Old Mexico, played some with them Mexican fellers' (Oliver, 1965). The sobriquet he part-shared with Sam Jones was strangely popular; there was also a Sweet Papa Stovepipe, who recorded a couple of vaudeville songs in 1926, and Stovepipe Johnson, who yodelled.

For songs of a more personal kind we may return briefly to Atlanta. Waymon 'Sloppy' Henry, who was associated with Peg Leg Howell's circle, sang a few semi-moralising pieces, such as *Canned Heat Blues*, about the effects of home-made alcohol, and *Bobbed Haired Woman Blues*, which reminds one of the popular white song *Why Do You Bob Your Hair, Girls?* He also declared that *The Best Cheap Car In The Market Is A Ford* – a favourite vaudeville theme, but one with surprising relevance to country musicians, for Henry Ford sponsored fiddling contests and even created his own record label for 'Henry Ford's Old Time Dance Orchestra'. Yet another theme which 'Sloppy' Henry touched upon was the topical tragedy; his *Royal Palm Special Blues* has connections, albeit slight ones, with the widely known *Wreck Of The Royal Palm*, one of the many compositions depicting railroad disasters. Quite why

26 Johnny Watson, known as Daddy Stovepipe, playing on Maxwell Street, Chicago, 1960

train crashes, child murders, robberies and assassinations should have been such popular subjects among Southerners is hard to say; no doubt it was a development of the eighteenth- and nineteenth-century broadside tradition, which spawned so many Laments, Confessions and Last Speeches. Certainly the new disaster ballads were produced in much the same way, by professional song-mongers; now, however, unlike Catnach's hacks, they eschewed anonymity. The prolific Carson Robison described the process to a *Collier*'s reporter in 1929: 'First, I read all the newspaper stories of, say, a disaster. Then I get to work on the old typewriter. There's a formula, of course. You start by painting everything in gay colours . . . that's sure-fire. Then you ring in the tragedy – make it as morbid and gruesome as you can. Then you wind up with a moral.' It certainly was sure-fire; Columbia's Frank Walker sold tens of thousands of copies of Robison's *The John T. Scopes Trial* (refrain: 'the old religion's better after all') in the courthouse square of Dayton, TN, where it all happened. The Rev. Andrew Jenkins ('Blind Andy'), an Atlantan Holiness preacher, did even better with *The Death Of Floyd Collins*, about a Kentuckian pot-holer who was trapped by a rock-fall and perished under the floodlights of journalistic ballyhoo in February 1925.

Such tragedies caused scarcely a flicker of interest in black musical circles; none of the ballads were recorded by Blacks, and they were only very occasionally referred to; the Memphis Jug Band, for instance, make a half-joking allusion to the Collins affair in their mainly sexual *Cave Man Blues*. Whites might sing about national disasters; for the black man his private tragedy was more than enough inspiration. And when a Black was caught up in some cataclysm, he pointed no moral; he simply mourned for himself and his family or friends. The Dixon Brothers sang of a *Wreck On The Highway*, and every verse tapered off into the moralist's sternly pointed finger: 'I saw the wreck on the highway, but I didn't hear nobody pray.' The black singer looked at the overwhelming floods of 1927, and his concern was solely for the homeless and death-depleted families. No talk of divine retribution. Is it too bold to see in the moralising songs of the white South an indirect expression of racial guilt?

Of course, it was possible to talk of your surroundings without dwelling on tragedy. Those north Georgian Whites of whom we spoke above had an especial fondness for topical songs and discussions about moonshining, taxation and cotton prices; the Skillet-Lickers' fourteen-part saga of the *Corn Licker Still In Georgia* was immensely well received. Possibly it was in an effort to popularise these skits with the black audience that Columbia had Barbecue Bob and his brother Charley Lincoln record a couple of double-sided 'happenings', *It Won't Be Long Now* and *Darktown Gamblin'*, but the Atlanta pair did little more than jive each other about their girlfriends in the former and quarrel over the dice in the other. There was no mention of the larger world of agricultural affairs and local politics, but this silence tells us less about the personalities of the brothers than about the suppression of free comment among Southern Blacks. A Tennessee farmer wrote in the middle of the nineteenth century, 'An employer should never ask a negro any questions whatever about the business of the plantation, or the condition of the crops; nor say anything in the presence of the negroes about the overseer, for they are always ready to catch any word that may be dropped, and use it if possible to cause a disturbance between the master and the overseer' (Patterson, 1922).

If Blacks were silent about agricultural work, they were not much more loquacious about other occupations. Many white singers found matter for dissatisfaction in the textile mills of Carolina where they worked long and disagreeable hours for low wages; from these grim surroundings grew Dorsey Dixon's *The Weaver's Blues, Weave Room Blues* and *Spinning Room Blues*; Dave McCarn's *Cotton Mill Colic*; J. E. Mainer's *Hard Times In A Cotton Mill*. On their farms they had been 'white trash'; they joined the South's industrial revolution, filed into the mills, and found themselves labelled 'factory trash'. Black workers had little to say on this theme, though they praised the economic opportunities offered by the steel mills of Pittsburgh and Chicago. Coal-mining offered a slightly more productive seam of song; the shafts of Birmingham, AL, were dug deep into Trixie Smith's *Mining Camp Blues* (1925) and Sonny Scott's *Coal Mountain Blues* and *Working Man's Moan* (1933). Alongside them we may place the Carter Family's celebrated *Coal Miner's Blues* (1938) and the less well-known *The Miner's Blues* (1928) of Frank Hutchison. Untypically, the black songs are more informative about the work:

Oh, I went on Coal Mountain,
     saw the men pulling coals from the mine;
Lord, I went on Coal Mountain,
     saw the men pulling coals from the mine;
I saw the men wearing their mine lamps
     where all the lights did shine.

Sonny Scott, Coal Mountain Blues

These blues are so blue, they are the coal black blues;
For my place will cave in, and my life I will lose.

Carter Family, Coal Miner's Blues

The Carters found their song on a collecting trip, in Lee County, VA; it was locally popular in the mining community. Whether its composer was black or white we have no way of knowing; Blacks were not numerous in the Virginias, but where they *were* to be found was in mining settlements. It is worth recalling that the Family often took a portable tape-recorder on their travels, in the form of one Leslie Riddles, a black singer/guitarist from Kingsport, TN. His job was to learn the tunes they collected, while A. P. Carter noted the words. Under his tuition, Maybelle picked up many of her instrumental ideas; and *Cannonball* came directly from him. Riddles had a friend in Brownie McGhee, who also lived in Kingsport during the thirties, and he too used to be visited by A. P. in search of songs.

Hutchison was probably a Virginian as well, possibly from Logan County. His repertoire seems to have been very broad; from the common stock came *Stackalee*, *Railroad Bill*, *The Deal* and *K. C. Blues*, a bottleneck guitar rendering of the *John Henry* tune. (Another hidden *John Henry* is Riley Puckett's *Darkey's Wail*, which the blind guitarist prefaces, rather incongruously, with the words 'I'm gonna play for you this time a little piece which an old southern darky I heard play, comin' down Decatur Street the other day, 'cause his good girl done throwed him down.') Hutchison was a stunning guitarist who probably heard black stylists; they seem to have something to do with his approach to *Railroad Bill* and the bottleneck-accompanied *Logan County Blues* and *Cannon Ball Blues* (which is not unlike Furry Lewis' song of

27 Frank Hutchison, 'The Pride of West Virginia'

the same name, also with bottleneck guitar). His singing, too, especially in *Worried Blues* and *Train That Carried The Girl From Town*, has some of the emotional force of black music. These two performances, recorded in April 1927 and issued as a coupling, have been suggested by Malone's informants as the first steel-guitar recordings in country music. This is difficult to interpret; there is, after all, an important difference between a steel (-bodied) guitar and a guitar (whether steel-made or not) played with a steel (or knife, or bottleneck). Malone appears to mean the latter, but his case is insubstantial; in the first place, this kind of playing is to be found on Hutchison's debut recordings of *circa* November 1926 – earlier versions of the same two titles – and secondly there are several black examples which predate all Hutchison's output: by Sam Butler, for instance, and indeed by Blind Lemon Jefferson, whose *Jack O' Diamond Blues* of May/June 1926 may well fill the required role.

Hutchison's versatility also embraced an automobile song, *The Chevrolet Six*; a cante-fable on the 'Titanic', widely different from the black treatments by 'Rabbit' Brown, Blind Willie Johnson and William & Versey Smith; a musical description, on the harmonica, of *The C & O Excursion Train*; and various stock figures of country humour like *The Burglar Man, Johnny And Jane* and *Old Rachel*, who far outstripped the Good Wyf Of Bathe by getting married forty-nine times. But where he stands out most from white traditions of 'nigger picking' – and 'nigger singing' too – is in his rhythmic approach; he talks and sings across the beat in a way that is at first disconcerting but adds great impetus to the already complex musical progression. Nor do any of his blues employ the heavy 4/4 rhythm which underlay all Jimmie Rodgers' blue yodels, and thus much subsequent white blues playing.

Black musicians from 'Hutchison country' and its environs – that is, from the Virginias and Carolinas – exhibit an extremely satisfying mixture of black and white traditions. Julius Daniels' *Can't Put The Bridle On That Mule This Morning* was very close to versions collected in the field years earlier; it is essentially one of the *This Morning, This Evening, So Soon* family. He also played *Crow Jane Blues*, a venerable piece found in the repertoire of the Knoxville-based Carl Martin and Sam Butler from the Carolinas. Lil McClintock of Clinton, SC, we know to have supplied material to a field researcher; *Delia* was collected from him in 1923. Seven years later he had a chance to record, and he sang *Furniture Man* and *Don't Think I'm Santa Claus*. The latter has segments of *Everybody Works But Father* and a coon-song refrain,

Lindy, O Lindy, you sweeter than sugarcane;
Lindy, Lindy, say you'll be mine;
While the moon am a-shinin',
And my heart am a-twinin',
Meet me, dear little Lindy, by the watermelon vine

which suggests that McClintock was out of the minstrel school. To the north, in Virginia, William Moore of Rappahannock played rags; and Luke Jordan, who worked round Lynchburg, sang *Traveling Coon* and *Look Up, Look Down*, the former a latter-day minstrel piece, also known as *Traveling Man* and so recorded by the fat medicine show singer Jim Jackson, the latter probably a variant of the ubiquitous *In The Pines/Black Gal* theme. His *Cocaine Blues*, with a typically fluent guitar part, incorporated elements of the *Furniture Man* motif. Jordan was well remembered by Brown Pollard and Percy Brown, who played with him at black and white functions; for the latter, they report, the group's book took in *Turkey In The Straw, Mississippi Sawyer* and *Soldier's Joy*. A recording unit which captured Jordan in Charlotte, NC, also documented fiddle–guitar tunes by Andrew and Jim Baxter. The racial identity of this pair has been questioned; Andrew's fiddling indeed has the high off-key sound of north Georgia playing, but his brother's interjections sound black enough, and the high proportion of blues in their repertoire is quite untypical of white fiddlers.

Artists like these are often hard to pin down to an area. Julius Daniels sang a *Richmond Blues* which may indicate Virginian provenance; *Richmond Virginia Blues* by Spark Plug Smith may do so as well, but guesswork becomes really hazardous here, for the piece is no more than an 'unissued' entry in the discographies. Smith's discography, though, is a fascinating one; it takes in *Sweet Evening Breeze, In A Shanty In Old Shanty Town* and *My Blue Heaven*. The last named is an engaging parody, sung in a light, dreamy voice with something of the throwaway quality of the white talking bluesmen.

Parody, of course, was ever a mainstay of the rural performer. One of its funniest exponents was Uncle Dave Macon. Born in Tennessee in 1870, Uncle Dave set up his 'Macon Midway Mule & Wagon Transportation Company' around the turn of the century, and became a familiar sight

28 Spark Plug Smith in 1933

on his Woodbury-to-Murfreesboro run. A fun musician until about 1918, he was then spotted by a talent scout of Loew's theatre circuit, and entered show business; at his death in 1952 he had still not retired. It is astonishing to realise that Uncle Dave was fifty-four when he first entered a recording studio – and he was one of the first country musicians on disc at that. His huge repertoire thus included songs far older than many of those recorded even in the earliest twenties, and his role as a preserver of the tradition is of the first importance. Most of the vaudeville-turned-folk pieces which we have mentioned in preceding pages are to be found in his songbag: *Shout, Mourner, You Shall Be Free, Sho' Fly, Don't Bother Me, Rockabout My Saro Jane, Jordan Is A Hard Road To Travel, Comin' Round The Mountain* and so forth. With his Fruit Jar Drinkers he made *Hold The Woodpile Down*, a variant of the piece which Sam Charters collected from the black Mobile Strugglers in Alabama in 1954, as *Raise A Rukus Tonight*; and the Strugglers harmonised on the refrain in just the same way as Macon's supporters did. *Over The Road I'm Bound To*

Go was more or less *Feather Bed*, as Cannon's Jug Stompers called it. There were blues, fiddle tunes transposed to the banjo, riverboat songs, lullabies, sentimental ballads. One of the latter stimulated Uncle Dave's most delightful parody; 'Now I'll sing you a beautiful song,' he announces, 'that a highly educated aristocratic broken-down aristocracy old-maid school-teacher sang to a wealthy old bachelor that called on her one Sunday afternoon on her guitar – and the words are simply *beau*tiful', and with that he goes into a crazily exaggerated *Nobody's Darling But Mine* which paints the prim schoolmarm's parlour overtures with hilarious fidelity. One gets no inkling of these joys from the record label, which simply lists *Two-In-One Chewing Gum*; the disc starts with that piece, but Uncle Dave moves, halfway through, into the other routine. This was one of his favourite techniques – a forerunner, indeed, of the extended-play, four-tune record. Oddly enough, the one black artist who did it at all frequently was a man who has other links with Uncle Dave Macon: the Texan songster Henry Thomas, who played guitar and panpipes on a list of tunes that includes *John Henry, Arkansas, The Fox And The Hounds, Jonah In The Wilderness, Shanty Blues* and *When The Train Comes Along* – *all* of which Macon recorded, virtually all earlier. Then there are the Maconesque medleys; *Arkansas* includes some of *Traveling Coon* and another song, while *Bob McKinney* takes the listener through *Wasn't He Bad?, Take Me Back, Make Me A Pallet On the Floor* and *Bully Of The Town*, though admittedly the changes in direction are not always very clearly signalled by Thomas' guitar. His playing had a country dance flavour, never more than in *Old Country Stomp* with its dance calls, and in this, too, he echoed the Macon spirit. It is hard to dismiss the suspicion that the Brunswick company, for whom Thomas made all and Macon the bulk of his titles, was attempting a sort of comparative issue programme – Macon for the Whites, Thomas for the race – but its advertisements make no reference to this, and the selling would have been on a subliminal level at best. Furthermore, Macon's discs appeared several years earlier (though they were reissued closer to Thomas' day); and of course the songs concerned were so old that Thomas need not have learned them from, nor even have heard, Macon's interpretations. It is curious all the same.

10 · LETTING OUT THE BLUES

> I've got the worried blues, God, I'm feelin' bad.
> I got no one, tell my troubles to.
> I'm gonna build me a heaven of my own.
> I'm gonna give all good-time women a home.
> Now fare thee, my honey, fare thee.

Single statements, each repeated twice to make a three-line stanza; they might have been selected at random from any of the early text collections; in fact they comprise about half of *Texas Worried Blues* by Henry Thomas, with whom we closed the last chapter. They show the blues at almost their most primitive; the lazy timelessness of the field holler has been lost, but the unconfined quality remains. The song could have had not eleven stanzas but fifty-one or a hundred and one; it is a close-up of the blues, a detail photograph from the whole blues landscape. In 1928, when Thomas was recorded, the form must have been not old-time but oldest-time; almost every singer, black and white, was experimenting with this marvellously elastic medium.

There was Blind Lemon Jefferson, also a Texan; more than a third of his recordings were made before ever Henry Thomas sat in front of a microphone, and from the start he forged blues with new words, clearly defined themes and carefully conceived accompaniments. His impact was immediate and tremendous. 'Up 'til then', recalls the Kentucky mountain musician Roscoe Holcomb, 'the blues were only inside me; Blind

Lemon was the first to "let out" the blues.' Hobart Smith of Saltville, VA, remembers seeing him about the beginning of the First World War. 'It was along about that time that Blind Lemon Jefferson came through, and he stayed around there about a month. He stayed with the other colored fellows and they worked on the railroad there; he'd just sing and play to entertain the men in the work camp. I think that right about there I started on the guitar' (Smith, 1965). Echoes of Jefferson can be heard in Smith's *Six White Horses* and *Railroad Bill*, both of which he learned from the older man, and in *Graveyard Blues*. Smith was inspired as guitarist, Holcomb rather as singer; the latter's high, penetrating voice has much of Lemon's acid tone. Hobart Smith had other experiences of black music: 'the first fiddle I ever heard in my life was when I was a kid. There was an old colored man who was raised up in slave times. His name was Jim Spenser. He played *Jinny*, *Put The Kettle On* and all those old tunes like that. And he would come up to our house and he'd play.' Leadbelly spoke of an old fiddler, too: 'Poor Howard . . . the first fiddler after Negroes got free, in slavery time.' His own association with Blind Lemon was particularly close, as his recollections and songs bear out.

Interviewing bluesmen who grew up in the twenties has a recurrent motif: guitarists nearly always cite Jefferson as the great formative influence, with occasional mention of Blind Blake and Lonnie Johnson. For all his formidable technique, Johnson was not popular among country Whites, but Blake's quick-fingered rags and delicately picked blues accompaniments were admired both sides of the colour line. The Kentuckian guitarist Asa Martin acknowledges his skill, while his fiddle-playing companion Doc Roberts can remember jamming with Blake in a hall adjoining the Paramount recording studio. One of Blake's sessions, in about May 1927, was interspersed with titles by the Kentucky Thorobreds, and the discographers Dixon and Godrich note that 'it is suggested that Blake may play on these'. Strangely enough, two other instances of integrated recording sessions also bring in Kentuckian musicians. The white singer Welby Toomey, recently interviewed at his home in Lexington, recalled travelling up to the Gennett studios in Richmond, IN, with a black one-man bandsman, Sammy Brown, also of Lexington. Brown, he said, had six fingers on each hand, and played guitar, drums and so forth (N. Cohen, 1969). Toomey's November 1927 recordings had guitar accompaniment, with occasional harmonica and 'jazzbow', and it sounds likely that Brown saw to all this. ('Jazzbow' I am taking to be a kazoo amplified with an old saxophone or trombone body; Brownie McGhee has such an instrument and gives it that name. Jazzbo Tommy Settles, too, was noted for his kazoo pyrotechnics. If the Gennett files mean literally a bow, that is a mouth-bow, like the ones used by the Ozark musicians Charley Everidge and Jimmie Driftwood, then Brown could not have done all the work, his extra fingers notwithstanding, for the mouth-bow, like the jew's harp, requires both hands.) Another local band was Taylor's Kentucky Boys, who employed a black fiddler named Jim Booker, but one would never guess his colour from the existing records.

White musicians did not listen only to the male black singers. Among Dock Boggs' most celebrated numbers are two from the 'classic blues' era, *Down South Blues* and *Mistreated Mama Blues*. At a concert he prefaced a performance of *Down South Blues* as follows: 'this is one of the songs that I heard a colored girl sing; she'd sung it and recorded it a few years before that, accompanied by piano. I'd never heard any blues played on a banjo before.' At another time he remembered the 'colored girl' as Sara Martin, OKeh recording star of the early twenties, who did indeed make the original *Mistreated Mama Blues*, with piano, in 1923. *Down South Blues*, however, was not hers but Clara Smith's – also a piano-accompanied 1923 performance. Another 'ruralised' Clara Smith piece was *31st Street Blues* of 1924, which turned up six years later in stringband form, the work of the Leake County Revelers.

If Dock Boggs had looked into Sara Martin's work more closely he *would* have heard blues on a banjo, for she was often partnered by Sylvester Weaver playing that instrument. Weaver's accompanying ideas, however, remained stolidly pianistic, and they have dated far more than Boggs' vivid, unusually melodic conceptions. Dock had heard other black music sympathetically: 'there was a colored string band playing for a dance in Norton (his native town, in Virginia). I stuck my head in at the door and I liked the way the banjo-player played, so I said to myself, I am going to learn to play that way' (Boggs, 1964).

29 Banjo player Dock Boggs, 1927

Another banjoist who learned from black sources was Sam McGee, a companion of Uncle Dave Macon and member of his Fruit Jar Drinkers. Sam and his brother Kirk were born in Franklin, TN, and heard black street musicians early in their career; their playing, Sam recalls, 'would just ring in my head'. A black banjoist and guitarist called Jim Sapp had particular influence upon Sam McGee, who quickly became skilful at reproducing raggy 'nigger picking' styles. His *Easy Rider*, played on the six-string banjo-guitar, is a stunning performance, as is *Railroad Blues*, a cleverly arranged and good-humoured blues with guitar accompaniment. In it he plays a break which he introduces with 'here come DeFord Bailey now with the harmonica'. Bailey was a fellow performer on Grand Ole Opry, the one exception to the programme's unwritten colour bar; he represents, I suspect, genial patronisation rather than genuine musical interaction. It was he, according to one story, who opened the first Opry broadcast when he blew *Pan-American Blues* into the WSM

30 De Ford Bailey, *c.* 1928

microphone; he was definitely among the Opry men who made the first Nashville recordings, for Victor in September/October 1928. (Country-music historians have so far been unable to pinpoint the first perform-ance recorded in Music City. It was the Binkley Brothers' Clodhoppers'

Watermelon Hanging On De Vine of 28 September 1928.) Bailey today has a shoe-shine pitch in Nashville and puts too high a price on his services for any record company to engage him. No doubt he is justified; Opry contemporaries have reported that he was often not paid for his appearances. His few records were issued largely in the old-time listings. But he made at least one mark on a black listener; Sonny Terry remembers a visit Bailey made to his home area of Rockingham, NC, and has enshrined the memory in a fine recording of Bailey's *Alcoholic Blues*.

We cannot leave Opry and its luminaries without one anecdote. A friend of his was talking one day to John Jackson, the fine black guitarist who is among the most pleasing discoveries of the 1960s. He recounted the story of DeFord Bailey and his unique position on the Opry. John was puzzled. The only black artist? What about Uncle Dave Macon?

One wonders if John would have had any difficulties about the Mississippi Sheiks; as we have already mentioned, they were marketed as both race and old-time artists. They came from the large and musical Chatman family of Jackson, MS; most of the eleven brothers who grew up in the teens and twenties could play at least one instrument. Bo Chatman was to attain fame as the dirtiest, and funniest, blues singer on the Bluebird label, but he played guitar and fiddle as a member of the Sheiks from 1930 to 1935, along with his brothers Lonnie (vocal and fiddle) and Sam (vocal and guitar) and their friend Walter Vincent, or Vincson (vocal, guitar and fiddle). Another prominent musical family in Jackson were the McCoys, Joe – who married Memphis Minnie – and Charlie. Between all these men there was much interaction, and they produced a large set of splinter-group recordings. Their most popular kind of music, on discs, was a verse/refrain blues, generally with a sexually metaphorical title: *Driving That Thing* (the Sheiks' first recording), *Pencil Won't Write No More*, *Loose Like That* (an answer, of course, to *It's Tight Like That*), *Your Friends Gonna Use It Too* (a two-sider), *It Is So Good* (another) and so on. There were some topical pieces, like Bo's Depression-era coupling with Charlie McCoy, *Mississippi I'm Longing For You* backed with *The Northern Starvers Are Returning Home*; the latter was to the tune of *Corrine Corrina*, a common-stock song the pair had recorded two years before. Then Charlie did *Times Ain't What They Used To Be*, which brother Joe followed with

31 A sentimental ballad by the Mississippi Sheiks. OKeh Records, 1930

The World Is A Hard Place To Live In. Bo also sang the startlingly titled *The Yellow Coon Has No Race,* unfortunately never issued, and a charming *Good Old Turnip Greens.*

> When I was a little bird, I always wanted to fly;
> I flapped my wings like a seagull and I flew up to the sky;
> When I got up in heaven, I seen somethin' I never have seen;
> There was a lot of curly-headed coons just a-scratchin' on the turnip greens.
>> He's a fool about his turnip greens, oh, yes indeed he are!
>> Corn bread and buttermilk, and the good old turnip greens.

> Mister Spencer went to Chicago, and I went to New Orleans;
> I got mad and walked all the way back home just to get my greasy turnip
> greens;
> Oh, the white man wears his broadcloth, and the Indian he wears jeans;
> But here comes the darky with his overalls on, just a-scratchin' on the
> turnip greens.
>   He's a fool about his turnip greens, oh, yes indeed he are!
>   Corn bread and it's greasy, and the good old turnip greens.
>
> White man goes to the college, and the Negro to the fields;
> The white man learns to read and write, and the nigger will learn to steal;
> Oh, the white folks in their parlours, just eatin' their cake and cream;
> But the darky's back in the kitchen, just a-scratchin' on the turnip greens.
>   He's a fool about his turnip greens, oh, yes indeed he are!
>   Corn bread and pepper sauce, and the good old turnip greens.

It reads like a minstrel song with sharpened points. Perhaps it was a parody of a non-racial original; versions without the 'darky' lines have been recorded by Whites like Pie Plant Pete and the Massey Family. Some of the phrases crop up in contemporary blues, like the parlour/kitchen couplet in Jefferson's *Piney Woods Money Mama* of 1928. Probably the piece was put together, like so many black and white songs, from both minstrel and folk sources.

A more successful Chatman production was the Sheiks' *Stop And Listen Blues*. Strongly reminiscent of the Jackson bluesman Tommy Johnson, it took its catchy title from the warning notice 'Stop – Look – Listen' on ungated level-crossings. Kokomo Arnold's 1935 *Stop Look And Listen* came nearer to the phrase, but was solidly based on the work of Johnson and the Chatmans; most other versions came directly from the Sheiks' hit, among them probably William Hanson's late 1930 recording. On the other side of this disc, Hanson – who was white – sang *Sitting On Top Of The World*, the original of which was, like *Stop And Listen Blues*, made at the first Sheiks session in February 1930. *Sitting*, the group's biggest seller, was a slow 8-bar blues, easy to learn and infinitely adaptable; its name was a defiant assertion of well-being, but its pace was usually funereal, and the odd clash probably added to the song's appeal. The Western Swing bands of the thirties grabbed it enthusiastically, and there were versions by Leon's Lone Star Cowboys (1932), Milton Brown and his Brownies (1934) and Bob Wills' Texas Playboys (1935). Black popularity has been constant from the obvious 'cover' by the 'Alabama Sheiks' in 1931 to the 1950s discs by Brownie McGhee & Sonny Terry and Howlin' Wolf. Slight revampings have been frequent – for instance, McGhee & Terry's *Better Day* – and the framework of the song is now established as a blues standard.

It is possible that the Sheiks intended the song to be a comment, of a sort, upon the earlier popular number, *I'm Sitting On Top Of The World* (*Just Rolling Along*), which emerged in 1925 and moved with an altogether more lively gait. (In the same year and from the same writers – Lew Brown, Ray Henderson and Sam M. Lewis – came *Five Foot Two, Eyes Of Blue*, which the Sheiks also played; 'in '28,' Sam Chatman told Paul Oliver, 'we got to playin' up at Leroy Percy Park for the white folks all the week. *Eyes of Blue*, that's what we played for white folks. *Dinah*, that's another'). From more traditional backgrounds came *Bootleggers' Blues*, which embraced lines documented many years before by collectors, and *Honey Babe Let The Deal Go Down*, the gambling song which virtually everyone knew, from Peg Leg Howell to Charlie Poole. These are airs from the common stock, but others of the Sheiks' songs betrayed one-way white influence, such as *Yodeling Fiddling Blues*. This was a neat marriage of blues fiddling and blue yodelling, and thus capitalised on country music's most exciting new sound. 'Go and learn to yodel', singer Walter Vincson urged his hearers, while a Chatman fiddle moaned behind him; 'that's the way to win a home'. One like the $50,000 'Yodeler's Paradise', perhaps, which marked the top of the ladder for the creator of this new sound: 'America's Blue Yodeler' – Jimmie Rodgers.

11 · 'THAT'S THE IDEA OF THE WHITE PEOPLE'

Much is made, in blues-collecting circles, of the Mississippi men – Charley Patton and Son House, Robert Johnson and Tommy McClennan, Muddy Waters and John Lee Hooker; the list runs into dozens. They are singers of sometimes frightening emotional power, and, if they are not – as some would have them – the creators of the blues, they certainly represent one of its most passionate strains. The man whose efforts crystallised the white blues form and ensured its future in country music was a Mississippian too. Jimmie Rodgers was born in Meridian in 1897, the son of an M & O gang foreman, and his father's work took the pair (his mother died early) to many Southern cities. Rodgers' musical environment has often been described; how he fetched water for the black gandy dancers in the Meridian yards; how he heard their songs and slang, and was taught the banjo by them. He travelled the line between his home town and New Orleans, as flagman or brakeman, and must often have met itinerant musicians looking for a free ride. Perhaps, musician himself, he gave them room in exchange for a song or a tune. (Listen to Jimmie Davis' 1931 recording *The Davis Limited*. Davis, narrating the events of a Southern railroad journey, adopts the role of brakeman to ask a guitar-carrying hobo: 'say, boy, can you play that thing?' 'Well, I can kind of strum a few tunes on it', comes the reply. 'Let's have it, boy', says Davis; 'if you can play that thing, you ride this train. Otherwise, you hit the ground.' 'Well, boy,' returns the hobo thankfully, 'I'm headed for home and here's your number.') Rodgers' career on the tracks was curtailed by tuberculosis in 1925, and he took up, full time, the musical life which he had for some years enjoyed as an amateur. His repertoire already included popular dance tunes, which he learned as rhythm guitarist in a local 'sweet' stringband, and blues, picked up from black musicians on Meridian's Tenth Street; and he branched out into minstrelsy when he became a blackface singer in a travelling medicine show. (Clarence Ashley was playing the same part in a Bristol, TN-based company as late as the middle fifties.) Moving to Asheville, NC, for the mountain air, Rodgers secured a radio engagement in early 1927; a quartet composed of himself, Jack Pierce and the Grant Brothers was billed as the 'Jimmie Rodgers Entertainers'. In July he heard of Ralph Peer's talent-seeking trip to Bristol and travelled there to see if Victor could use him. On 4 August he made his first recordings.

It was a momentous stay for the Victor team, since they also captured the Carter Family (A. P., Sara and Maybelle), who, with Rodgers, were to subsidise the company through the Depression years. Musically, the twelve days in Bristol were amazingly rewarding; there were sessions by Ernest Stoneman and the Johnson Brothers, Henry Whitter and Blind Alfred Reed; the tremendous gospel singer Alfred Karnes, from Corbin, KY; a superb black harmonica player named El Watson, accompanied by Charles Johnson of the Brothers – another integrated session; and many other historic banjoists, fiddlers and stringbands. Rodgers' two pieces were moderately successful, and he was invited to come to Victor's Camden, NJ, studios in November. The session there was a watershed in country music history, producing the undying *Blue Yodel* ('T for Texas').

'The identifying characteristics of the "blue yodel"', John Greenway has written, 'are (1) the slight situational pattern, that of a "rounder" boasting of his prowess as a lover, but ever in fear of the "creeper", evidence of whose presence he reacts to either with threats against the sinning parties or with the declaration that he can get another woman easily enough; and (2) the prosodic pattern, the articulation of Negro maverick stanzas dealing with violence and promiscuity, often with double meaning, and followed by a yodel refrain'. This is true enough of many

RODGERS, JIMMIE

Born into a family of railroaders, at Meridian, Miss., Jimmie Rodgers, when little more than a child, went to work on the road as a common laborer. Curiously enough, the music which was to cause his rise to affluence, began simultaneously with his first employment. The old songs and ballads of the railroad, some born of pioneer toil on the railroads, some the crooning songs of the hoboes who were attracted to the new railroads like crows to a farmer's fence —these constituted the music that Jimmie Rodgers first knew. He learned to play the guitar, and to sing in a naturally appealing voice the songs of the road. Later Jimmie became a brakeman but his health failed. He wandered about the country, his guitar and his voice providing the necessities of life.

JIMMIE RODGERS

A Victor recording expedition into the mountains of Tennessee discovered Jimmie Rodgers, quite accidentally. From the first impromptu recording, Jimmie's Victor records have been tremendously successful. He is now a headline vaudeville artist, and his Victor success grows greater with each succeeding record.

RECORDS BY JIMMIE RODGERS

Away Out On the Mt.	21142	Desert Blues	V-40096	My Little Old Home	21574
Ben Dewberry's		I'm Lonely and		My Old Pal	21757
Final Run	21245	Blue	V-40054	Never No Mo' Blues	21531
Blue Yodel	21142	I'm Sorry We Met	22072	Sailor's Plea, The	V-40054
Blue Yodel—No. 2	21291	In the Jailhouse		Sleep Baby Sleep	20864
Blue Yodel—No. 3	21531	Now	21245	Soldier's Sweetheart	20864
Blue Yodel—No. 4	V-40014	Lullaby Yodel	21636	Treasures Untold	21433
Blue Yodel—No. 5	22072	Memphis Yodel	21636	Waiting for Train	V-40014
Brakeman's Blues	21291	Mother Was a Lady	21433		

32 Victor catalogue list of records by Jimmie Rodgers

of Rodgers' thirteen blue yodels, and associated pieces like *Memphis Yodel*, though generally the boasting rounder takes second place to the rejected lover. An exception, in which the fear of rivalry is quite absent, is – oddly – *Jimmie Rodgers' Last Blue Yodel*, a jaunty composition recorded only eight days before his death.

Striking features of the blue yodels include the very frequent railroad references: 'I can get more women than a passenger train can haul'; 'I've got my ticket, I'm sure gonna ride this train, I'm goin' some place where I won't hear them call your name'; 'Look-a-here, Mister Brakeman, don't put me off your train, / 'Cause the weather's cold and it looks like it's goin' to rain'. If one did not know the man's early life one could still guess its railroad associations. Then there are the 'Negro maverick stanzas dealing with violence and promiscuity': 'Won't you tell me, mama, where you stayed last night? / 'Cause your hair's all tangled and your clothes don't fit you right', in *Blue Yodel No. 3*, comes two verses before 'I hate to see this evening sun go down, / 'Cause it makes me think I'm on my last go round' – and both verses are so common in black blues that it is unnecessary to cite examples. Or there is that beautifully concise couplet, 'When a man's down and out, you women don't want him round; / But when he's got money he's the sweetest thing in town', which was still in use in 1950; Baby Face Leroy Foster put it into his moving *My Head Can't Rest Anymore*. Another recurrent element is the city of Memphis, and it may be that Rodgers picked up some ideas from black singers there. 'I woke up this mornin', the blues all around my bed', from *Memphis Yodel*, is a favourite Furry Lewis line, and there are street references in *Blue Yodel No. 9*, in which piece Rodgers was accompanied by Louis Armstrong and Earl Hines. Lewis also adapted the famous 'T for Texas, T for Tennessee' line to make 'M for Memphis, B for Birmingham' (*Skinny Woman*). The connections are tenuous; lines used by Rodgers in this group of songs occur in several areas, and they were often recorded by Memphis singers because a lot of Memphis singers made records. On the other hand, Jimmie's medicine show tours must have taken him to the city; on one such trip he worked on the same bill as Memphian singer/guitarist Frank Stokes, and was remembered for it as far west as Fort Worth, Texas. Whether or not he had much truck with the Memphians, he heard plenty of south Mississippian black music on his Meridian-to-New Orleans trips. One of the last titles he recorded was a *Mississippi Delta Blues*, and *Mississippi River Blues* was a touching evocation of those muddy waters. But like every artist with an acute commercial sense (or a good manager) he sold himself to as wide an audience as possible, with *Jimmie's Texas Blues*, *Peach Pickin' Time Down In Georgia*, *My Little Old Home Town In New Orleans*, *Roll On Kentucky Moon*, *In The Hills Of Tennessee*, *My Carolina Sunshine Girl* and – a blanket coverage of his southern market – *Somewhere Down Below The Dixon Line*. Of course, the undeniable magic of these regional titles further sold the records to Rodgers' fans in England and Australia, India and Ireland, even Japan. (Nearly all his discs appeared in England and Australia during the thirties.)

The blue yodels were a foundation upon which countless white country singers built. Their great strength lay partly in their similarity to, partly in their difference from, black blues. Some Whites would sing the blues in very black fashion, though few imitated the vocal tone and speech patterns deceptively well. Other singers may have found such re-creation unacceptable. For them the blue yodel, as a vehicle of blues feelings, was an attractive compromise. The 12-bar structure was fashionable, easily manipulated and aesthetically satisfying; the yodel drew listeners who had heard Swiss virtuosi on travelling shows; and the Hawaiian guitars which Rodgers and many of his successors often added caught a third section of the market. The style was a very happy compendium of popular rural motifs.

But one must not distort Jimmie Rodgers' work; his blues, blue yodels and blues-like songs were only a part of his repertoire. The first two sessions, for example, had all the diversity which was and is typical of white country music. *Sleep, Baby, Sleep* was an old lullaby (which the black vaudeville singer Charles Anderson recorded, with yodelling, in 1923); *The Soldier's Sweetheart* was a reworked ballad. *Mother Was A Lady* (*If Brother Jack Were Here*) was a popular song of 1893, while *Ben Dewberry's Final Run* came from the hand of the Rev. Andrew Jenkins, of *Death Of Floyd Collins* fame. By songs of this kind as much as the bluer ones, Rodgers' memory was kept alive amongst his own people. The Western Swing bands of the thirties were great fans of his work; Bob Wills' Texas Playboys, for instance, successfully remade many Rodgers tunes, from *Gambling Polka Dot Blues* – Jimmie's original of which, with its solo piano accompaniment, had a touch of the vivacious female blues style – to the Depression-inspired *Never No More Hard Times Blues*.

Black interest took many forms. First, there were textual reminiscences. The opening stanza of his *Waiting For A Train* turned up in Peg Leg Howell's *Broke And Hungry Blues* and *Away From Home*, both made some six months after Rodgers' song was recorded; and a verse from *Blue Yodel No. 4*, the reverse side of *Waiting For A Train*, appeared in *Broke And Hungry Blues* too. The whole of *Waiting For A Train* has been recorded by Snooks Eaglin and Furry Lewis; Furry's version – which he calls *The Dying Hobo* – includes the yodel, which he introduces with 'I'm gonna try somethin' now – I may make a failure.' (He does. However, he is over seventy, and as a young man may have been more accurate.) That 'T for Texas' line which we have mentioned also cropped up in Frank Stokes' *Nehi Mama Blues* of 1928, neatly elaborated:

Ah, now, T for Texas, T for Tennessee,
S is a mighty bad letter for she stole away from me.

– and it was still recalled by J. B. Lenoir in 1960. Small borrowings, but they show that Blacks listened to Rodgers' records. Some may even have regarded him as an honorary Negro; he certainly had ways which his acquaintances thought rather black, as Cliff Carlisle recounted to Eugene Earle: 'He crossed that leg – well, his leg didn't do like mine does; *my* leg won't hang down . . . he put one leg over the other, and it was hangin' right down . . . And he opened that mouth – and he had a long face, you know, long jaw, like; anyhow, it just flopped! Jimmie, he reminded me more of a colored person, or a negro, or whatever you want to call 'em . . . [another voice: "he played that part a whole lot"] . . . than anybody I ever saw, in a way. He had that old southern, long southern drawl, you know.'

33 Jimmie Rodgers. Still from his movie *The Singing Brakeman*

Though black singers might borrow from Rodgers' recordings, yodel – with a few exceptions – they could or would not. They had a similar device, however, in the falsetto. The voice was raised an octave, generally in the last syllable of a word, often at the end of a line; the effect was rather of a whoop or howl than of the seesawing about the voice's breaking point which makes a yodel. It is difficult to tell what relationship there was between the two devices. David Evans has suggested, very reasonably, that the blue yodel synthesised Swiss (yodelling) and African (falsetto) traditions; the falsetto 'leap' was established among Blacks since the days of the field holler – consider Vera Hall's *Wild Ox Moan* – and Rodgers, hearing it, thought it analogous to the yodel and inserted both into his blues. His minstrel experience may have helped too; yodelling was heard from blackface 'coons' as far back as 1847, when one Tom Christian introduced it on a Chicago stage. The full version of *Lily of Laguna* has a yodelled chorus. Evans has investigated the late Jackson bluesman Tommy Johnson, whose trademark the falsetto 'leap' was, and he reports that Jackson-based singers like Ishman Bracey and Rubin Lacy saw Rodgers often in the twenties; it is interesting to speculate on the interchange between the white singer and Johnson's 'school'. Chester Burnett, whose powerful whooping owed a little to Johnson, claims he met Rodgers in the twenties and was given by him the nickname of 'Howlin' Wolf' which he has used ever since.

Among the other Mississippians through whom Evans has traced various threads of blues history was Skip James of Bentonia, not far out of Jackson. Skip's *Yola My Blues Away* (also known as *Four O'Clock Blues*) was sung – like all his material – entirely in falsetto; apparently Blacks use 'yodeling' or 'yolaing' to denote both the techniques. Evans also recorded him singing *Waiting For A Train*. Yet another singer in this area was John Hurt, who sang an occasional Rodgers number in his latter-day stage act. Hurt first recorded through the recommendation of two white musicians in his home town of Avalon, Willie Narmour and Shell Smith. This fiddle-and-guitar duo had a longer recording career than Hurt, thanks chiefly to their *Carroll County Blues* hit.

The sympathetic listener will find, I think, that Rodgers was a very great artist, and men of that stature, given a certain amount of circulation, do tend to cross social barriers; witness the impact of Blind Lemon. His delicate though masculine baritone could draw the best from a song, whether it was sentimental, like *Old Pal Of My Heart*, mournful, as in *Why Should I Be Lonely?*, gay – *My Little Lady*, *Everybody Does It In Hawaii* – or resolute and self-assured, like some of the blues. There were pieces about *Daddy And Home* and *Hobo Bill's Last Ride*, but Rodgers scarcely ever yielded to gross sentiment, and his tragic ballads have a refreshing simplicity and control. As if rejecting the formula-ridden disaster songs of Robison & Co., he ended his buoyant version of *Frankie And Johnny* with the words 'this story has no moral, this story has no end, This story just goes to show that there ain't no good in men.'

When the blue yodels caught on, both citybillies, like the prolific and polypseudonymous Frankie Marvin, and countrymen – Riley Puckett, for one – recorded songs in the new form. Puckett for some years attended the State Blind School in Macon, GA, and while there he may have encountered the black singer Willie McTell, who was a pupil from 1922 to 1925. It may even have been McTell from whom he learned his interpretation of *John Henry*. Blind Willie enjoyed a long recording career, but had returned to street busking when he was found by folklorist John A. Lomax in November 1940. In an Atlanta hotel room he talked to Lomax about the development of the blues.

'I'm talking about the days of years ago – count from 1908 on up, to the 'riginal years. Back in the years of those days blues had started to be original, in 1914. From then until the war time, people always had times – from blues on up to original blues. Then on up to 1920 – the changed blues. After then there was more blues. After then there come the jazz blues – some like this . . . And after then there's more blues – come to fast pieces . . . And after then it come the blues of changed things – gettin' in the alley low. People call it the alley, calls it in the colored race of blues. Now we take our white race of the southern states; they plays a little different from we colored people. Now here's some of their pieces . . . That's the idea of the white people. Now you come back to the colored; they have a different type of playing. Now we have some pieces goes like this . . . now that's the colored. Here's our colored again . . . And still we have still down in the alley of blues, just like the white, when they play their yodelin' songs. But we have our blues, a little different – I thinks.'

34 Tom Darby (right) and Jimmie Tarlton

McTell illustrates his points now and then with tune fragments on his resonant 12-string guitar; unfortunately he didn't have time to give any very good idea of the tunes' identities, though the 'colored' excerpts can be tracked down, for the most part, to various of his earlier commercial recordings. He appears to think that the bluest of the white blues are their 'yodelin' songs', and he may have had Rodgers in mind, but there was music closer to his home which had the essence of the blue yodel with a more searching emotional strength. It was provided by Tom Darby and Jimmie Tarlton, who had a resounding success with their second release, *Columbus Stockade Blues* and *Birmingham Jail*. The refrain of the former, 'Go and leave me if you wish to, / Never let me cross your mind; / In your heart you love some other, / Leave me, darling, I don't mind', came from an old Irish song, and can be heard even now from English traditional singers. *Birmingham Jail* was also a reworking of an old theme, but it derived its particular success, apparently, from the fact that both artists had done time in that prison, and were felt to be singing from the heart. The pair's early recordings owe little to black song, the darkest element being Tarlton's steel guitar playing, which he says he taught himself before ever seeing Hawaiian guitarists, let alone black ones. Its lyrical figures nevertheless have a Hawaiian air rather than any other, but in some performances Tarlton shows considerable knowledge of black phrasing. His singing was always excellent, and attained a depth of feeling in their blues which was rarely matched among white country singers. *Traveling Yodel Blues* and *Touring Yodel Blues* indicate a fellowship with Rodgers; *Heavy Hearted Blues* and *Slow Wicked Blues* are fragmentary pieces which sound wholly improvised. Probably the recording director simply asked for 'some blues', as much for the lightning guitar work as for the words, and was rewarded with off-the-cuff performances. The duo were not primarily bluesmen, and a lot of the songs they called blues were only loosely so – *The Weaver's Blues*, for instance, which Tarlton learned from Dorsey Dixon when the two were working in the East Rockingham, SC, textile mills. However, Jimmie has recorded some earthy items; *Ooze Up To Me* is a bouncy song-with-refrain out of the Mississippi Sheiks' mould, and he still plays a speedy *Red Hot Daddy Blues* along similar lines. He is as likely, though, to play *Vaya Con Dios* or *Sidewalks Of New York* or *Old Black Joe*; eclecticism is the spirit of his music.

One of Darby and Tarlton's records had an odd sequel. *Black Jack Moonshine* (April 1929) was a piece of some antiquity; White, who quotes a black version heard in North Carolina, says that it 'is related to a song of the white people, the tune and a few words of which I can remember from my childhood'. (He was born in 1892.) His text has a refrain beginning 'coon shine, ladies, coon shine', which seems to refer to the 'coonjine' dance popular in the 1870s. Darby and Tarlton's tune has an appropriately jerky rhythm – 'coonjining' was a sort of shuffling – but they change the key word to 'moonshine' for a joke. There were jokes galore eight months later when Tampa Red, Georgia Tom and female impersonator Frankie 'Half-Pint' Jaxon gathered in a Chicago studio to record – under the sobriquet of 'The Black Hillbillies' – *Kunjine Baby*. Its tune was very close to the white pair's, but they stuffed the piece with comic stories and puns.

'Well, say, boy!'
'What?'
'You know, I feel kinda sick!'
'What you been eatin'?'
'Oh, I ain't been eatin' nothin' but eggs.'
'You got egg-zema!'

Is this true to the spirit of the medicine shows? Probably it is. Here is another of the trio's routines:

'What is all that round your mouth there?'
'You talkin' 'bout on my upper lip? That's my mustache!'
'Oh, beg pardon! Look like you swallowed a mule and left his
        tail stickin' out!'

And that particular joke was also told on record by Uncle Dave Macon (*I've Got The Mourning Blues*).

Interviewer Norm Cohen has reported that Jimmie Tarlton 'feels strongly that the treatment of Negroes in the south is unjust and not according to God's intentions. He feels that the troubles the Whites in the south are now having are their punishment for many years of mis-treatment of Negroes' (N. & A. Cohen, 1966).

Blind Willie McTell found it difficult to explain to John Lomax why he had no 'songs about colored people havin' hard times there in the south'. 'Why', asked Lomax, 'is it a mean world to live in?' 'Well, I don't know', said McTell; 'it's not altogether. It has reference to everybody.' 'It's as mean for the Whites as it is for the Blacks. Is that it?' 'That's 'bout it.' It must have been difficult for even so experienced a field collector as Lomax to elicit unfettered replies from his black informants on this topic; certainly McTell sounds very uncomfortable in the con-versation. But it was quite true that, economically, it was as mean a world for the Whites, in many parts of the south, as for the Blacks. (And in some northern areas too.) Economic and social lowliness or depriva-tion are not the only qualifying ingredients of the blues, but they are important, and in songs about poor living standards there is consider-able similarity in black and white treatments. Jimmie Tarlton's New Deal *Administration Blues*, with its closing stanza

> So hold up your head now,
>   Come fall in our line;
> We're gon' elect Franklin D. Roosevelt
>   For a mighty long time,

chimes in the same tone as, say, Champion Jack Dupree's *God Bless Our President*. McTell, too, had a Roosevelt song:

> Roosevelt is a mighty fine man, darlin', (*twice*)
> Roosevelt is a mighty fine man,
> Got to be president of our land, darlin'.
>
> Moonshine been here long enough, darlin', (*twice*)
> Moonshine been here long enough,
> Let's get right and drink up this stuff, darlin'.
>
> I got a gal in the white folks' yard, darlin', (*twice*)
> I got a gal in the white folks' yard,
> She don't drink liquor but she do play cards, darlin'.

The structure is that of an old song sometimes called *Sweet Thing*, collected from Mississippi Blacks in 1909 as beginning 'What makes a Frenchman grow so tall, sugar-babe?'; perhaps more to the point, both the pattern and a similar melody had recently been used on a recording by the white singer Bill Cox, a topical one at that: *N. R. A. Blues*. Cox – who also celebrated FDR's re-election in 1936 with *Franklin D. Roosevelt's Back Again* – used the repetitive little *Sweet Thing* tune to put over a unionist message – 'When you all join the NRA, we'll all feel happy and we'll all feel gay' – which would never have appeared in a black song. McTell's version, incidentally, went out under the title *Hillbilly Willie's Blues*, which shows us the progress of the stratification imposed by recording companies (and perhaps record-buyers too) upon the old common stock.

We have already looked at the 'nigger' / 'white man' antitheses of *Good Old Turnip Greens*; another stanza sometimes found in this song ran

> White man in the parlor reading latest news,
> Negro in the kitchen blacking Roosevelt's shoes.

And a more popular contrast was incorporated in the song of which this is a fragment:

> Well, a white lady smells like toilet soap,
> A yaller gal tries to do the same;
> But a poor black gal smells just like a ram billy goat –
> But she's smelling just the same!

The refrain to this gives the piece its commonest titles, *Charmin' Betsy* and *Do, Lord, Remember Me*; it appears to have started life as a parody of the spiritual with the latter name. In white hands it was often a fiddle or banjo breakdown, but the salty words occur in both race and hillbilly records, such as the Delta Boys' *Black Gal Swing* or Clarence Ganus' *All Night Long*. However, within the race the song was often used to express internal colour prejudice; the three types contrasted would be black, brown and yellow. For black/white antipathy we must look long, among the commercial discs. Working in the field, Paul Oliver recorded an extraordinary *Kill That Nigger Dead* from Butch Cage and Willie Thomas:

> Black nigger baby, black feet and shiny eyes,
> Black all over to the bone and india-rubber thighs,
> > Turn that nigger round and knock 'im in the head,
> > 'Cause white folks say 'We're gonna kill that nigger dead.'

A black man might have composed the song in a spirit of bitter summing-up, and it was collected from Alabamian Blacks around 1915, but it was also recorded by a white stringband in the late twenties, so its race-of-origin is in doubt. As a rabble-rouser among nigger-haters it could doubtless have done an effective job.

So too, perhaps, could some of the early recordings of racist-sounding material, of which – since I have been unable to hear them – I can only offer the reader the titles; Fisher Hendley's *Nigger, Will You Work?* of 1925, Herschel Brown's *Talking Nigger Blues* (1928), Uncle Dave Macon's *Run, Nigger, Run*, probably the most famous version of this old slavery-days coon-hunt hymn, which was widely sung by Blacks too. Uncle Tom Collins – despite his name, a white man from Georgia – sang *Every Race*

Has A Flag But The Coons, a popular song of 1900. (*All Coons Look Alike To Me* had appeared four years earlier; and that one was written by a *Black*.) The year 1900 also saw *Just Because She Made Dem Goo-Goo Eyes*, which may have contributed to, or come from the same root as, Gus Cannon's *Can You Blame The Colored Man*, which described Booker T. Washington's dinner at the White House with Theodore Roosevelt, in 1901. Both Washington and the President were bitterly criticised by Southerners for this disgraceful breach of racial propriety, and Cannon's depiction scarcely dignifies the episode . . .

> Now could you blame the colored man for makin' dem goo-goo eyes?
> And when he sat down at the President's table he began to smile;
> > Eatin' lamb, ham, chicken roast,
> > Chicken, turkey, bread or toast,
> Now could you blame the colored man for makin' dem goo-goo eyes?

Newman Ivey White, at the close of his remarks on 'Race-Consciousness', wrote 'if he (i.e. the Negro singer) is consistent in contrasting raccoon, 'possum, and rabbit, the yaller gal and the black gal, the ladybug and the bedbug, sometimes in the very same song in which he contrasts Negro and white man and always in the same manner, I am led to suppose that the real importance of the circumstance is not self-pity, but a fondness for the rhetorical device of antithesis, let the sentiments be what they may. Of course the Negro laborer is sometimes . . . dissatisfied with his lot. But the real significance of his songs expressing race-consciousness is the fact that they show so little of this mood.' And the real significance of *that* fact, surely, is that it masked from White, and from many commentators upon black song, the true feelings of the black population – feelings that were sublimated in animal antitheses because there was no other safe way of expressing them. Despite his obvious humanity and perceptiveness, White failed to see beyond the 'happy darky' superstructure; he fell a victim, as had those earlier slave-owners who thought 'coon songs' authentic black music, to minstrel stereotypes. 'To the folk Negro the music, and not the words, is the important matter'; perhaps he would have seen the fallacy of this belief if he had listened more closely to the blues, but unfortunately he thought that

35 Medicine show, Huntingdon, Tennessee, with blacked-up black artist

'the value of the blues as an expression of the folk-Negro's mind is somewhat impaired by the fact that the folk blues and the factory product are
to-day almost inextricably mixed'. (This was half true, but much less
harmful than he imagined.) He did see that the blues 'illustrate the singer's
desire to comment upon himself', but he supposed that they 'do not speak
for the groups, but only for the singer. They sometimes show self-pity,
but it is most distinctly personal and without racial tinge. The white man,
and the Negro *as* Negro, have no place in them.' Of course, the mass
of blues give him superficial support; well-known lines like 'I'm blue,
black and evil, and I did not make myself', or 'I can hear my black name
ringing', are exceptions rather than representatives. Yet racial consciousness underlies even the most explicitly personal blues; the peculiar savour
of the music rises from something more than individual emotion about

love affairs and hunger and joblessness and solitude. In the commercial recordings, blues are often a dragon, and the blues singer who goes out to meet it a St George on the black community's payroll; the race record is a three-minute film of the battle. If the dragon were only a personal demon, like Robert Johnson's 'hell hound on my trail', or the voodooesque 'Mr Blues' who comes 'walking through the wood' in Little Brother Montgomery's song, then the singer might, in his five or six verses, begin to exorcise it; but too often St George is forced back against the wall, or the fight ends in an uneasy draw. For the dragon represents many public interests, particularly segregation. 'When I sing the blues,' says John Lee Hooker, '. . . it's not . . . that I had the hardships that a lot of people had throughout the South and other cities throughout the country, but I do know what they went through . . . it's not only what happened to you – it's what happened to your foreparents and other people. And that's what makes the blues.' One of Charley Patton's songs was *Mean Black Moan*; the three words make a concise definition of the blues, but the central one, in *every* sense, is 'black'.

12 · OUT WEST

'The blues come to Texas,' sang Blind Lemon Jefferson, 'lopin' like a mule.' This is poetry, not history; cowboy song, however, did lope out of Texas, and white country music has worn a saddle ever since. The uniform of the country artist is the cowboy's – albeit a grotesque, besequinned version; the music that blares out of the Opry and from other radio stations is called country-&-western, and the Western Swing of Texas and Oklahoma is one of its strongest strains. The Old West myth appeals more than any other because it embodies so many traditional American virtues: self-reliance, rugged individuality, respect for women, love for mother – in short, the pioneer spirit. (How astute the decision to locate the US space programme in Houston!) Cowboy song has no black affiliations, though there have been black cowboys, and Leadbelly – an exception to every generalisation about race music – used to sing *Out On The Western Plains* and other such. Indeed, there is not much of real western music in modern C & W, for confusion rose very early between genuine material, by men like Jules Allen and Carl T. Sprague, and nostalgic recreations like Jimmie Rodgers' *Yodeling Cowboy*.

Black and white traditions have not often drawn together in Texas, but Louisiana, lying between it and Mississippi, has been something of a melting-pot for styles from east and west. Southern Louisiana enjoys a strong tradition of cajun music, which has created a vivacious substyle among the local Blacks: 'zydeco'. The distinguishing characteristics of cajun and zydeco are the instrumentation – accordion and fiddle are most

favoured – and the repertoire of old French dance tunes, now much augmented by Western Swing, blues, country ballads and pop. Cajun music
was very much a localised tradition in the twenties and before, but the
success of the Riverside Ramblers, who reputedly sold a million copies
of the wailing, sentimental *Wondering* in the late thirties, helped to focus
interest from the larger world; and similar attention came in the fifties when
a fiddler named Harry Choates put out a raw 'French Western Swing', which
popularised the steel guitar among cajuns and showed that the old one-
steps, two-steps and waltzes were commercially viable. Black music was
always quite well received along the bayous, and blues standards like *Trouble
In Mind*, sung in either English or French, or both, established themselves
in everyone's repertoire. (The Hackberry – i.e. Riverside – Ramblers have
recorded a bilingual *Trouble In Mind*, as *Fais Pas Ca*.) The long-drawn
moaning of the accordion may be adapted surprisingly well to blues, and
artists like Iry Le June – one of the best-loved of all cajun figures – could
put over *Grand Bosco* and similar slow blues with powerful impact. Moreover, the constricted, high-pitched singing style of the cajun has great blues
'feel', and can be very reminiscent of Blind Lemon. Indeed, Jefferson's
Black Snake Moan has been recorded by Clifton Chenier, a popular accor-
dionist whose tough singing and amplified playing are well known in the
bars of Louisiana and East Texas. Chenier's repertoire includes the country ballad *I Can't Stop Loving You*, Louis Jordan's *Let The Good Times Roll*
(as *Bon Ton Roulet*) and, of course, the theme which gave his music its name,
Zydeco Et Pas Sale – 'no salt in your snap-beans!' Such pieces, interspersed
with dance-tunes catering for waltzers, one- and two-steppers, stompers
and breakdowners, make up a wide and exciting programme, which, nowadays, has probably more acceptance within the race – in this part of the
world – than any other black tradition anywhere else. Zydeco is not the
striking instance of interaction it may seem to be, for its exponents are usually doing no more than reproducing an inherited collection of tunes and
songs; but it is an outstanding example of a common stock like that which
I have described as existing in the 'pre-blues' era, towards the end of the
nineteenth and in the early years of the twentieth century, for the evening's
entertainment which a zydeco group will give you is not easily distin-
guishable, in selection or treatment, from that of a cajun band.

Those are the sounds of southern Louisiana; further north French music has less hold. Shreveport, for one, was a strong blues town in the forties and fifties, with many black artists playing the cafés and pavement of Texas Avenue. John Lomax visited the place in October 1940 to make some recordings for the Library of Congress, and he wrote in his field notes of three musicians he found: 'Oscar (Buddy) Woods, Joe Harris, Kid West are all professional Negro guitarists and singers of Texas Avenue . . . The songs I have recorded are those they use to cajole nickels from the pockets of listeners. One night I sat an hour where the group was playing in a restaurant where drinks were served. I was the only person who dropped a contribution in the can. I doubt if the proprietor paid them anything.'

Harris and West played Lomax a selection of blues and rags, also *Nobody's Business If I Do*, *Bully Of The Town* and *Old Hen Cackle*, West's mandolin complementing Harris' guitar. Woods sang *Boll Weevil* and some blues, as well as his own composition *Don't Sell It – Don't Give It Away*, which he had twice recorded a few years earlier. Lomax may not have known that in Oscar Woods he had traced a musician of considerable interest, both as bluesman – he inspired Babe Kyro Lemon Turner, 'The Black Ace', to follow his steel guitar style, so that we can today hear his music in another guise than on his scarce recordings – and as that rare phenomenon, the black artist who worked with Whites. For Woods not only played on a white man's records, but even sang with him – a circumstance without parallel, I think, in country music discography. This would not be more than a scholar's footnote, were it not that the affair was quite informative about the appeal of the blues to white Southerners.

The white man was Jimmie Davis, who has been enshrined in the relevant history books as the composer–singer of *You Are My Sunshine*, which – it is said – propelled him firmly to the State Capitol in Baton Rouge, where he served as Governor in 1944–8 and 1960–4. ('How', his opponents asked, 'can you fight a song?') He had worked his way through school, partly by teaching yodelling, and during the late twenties and thirties built a large following with numerous records and personal appearances. While touring he safeguarded his voice with goat's milk. The middle and late thirties saw him a stalwart of the Decca list, both as singer of sentimental and novelty songs and as song writer for Buddy

36 Jimmie Davis and his band on radio station KWKH, Shreveport, Louisiana, 1930s

Jones and others. His earlier work has been dismissed by Shelton as Rodgers-imitation, but this is not the half of it. Though he was fond of pieces in the blue yodel vein, he made a distinct, if less influential, contribution to white blues, by exploring the world of sexual symbolism with a wit and metaphorical command that were typically black. Songs like *She's A Hum Dum Dinger From Dingersville, Sewing Machine Blues, Bear Cat Mama From Horner's Corners, Yo Yo Mama* and *Triflin' Mama Blues* must have been dubious recommendations for public office, and it is said that Davis, while campaigning, had frequently to answer accusations of mixing with Blacks. Some of the songs do rather support the suggestion.

I got the world in a jug, stopper in my hand, (*twice*)
And I got a triflin' mama, tom-cattin' with another man.

You ain't foolin' me, pretty mama, 'cause I got your lowdown; (*twice*)
You've got another sidetrack, and you sure Lord are switchin' around.

Now you triflin' women sure do make me tired; (*twice*)
Got a handful o' gimme, mouthful o' much obliged.

Went home this mornin', as the clock was strikin' five; (*twice*)
And I found another daddy gettin' honey from my beehive.

It could easily have been a black man's song; indeed, the opening line and the third stanza are very common in blues. It seems certain that Davis had been listening either to black records or to black musicians in his home area – Shreveport – or both. The railroad image in the second verse may have come from Rodgers' *Let Me Be Your Sidetrack* of two years earlier, or from tradition; Leadbelly used it about this time in his *See See Rider*. (Unissued takes of Rodgers' *Sidetrack*, incidentally, featured a black accompanist, the Mississippi guitarist Clifford Gibson, but on the take used for release only Rodgers' guitar can be heard. Five days later Jimmie recorded with the all-black Louisville Jug Band – a selection which *was* issued, *My Good Gal's Gone Blues*.) Though the yodel which follows each stanza puts us in familiar territory, Davis differed from Jimmie Rodgers in his explicitness; the more famous artist applied a paler shade of blue, and would not often have sung, as Davis did in *Sewing Machine Blues*,

> It ain't your fancy walk, gal, it ain't your vampin' ways;
> It's the way you do, just before the break of day.

This blues gained considerably from the full steel guitar accompaniment of Woods, who was present throughout this Dallas session of February 1932 but may not have played on all Davis' pieces. (The report that he also accompanied Jimmie Rodgers' *Down The Old Road To Home*, made at the same location a few days earlier, is not confirmed by the issued record.) *Sewing Machine Blues* comes from a notable group of titles; the others made on that day were *Red Nightgown Blues*, *Davis's Salty Dog* and *Saturday Night Stroll*, on the last of which the two men sang in duet. *High Behind Blues*, from the previous day, is an intriguing phrase; Mississippi bluesman Jack Kelly used it to name a blues a few years later, and one wonders if he derived from Davis or invented for himself such verses as

> She turned around and she began to grin;
> 'I ain't had none of this, Lord, in God knows when!'

On the same day as he played with Davis, Oscar Woods joined a singer guitarist called Ed Chafer, or Schaffer, to make a couple of blues, one the Texas classic *Flying Crow*. They had recorded together before, in 1930, naming themselves the 'Shreveport Home Wreckers' – which fits neatly with a Davis line in *Pea Pickin' Papa*, 'I'm an old home-wrecker from down in Texas.'

It seems certain that Woods was one of the black musicians closest to Davis, and perhaps their association was extended to travelling shows; both had found their way to Memphis in May 1930 when the Victor team was there. (So had David McCarn, a North Carolinian who had worked in textile mills and sang disillusioned compositions like *Cotton Mill Colic* and *Serves 'Em Fine*. He was despairing of a future in music, too, but a black artist whom he met in Memphis advised him to try the recording men at the Auditorium. It was a moderately successful move, and one would like to know who the acute acquaintance was; one of the Memphis Jug Band, perhaps, or Georgia-born Kokomo Arnold, who made his recording debut two days earlier.) Unfortunately, mist hangs over the past of Davis, Woods, Schaffer and the rest, and a chapter of potentially immense interest lies beyond our sight range. Most of Jimmie Davis' early, bluer discs are rare, which suggests that his material was a little too outrageous for the market, but *Bear Cat Mama* and *Hum Dum Dinger* were re-released as a cheap Bluebird coupling and stayed in catalogue well into the war years, spurring 'cover' versions by Gene Autry and others.

A noteworthy feature of his work was the retention of black and brown gals in the lyrics of his black-derived songs. Jimmie Rodgers was usually careful to give no racial hints, but Davis – who was not best known for his liberal views when in office – could cheerfully declare

> Gonna telephone to Heaven, to send me an angel down;
> If you haven't got an angel, Saint Peter, send me a high-steppin' brown.

Similarly Dick Justice's *Brown Skin Blues*, a melee of stock phrases and verses from Blind Lemon's *Black Horse Blues* and *Stocking Feet Blues*, expresses a wish to 'laugh . . . and talk with that long-haired brown o' mine'; while Goebel Reeves' catalogue of sexual experiences, *I Learned About Women From Her*, tells how he stole 'the wife of a nigger', who 'stabbed me one night when I wished she was white'. This sort of thing can be quite unremarkable, for many Whites, in performing 'nigger blues', are going through an accepted act, and have no reason to bleach the female characters who occur in such songs; on the other hand, Reeves' composition, and no doubt others, suggests that the sociologist might unearth useful information in this field concerning the attitudes of the poor white.

He would find good things, too, in the topical and occupational compositions of the thirties. Decca's Buddy Jones put out *Taxicab Driver's Blues*; Ted Daffan wrote *Truck Drivers' Blues*; Fiddlin' John Carson came back to the studios and remade *Taxes On The Farmer Feeds Them All*. Now and then the black community came out in sympathy; there were Peetie Wheatstraw's *Truckin' Thru' Traffic* and *Chicago Mill Blues*, while his *Working On The Project* was only one of dozens of black comments on the New Deal. But the recording activity in northern cities which stimulated these observations was not matched by any 'urban hillbilly' development; to stock their old-time lists Bluebird and Decca and A.R.C. had to go south. Not, as once, to the southeastern states, or at least not so much; the big new sound came from Texas and Oklahoma, an amalgam of blues, jazz and the south-eastern string band tradition with the local cowboy songs. It was called Western Swing.

It is an enigma to many followers of country music. Some solve it by deciding that authentic hillbilly sounds died in the middle thirties for want of sustenance. How else can they face bands which throw at them, successively, *St Louis Blues, Love In Bloom, Fan It, Spanish Fandango* and *I Like Bananas Because They Have No Bones*? The Western Swing musicians rejoiced in an eclecticism more extreme than any other school's, and in doing so captured a wider audience than native folkmusic had ever had. To be just, we should probably call Western Swing a folk-*like* music – a precursor, in that sense, of rock-and-roll (which picked a few ideas from it too). The Western Swingers offered pops, new and venerable; jazz standards and boogies; classic blues and rural blues hits; instrumental rags and waltzes; music-hall and novelty songs; Mexican dance tunes and cowboys' songs of the range. Among the prominent orchestras were Bob Wills' Texas Playboys, famous for their leader's cigar, steel guitarist Leon ('take it away, Leon!') McAuliffe, and their radio show over KVOO, Tulsa, OK. The Playboys' popularity was equalled in Texas by Milton Brown's Musical Brownies, whose fame grew apace from about 1934. The Brownies were perhaps a little less concerned with traditional country tunes, and slightly more with black material, than Wills' outfit; their records included versions of *Joe Turner Blues, Sitting On Top Of The World, You're Bound To Look Like A Monkey, Somebody's Been Using That Thing, Mama Don't Allow It* and so forth. Their *Louise Louise Blues* followed a few months after the original by black singer Johnny Temple, a solitary example of the flourishing 'cover' industry; many of the mid-thirties blues successes were quickly made available in white form, often under the auspices of the same company. Kokomo Arnold's *Milk Cow Blues* reappeared in Decca's hillbilly series, performed by Bob Wills' brother Johnny Lee; it also contributed distinctive touches to Bob's own *Brain Cloudy Blues*, among others. Likewise, *Kansas City Blues* was reworked by Leon's Lone Star Cowboys. And the longest-selling Western Swing hit of all was Wills' *Steel Guitar Rag* backed with *Swing Blues No. 1*, which could hardly have owed more to black music. The instrumental side was a modernised treatment of Sylvester Weaver's 1923 *Guitar Rag*; *Swing Blues No. 1* took at least one of its verses from a hiding place ten years deep: Blind Lemon's *Long Lonesome Blues*. There was nothing accidental in this. 'Sleepy' Johnson, who played guitar and banjo with the Playboys, remembers how the Fort Worth musicians used to gather round the phonograph in a local store and learn all the latest race hits. Lead singer Tommy Duncan had a mellow, sun-warmed voice, like a hillbilly Bing Crosby; and sure enough Bing 'covered' the Wills–Duncan *San Antonio Rose* and far out-sold their version.

In its line-up the Western Swing Band was just a string band. Two fiddles, at least two guitars (one steel), bass, tenor banjo – not the 5-string instrument – with sometimes a piano, but no drums for the first few years. Brass and reeds were optional, but the successful groups normally employed them. Lead voice, after the singer, was either fiddle or steel guitar; in this respect there were some similarities with contemporary Chicago blues. Casey Bill Weldon ('The Hawaiian Guitar Wizard') and Kokomo Arnold were noted steel-men; the former was for a time member of a group called 'The Brown Bombers Of Swing'. This may have been one of those combos that followed Western Swing tactics and indulged in broad repertoires of jazz, blues, hillbilly song and religious material – like the Blue Chips or Norridge Mayhams' Barbecue Boys. Weldon was

37 *Swing Blues* 1, by Bob Wills, a Western Swing hit of the mid-thirties

also one of the Hokum Boys, with Big Bill Broonzy and others, and one remembers with pleasure his gaily bawdy *Caught Us Doing It* and *Keep Your Mind On It*. Broonzy, with Carl Martin and the harmonica-player Jazz Gillum, made some interesting discs in the same year (1935) with a somewhat Western-Swing-like line-up of fiddle, harmonica, guitar, piano and string bass; the State Street Boys, as they called themselves, made one of the very few black recordings of *Midnight Special*.

The Western Swing fiddle, however, was not much copied by Blacks; the instrument was little heard in urban blues, and kept its place only in down-home string and jug bands, like Jack Kelly's. The Memphis Jug

Band, led by Will Shade, ceased to record after 1934, when it made a
set of spirited tunes that may have owed some ideas to Western Swing;
the cross-talk and encouragements which the musicians threw in remind
one of Bob Wills, while Charlie Burse's lunatic scat singing was closer
to Cab Calloway. Burse had another recording chance in 1939, when he
and another Memphian singer, James DeBerry, led swinging bands that
featured trumpet and saxophones. Burse's 'Memphis Mudcats' played
It Makes No Difference Now, a country ballad written by Floyd Tillman;
this was also recorded by Piano Red (backed with *Hey Good Lookin'*).
(Blues pianists delved into hillbilly music quite often in the postwar years;
Albert Ammons, for instance, made an amazing boogie transformation
of *You Are My Sunshine!*)

As Western Swing gathered momentum there came palmy days for
other country artists: Gene Autry, Roy Acuff, Wilf Carter ('Montana
Slim'), Bill and Cliff Carlisle. Acuff's *Wabash Cannonball* did well, and
crept, for a time, into at least one black artist's repertoire: 'I didn't know
too much about many blues; we had a radio down there but they all played
big band stuff and country and western music. Well, hillbilly music was
popular there and so I played hillbilly music on guitar and sung, like *She'll
Be Comin' Round The Mountain*, and *It Ain't Gonna Rain No More* and
Wabash Cannonball . . . At that time I didn't have no knowledge of music.
I even liked those – as I call it – hillbilly music . . . And when I played
out on street-corners, well, I'd be playing for white folks mostly and that
was the music they seemed to like better' (Titon, March 1969); thus Lazy
Bill Lucas, talking of his early days in Cape Girardeau, MO, around
1936–40. When he moved to Chicago he found different audiences –
'They tell you right away, "What you think I am, a hillbilly? I ain't no
hillbilly."' – and turned to piano, accompanying local bluesmen; but he
has not shut his ears to country music, and a recent LP shows him at
work on *Blueberry Hill* and similar stuff.

Not long after Lucas came to Chicago, a Library of Congress team
supervised by Alan Lomax and John Work journeyed to Nashville, where
it found a washboard band whose members included James Kelley
(mandolin), Frank Dalton (guitar), Tom Carroll (tin can) and Theobald
Stokes (washboard). Kelley may just have been the Jack Kelly who led

the South Memphis Jug Band back in 1933; the Nashville group recorded a *Kohoma Blues*, and Jack Kelly is known to have been from Mississippi, possibly from Coahoma County. The band played *Soldiers Joy* and *Arkansas Traveler*, also *You Rascal You* (for some reason always a favourite with small bands); then the washboard player demonstrated various dance tempi: breakdown, blues and swing. One cannot say, without hearing this recondite material, whether 'swing' meant, to Theobald Stokes, Western or jazz – Bob Wills or Benny Goodman. The second alternative is not so unlikely as it may seem; one of Doctor Ross' favourite breakdowns is called *Tommy Dorsey's Boogie*. (As Ross went to some pains to explain to the author, this piece is substantially the same as Walter Horton's celebrated harmonica showcase *Easy*.) Bourgeois semi-jazz did not generally make much impression upon rural Blacks, though *Blues In The Night* (Mercer-Arlen, 1941) 'convincingly suggested', as Spaeth puts it, 'the mood and style, if not the actual form, of true Negro folk-music', and was adopted by some black artists with appropriate affection. (Doctor Ross was one.)

It would be useless to try and find extensive deposits of Western Swing in black music of the forties; the hard driving jazz of Kansas City had much more to offer the race, and in any case the Southern audiences were moving back to a simpler sort of country blues, 'down-home' music. Economic difficulties encouraged solo performers and two- or three-man groups, while electrification could make an orchestra out of a guitar. Texan Blacks emigrated westwards to the ghettos of San Francisco and Los Angeles; men like Lightnin' Hopkins covered both the back-home and the transported market by working for Gold Star in Houston and then Aladdin and Imperial in LA. Southwestern Whites showed equal fidelity to their music when they made the great trek, as *Rolling Stone* reporter John Grissim, Jr, learned when interviewing a San Francisco newscaster about those years (the quotation has been slightly and insignificantly edited): 'KLX's manager called all the staff announcers together and said "I know you all hate the music but one of you guys is going to have to do a Western show – I don't care who does it." Two days later "Cactus Jack" (Cliff Johnson) started playing Western stuff off tapes (you couldn't get records because of the war shortage) and the few records we had around the station. A lot of people from Oklahoma, Texas and Arkansas kept asking him to play records by Bob Wills and his Texas Playboys. He'd never heard of him but they all insisted Wills was their little tin Jesus back there in the Southwest.' Grissim goes on to reveal that Wills' appearances in the area often outdrew those by the Dorsey, Goodman and Miller orchestras. For all that, they did not touch the black musicians, who developed a jazzy blues style with moaning vocals and prominent electric guitar solos; it drew upon KC sounds and employed the riff, but it had native Texan roots which can be heard in, for example, the 1939 recordings of Dusky Dailey and his Band.

However, Western Swing did not dominate country music in the thirties and forties. Plenty was happening in the east.

13 · OUT EAST

Once again, country music bloomed in eastern Tennessee and the areas encircling it, but the stringbands of Georgia and North Carolina were not surviving the Depression years at all well. Charlie Poole died of a heart attack in 1931, and his fiddle-playing companion Posey Rorer followed in 1936. Clayton McMichen left the Skillet-Lickers to form a modernist group, Riley Puckett devoted himself entirely to solo work, and Gid Tanner went back to his chicken farm. At their last Victor session in 1932 the Original Carolina Tar Heels sang *Times Ain't Like They Used To Be*, which exactly described both the economy and the music of the South.

For one thing, there was a fashion for duets. The Allen Brothers (Austin and Lee), probably from east Tennessee, sang a series of blues accompanying themselves on banjo, guitar and kazoo; but their chief success was with the old *Salty Dog* and *Next Week Sometime* themes. Victor kept *A New Salty Dog* in catalogue for years, but partly because of the reverse side, Alton and Rabon Delmore's *Brown's Ferry Blues*.

> Hard luck papa countin' his toes; you can smell his feet wherever he goes;
>   Lord, Lord, got them Brown's Ferry blues;
> Hard luck papa can't do his stuff; the trouble with him, he's been too rough;
>   Lord, Lord, got them Brown's Ferry blues.

The Delmores were from Elkmont, in Limestone County, AL, only a few miles from the state boundary with Tennessee. Adept guitarists, they were fond of the complex boogie patterns which east-coast Blacks were

38 The Allen Brothers,
Austin on banjo and Lee
on guitar, 1930

developing; their songs often fell into the verse/refrain form of, say, Blind Boy Fuller's *I'm A Rattlesnakin' Daddy*. They sang in soft-toned, bland harmony, appropriate enough in melancholic airs like *Gonna Lay Down My Old Guitar* (which John Jackson has neatly reproduced in a half-whisper), but monumentally unsuitable for any sort of blues but novelties, to which they largely confined themselves.

Novelty blues, indeed, were one of the most striking innovations of the thirties. The method was to set elaborate, witty lyrics to equally elaborate guitar parts; sometimes the yodel appeared, but often things were happening so fast that it couldn't be fitted in. Among the best exponents of the style were Bill and Cliff Carlisle and their associate Fred Kirby; typical productions were Bill's *Rattlin' Daddy*, Kirby's *I'm A Gold Diggin' Papa* and Cliff's *A Wild Cat Woman And A Tom Cat Man*. All three men owed a good deal to Jimmie Rodgers, but in their bawdy songs they progressed considerably further; Cliff's *Mouse's Ear Blues*, for instance, was about defloration, as was *Sal's Got A Meatskin* (which one of White's informants had heard among railroad gangs of Alabama Blacks some twenty years before). Neither Rodgers nor even Jimmie Davis would have chosen to sing

My gal, she's got a mouse's ear,
But she's gonna lose it when I shift my gear,

or

Place the needle in that hole and do that nasty swing,

from Cliff's *That Nasty Swing*, recorded about three months before Robert Johnson's not dissimilar *Phonograph Blues*. Carlisle's instrument was the dobro, a steel resonator guitar which he played in the bottleneck fashion, drawing long, clean lines of sound behind his or his brother's vocals. Fred Kirby used one too, as in his *Deep Sea Blues*, a sturdy revamping of *Trouble In Mind*. Bill Carlisle, on the other hand, favoured the conventional guitar, which he played with stunning speed and accuracy, often recreating on his own the complete two-guitar patterns of a Carter Family performance. His *Rattlin' Daddy*, which we have mentioned, was a popular theme; Jimmie Rodgers' cousin Jesse made one of the earliest recordings. It seems

CARLISLE, SMILING BILL
—Vocal (Old Time)

02819	Bachelor's Blues
02529	Barnyard Tumble
02839	Beneath the Weeping Willow Tree
02528	Blue Eyes
02831	Copper Head Mama
02839	Cowboy Jack
02529	Don't Marry the Wrong Woman
02831	Duvall County Blues
25021	Final Farewell, The
25021	Little Dobie Shack
02528	Lost on Life's Sea
02819	Penitentiary Blues
25020	Rattle Snake Daddy
02797	String Bean Mama
02797	Sugar Cane Mama
25020	Virginia Blues

39 Bill Carlisle, with some Vocalion titles

associated with, though not the same tune as, Blind Boy Fuller's composition (see above). The Carlisles sometimes worked in the Carolinas, and may have seen Fuller, but they and their ilk had no reciprocal influence upon him; his only excursions into white territory were *Cat Man Blues*, which was a version of *Our Goodman*, and *She's Funny That Way*, a tentative stab at the popular song of the same name.

The Carlisles came originally from Wakefield, KY. Cliff had early experience of blues playing with a young relation, Lillian Truax, who sang low-down blues and could also play guitar. He toured with shows as a yodeller and Hawaiian guitarist, and his recorded repertoire embraces every kind of country song: sentimental, western, religious and novelty. Pieces like *Ash Can Blues* and *Rooster Blues* owed their notions to black music, but often he used an ingenuity and turn of phrase foreign to that tradition, and closer to Jimmie Rodgers. This is not to say that black song in the thirties was less inventive; but it aimed either for a tough, jivey language or for subdued lyricism. The two approaches are well exemplified by, respectively, Peetie Wheatstraw and Leroy Carr. Each of these artists

40 Cliff Carlisle, *c.* 1930

also illustrates a link with the white singers; Wheatstraw, in *Third Street's Going Down* and others, commented upon his urban surroundings and on the post-Depression relief programmes rather as southerners described their industrial revolution (cotton-mills especially) or supported local politicians against the Washington machine (as they thought of it); Carr, on the other hand, occasionally sang melancholy ballad-like compositions, his accompanist Scrapper Blackwell filling in with dreamy mock-Hawaiian work on guitar.

Carr and Blackwell were one of the few blues duos of the thirties. The prevailing sound was that of the urban group; migration patterns had made the northern cities of New York, Chicago and Detroit the centres of black musical development. Unlike white singers, the Blacks had no attachment to down-home country, and their songs reflect the confrontation with city life and, sometimes, with self-betterment.

I have my books in my hand, I'm goin' 'cross to the Booker T.;
I'm goin' to get Mr So-and-So to teach me my ABC.

                                        Washboard Sam, *Booker T. Blues*

If a musician had the country twang in his voice, it soon disappeared.
William 'Jazz' Gillum, from Bessemer, AL, sang a *Sarah Jane* which came
from the same root as the white song *I Was Born Ten Thousand Years
Ago* (compare also Charlie Poole's *I'm The Man That Rode The Mule
'Round The World*); that was at his second session, and he was never to
go so far from the blues again.

   This urbanising of the blues may be contrasted with the efforts of many
eastern Whites to revive old-time traditions. The brothers Bill and Earl
Bolick, from Hickory, NC, did a great deal to repopularise the ballads
and broadsides of the two previous centuries, such as *The Butcher's Boy*
and *Mary Of The Wild Moor*. Calling themselves the Blue Sky Boys, playing guitar and mandolin, and singing in delicate harmony, they quickly
made a name in North Carolina, aided by exposure over WBT, Charlotte.
This work came their way through J. W. Fincher, the local representative
of the Crazy Water Crystals Co. (a patent medicine manufacturer) and
an enthusiastic hirer of hillbilly musicians. He also employed Howard
and Dorsey Dixon, who played steel and conventional guitar respectively,
in the manner of Darby and Tarlton (whom they knew well). Like the
Bolicks, they sang much religious material; *What Would You Give In
Exchange For Your Soul?* was recorded in Parts 1 to 5, and *Maple On The
Hill* – which Jimmie Tarlton says he wrote – stimulated several versions,
as well as an *Answer To . . .* The best-known *Maple On The Hill*, though,
was by Mainer's Mountaineers.

   J. E. Mainer was doffing and piecing-up in a Concord, NC, cotton-
mill about the same time as Blind Boy Fuller was busking in the tobacco
town of Winston-Salem. A fine old-time fiddler, he drew about him a
band which included many musicians who went on to considerable fame
on their own. They drew from the stringband tradition, recording – as
Charlie Poole and the Skillet-Lickers had done – *Watermelon On The Vine*,
Take Me Home To The Sweet Sunny South, *John Henry* and others; but
they imitated the action of the Western Swingers in combining this

common stock material with newer sentimental and religious composi-tions. The 'Crazy Mountaineers' came to the attention of bandleader Fisher Hendley, whose 'Aristocratic Pigs' were advertising sausage-meat over WBT; soon Mainer and his men were on the Crazy Water payroll. They made their recording debut in August 1935 – some two weeks after Blind Boy Fuller did – and they have been playing, though with changes in personnel, ever since. Now seen as exponents of what might be called proto-bluegrass, they are popular among folksong enthusiasts.

The band had an excellent singer, yodeller and guitarist in 'Daddy' John Love, who sounded like a cross between Jimmie Rodgers and Bill Carlisle. *Broken Hearted Blues* took its refrain – 'my woman's done made a fool out of me' – from Jimmie's last blue yodel, but was an affecting personal creation. Similar neo-Rodgers performances were to be heard now and then from Byron Parker's Mountaineers, who made an amusing *Married Life Blues*; the quartet's reputation at present stems from the acknowledged influence of its banjoist Snuffy Jenkins upon Earl Scruggs, and thus upon the whole bluegrass movement. Scruggs' early work, which was, without exaggeration, epoch-making, was under the aegis of Bill Monroe, who also showed a fondness for crisp reworkings of Rodgers' material and similar yodelled blues. Monroe was born in 1911, a Kentuckian, and he learned much of his technique from a black fiddler and guitarist, Arnold Schultz. 'Arnold and myself,' he recalls, 'we played for a lot of square dances back in those days.' (It was Schultz' 'choke' style of guitar picking that was to influence Merle Travis.) John Cohen has written that 'stylistically speaking, Bill Monroe's Bluegrass was probably the finest merging of the blues and the old Anglo tradition to make a new music incorporating qualities from both', but early Monroe recordings, with his brother Charlie's guitar backing up the mandolin, show only passing references to black music, as in *Nine Pound Hammer Is Too Heavy*, with its worksong phrases. (The story of bluegrass, and its black associations, must be left to the second volume of this study.)

Most of the above-mentioned artists worked, travelled and recorded only in the South; black musical activity outside the northern cities, how-ever, was remarkably poorly documented during the thirties. The Victor recording trip to Charlotte, NC, in June 1936 gives a striking example of this. In nine days the company recorded the phenomenal total of 224 titles, of which less than a quarter – 54 – were by black musicians. Of the rest, 38 were of jazz or religious material; the remainder was made up of half-a-dozen by pianist 'Peg Leg' Ben Abney – one of whose songs was Fuller's *Rattlesnakin' Daddy* again – and ten by an odd singer–guitarist named Philip McCutcheon, the 'Cedar Creek Sheik', who concentrated on bawdry; 'cock for sale, buy it from the poultry man', sung in a high, almost expressionless voice, was one of the more extraordinary black offerings of the decade.

In the same town, the following year, one of the last pre-war black bands had a little session. Eddie Kelly, 'Bill' and 'Walter', playing washboard, harmonica, kazoo and guitar, made eight brisk titles, including *Come On Round To My House, Baby* and *Mama Don't Allow* (as *Shim Shaming*). They may have been from Polk County, but nothing else is known of them, and they remain an anachronism in the blues milieu of 1937. So, at least, one is tempted to think, considering the flood of urban blues; but it is true that black country music may have changed more slowly. Evidence is scanty. The first generation of blues singers was dying out; Blind Lemon passed in 1930, Charley Patton in 1934, Blind Blake sometime round the mid-thirties. Those that followed were open to sounds from the north, whether they lived there or stayed in their Southern homes. So Robert Johnson drew elements of his work from Lonnie Johnson and Leroy Carr, while Mississippian neighbours of his, like Robert 'Baby Boy' Warren or Willie '61' Blackwell, experimented with words and produced cool, almost hip, blues.

Robert Johnson is a good example of the black musician who seems, during the thirties, to be asserting the existence of the colour line and its social consequences. This was already reflected in small things; for example, family groups, particularly pairs or trios of brothers, were as common in white music as they were scarce in black. And only rarely would one find a race artist singing both secular and religious material; the black listener, if he wanted church music, did not look for it from Roosevelt Sykes or Tampa Red; he went to church. Sentimental pieces about silver-haired daddies or sweethearts of yesteryear held nothing for a black man who might never have known his father and was more concerned about the sweetheart of today. White Southerners used their songs to affirm the ideals of friendship, family loyalty and old time religion – concepts outside the experience of most black people. To some extent it had always been so, but now there were more rootless, jobless and luckless Blacks, the proper function of whose music was to express, and thus ease, the new hard times – not to reminisce about the old.

Yet, though the common-stock tunes and songs were being somewhat neglected, black and white traditions still met here and there. Though their records did not reflect it, many black musicians continued to play for Whites and to keep their ears open to hillbilly developments. Some of country music's most influential new sounds, on the other hand, were adaptations of black models. And, underlying all the changes in musical fashion, there was a parity in the living conditions of black and white southerners; they ate the same food, spoke substantially the same language, endured the same poverty and found relief from it in similar ways. There was always an escape route in the blues for every man, since the blues could 'creep up on you and carry your mind away' whatever your colour. Not exactly the same blues; count up the troubles of the white man and then those of the black, and the second list will always be longer by one entry. But blues about 'plain old bein' lonesome . . . for a job, spendin' money, good whiskey', as Woody Guthrie put it – these blues were universal. In singing them the races almost attained a sort of union. But the barriers were not to fall; what God, in the eyes of the Southern white man, had put asunder, no musical communion could join together. Which is not to say that the blues failed in anything; they had never set themselves such a task. If it is of any value that we know, from their songs, something of the lives and emotions of the blues singers, black and white, then the blues have done their business. Through them we can begin to understand what it was to be alive in that troubled world, in those troubled times. And that is a legacy we should cherish.

BIBLIOGRAPHY

BOOKS

Allen, Frederick Lewis. 1931. *Only Yesterday: An Informal History Of The Nineteen-Twenties*. New York: Harper and Brothers.

Blesh, Rudi, and Janis, Harriet. 1966. *They All Played Ragtime*. Rev. edn. New York: Oak Publications.

Charters, Samuel B. 1959. *The Country Blues*. New York: Rinehart and Co., Inc. 1960. London: Michael Joseph Ltd.
  1967. *The Bluesmen*. New York: Oak Publications.

Dorson, Richard M. 1959. *American Folklore*. Chicago: University of Chicago Press.

Doyle, Bertram Wilbur. 1937. *The Etiquette Of Race Relations In The South: A Study Of Social Control*. Chicago: University of Chicago Press.

Godrich, John, and Dixon, Robert M. W. 1969. *Blues & Gospel Records 1902–1942*. Rev. edn. London: Storyville Publications and Co.

Greenway, John. 1953. *American Folksongs Of Protest*. Philadelphia: University of Pennsylvania Press.

Keil, Charles. 1966. *Urban Blues*. Chicago and London: University of Chicago Press.

Lawless, Ray M. 1960. *Folksingers And Folksongs In America: A Handbook Of Biography, Bibliography, And Discography*. New York: Duell, Sloan and Pearce.

Laws, Jr, G. Malcolm. 1950. *Native American Balladry: A Descriptive Study And a Bibliographical Syllabus*. (Publications of The American Folklore Society, Bibliographical and Special Series, volume 1.) Philadelphia: The American Folklore Society. 1964. Rev. edn.

Leadbitter, Mike, and Slaven, Neil. 1968. *Blues Records: 1943–1966*. London: Hanover Books Ltd; New York: Oak Publications.

Logan, Rayford W. 1957. *The Negro In The United States: A Brief History*. Princeton, NJ: D. Van Nostrand Co., Inc.

MacInnes, Colin. 1967. *Sweet Saturday Night: Pop Song 1840–1920*. London: MacGibbon and Kee Ltd 1969. Panther Arts.

Malone, Bill C. 1968. *Country Music, USA: A Fifty-Year History*. (Publications of The American Folklore Society, Memoir Series, volume 54.) Austin and London: University of Texas Press for the American Folklore Society.

McCarthy, Albert, *et al.* 1968. *Jazz On Record: A Critical Guide To The First 50 Years: 1917–1967*. London: Hanover Books Ltd; New York: Oak Publications.

Oliver, Paul. 1960. *Blues Fell This Morning*. London: Cassell and Co., Ltd; 1963. New York: Collier Books (retitled *The Meaning Of The Blues*).

    1965. *Conversation With The Blues*. London: Cassell and Co., Ltd; 1965. New York: Horizon.

    1968. *Screening The Blues*. London: Cassell and Co., Ltd; 1970. New York: Oak Publications.

    1969. *The Story Of The Blues*. London: Barrie and Rockcliff, The Cresset Press; Philadelphia: Chilton Books.

Patterson, Caleb Perry. 1922. *The Negro In Tennessee, 1790–1865*. (University of Texas Bulletin No. 2205.) Austin: University of Texas Press.

Randel, William Peirce. 1965. *The Ku Klux Klan: A Century Of Infamy*. London: Hamish Hamilton Ltd.

Rust, Brian. 1969. *The Victor Master Book: Volume 2 (1925–1936)*. Hatch End, Middx.: published by the author.

Scarborough, Dorothy. 1963. *On The Trail Of Negro Folk-Songs*. Hatboro, PA: Folklore Associates, Inc. (facsimile reprint of original 1925 edition).

Shelton, Robert, and Goldblatt, Burt. 1966. *The Country Music Story*. New York: Bobbs-Merrill Co., Inc.

Spaeth, Sigmund. 1948. *A History Of Popular Music In America*. New York: Random House, Inc.; 1960. London: Phoenix House.

Strachwitz, Chris [ed.]. 1964. *American Folk Music Occasional No. 1*. Berkeley, CA: AFMO.

White, Newman I. 1965. *American Negro Folk-Songs*. Hatboro, PA: Folklore Associates, Inc. (facsimile reprint of original 1928 edition).

ARTICLES

Boggs, Dock. 1964. 'I Always Loved The Lonesome Songs', *Sing Out!* 14:3 (July), 32–9.

Carter, June. 1967. 'I Remember The Carter Family', *Sing Out!* 17:3 (June/July), 6–11.

Cohen, John. 1964–5. 'The Folk Music Interchange: Negro And White', *Sing Out!* 14:6 (December/January), 42–9.

   1966. 'Country Music Outside Nashville', *Sing Out!* 16:1 (February/March), 40–2.

   1966. 'Roscoe Holcomb: First Person', *Sing Out!* 16:2 (April/May), 3–7.

Cohen, Norm. 1969. 'Tapescript: Interview with Welby Toomey (T7–197)', *JEMF Quarterly*, 5:2 (Summer), 63–5.

Cohen, Norm, and Cohen, Anne. 1966. 'The Legendary Jimmie Tarleton', *Sing Out!* 16:4 (September), 16–19.

Green, Archie. 1961. 'The Carter Family's "Coal Miner's Blues"', *Southern Folklore Quarterly*, 25:4 (December), 226–37.

   1965. 'Hillbilly Music: Source And Symbol', *Journal Of American Folklore*, 78:309 (July–September), 204–8.

   1966. 'Dorsey Dixon: Minstrel Of The Mills', *Sing Out!* 16:3 (July), 10–13.

Greenway, John. 1957. 'Jimmie Rodgers – A Folksong Catalyst', *Journal Of American Folklore*, 70:277 (July–September), 231–4.

Grissim, Jr, John. 1969. 'California White Man's Shit Kickin' Blues', *Rolling Stone*, 36 (28 June), 13–14, 17–19, 22, 24–8.

Groom, Bob. 1968– . 'The Legacy Of Blind Lemon', *Blues World*, 18 (January 1968), 14–16; 20 (July 1968), 33–7; 21 (October 1968), 30–2; 23 (April 1969), 5–7; 24 (July 1969), 9–10; 25 (October 1969), 9–10.

Hickerson, Joseph. 1965. 'Alan Lomax's "Southern Journey": A Review-Essay', *Ethnomusicology*, 9:3 (September), 313–22.

Kent, Don. 1969. 'On The Trail Of Luke Jordan', *Blues Unlimited*, 66 (October), 4–6.

Lomax, Alan. 1959. 'Folk Song Style', *American Anthropologist*, 61:6 (December), 927–54.

Mainer, J. E. 1968. 'J. E. Mainer Of Concord, North Carolina', *Sing Out!* 18:1 (March/April), 22–7.

Odum, Howard W. 1911. 'Folk-Song And Folk-Poetry As Found In The Secular Songs Of The Southern Negroes', *Journal Of American Folk-Lore*, 24:93 (July–September), 255–94; 94 (October–December), 351–96.

Pankake, John. 1964. 'Sam And Kirk McGee From Sunny Tennessee', *Sing Out!* 14:5 (November), 46–50.

Perrow, E. C. 1912–15. 'Songs And Rhymes From The South', *Journal Of American Folk-Lore*, 25:96 (April–June 1912), 137–55; 26:100 (April–June 1913), 123–73; 28:108 (April–June 1915), 129–90.

Russell, Tony. 1969. 'The Kansas City Dog Walkers', *Jazz Monthly*, 168 (February), 8–10.

1969. 'Key To The Bushes: Johnson Boys', *Blues Unlimited*, 67 (November), 19.

Smith, Hobart. 1965. 'I Just Got The Music In My Head', *Sing Out!* 14:6 (January), 8–15.

Spottswood, Richard, and Jason, David A. 1968. 'Discoveries Concerning Recorded Ragtime', *Jazz Journal*, 21:2 (February), 7.

Titon, Jeff. 1969. 'Calling All Cows: Lazy Bill Lucas', *Blues Unlimited*, 60 (March), 10–11; 61 (April), 9–10; 62 (May), 11–12; 63 (June), 9–10.

Welding, Pete. 1968. 'Interview With Carl Martin', *78 Quarterly*, 1:2, 27–31.

14 · AFTERWORD

The point of *Blacks, Whites and Blues* was to suggest different ways of listening to, and thinking about, black and white vernacular musics and their relationship to each other. It was an attempt to reshape the terrain: a big job, but there are places where I might have operated the earth-mover more subtly. *Blacks, Whites and Blues* is obviously a young man's book. Its tone is earnest, even preachy. Too many of its ideas were acquired in the library rather than learned in the field – and even at that, the library, or at least its record shelves, had not been large enough: there was a great deal I ought to have heard and had not. That said, it has become clear to me that such a book cannot be written only on the basis of recordings. A central fact about this line of enquiry is that much of the evidence has to be looked for in the cracks between the sources: in the records not made, the encounters unsuspected, the questions not asked.

It was a quirk of the book, too, that in throwing grappling hooks back and forth between the brigantine *Blues* and the good ship *Country Music*, I spent what might seem a disproportionate amount of time on the decks of the latter. There were practical reasons for that. *Blacks, Whites and Blues* was commissioned for a series directed explicitly at blues enthusiasts, most of whom had little knowledge of, or interest in, country music. In those days, blues musicians undergoing the peculiar grilling to which they were subjected the moment their feet hit European soil were rarely asked about white musicians in their background, and any reminiscences of that kind which they might volunteer would be printed – if they *were* printed – with an implied 'Just fancy that!' One of the seeds of *Blacks, Whites and Blues* may have been sown in 1965 when I met the black musician Doctor Ross and learned that his harmonica mentors included Wayne Raney and Lonnie Glosson. They were a white duo, popular on rural radio, and I knew just enough to have heard of them.

So it was necessary, in order to interest blues enthusiasts in notions of how black musical traditions had interacted with those of white contemporaries, to be more expansive about the latter, who had been less, or less accessibly, charted by historians, and scarcely at all by discographers. I stress this not only to explain the structure of the book but because the landscape of American vernacular music studies now looks so different, not least that border-country which I tentatively mapped. Personalities and ideas that were obscure in 1970 have emerged, or been hauled, into at least a half-light. Many seem to have been absorbed into the received history of the subject.

To take an example almost at random, James Sallis' *The Guitar Players*, a study of the major exponents of twentieth-century American guitar music, not only discusses Eddie Lang, Lonnie Johnson and Charlie Christian but devotes a whole chapter to the country musician Riley Puckett: so capacious a brief would have been unthinkable in the 1970s. Standard jazz histories now take account of Western Swing and its creative figures like Bob Dunn and Eldon Shamblin; the Dunn/Milton Brown recording *Taking Off* is included in the CD accompanying Richard Sudhalter's revisionist survey *Lost Chords: White Musicians and Their Contribution to Jazz*. Bill Monroe and Bob Wills, though by no means obscure in 1970, have come to be recognised as colossal figures, key elements in the fusions that created two all-American musics (Rosenberg, 1974; Townsend, 1976). Dock Boggs, thanks to the imaginative if not wholly persuasive pleading of the cultural historian Greil Marcus, may be destined for a kind of apotheosis – or should it be demonisation? – alongside Robert Johnson, twin Mr Kurtzs at the heart of downhome darkness (Marcus, 1997).

So the subject has come a long way as a scholarly discipline. (This is not to say that it is always pursued with scholarly rigour. An entire book has been devoted to the proposition that Western Swing simply *is* a form of jazz, not country music at all: a mistaken notion, and no wonder, since the author was unaware of almost all the thirty-year literature of Western Swing, a shortcoming that evidently did not trouble her publisher, a university press.) The serious literature of early country music has grown, not quite apace with blues studies, but not too far behind them. In addition to reliable histories like Bill Malone's *Country Music, USA*, which has been considerably updated since the 1968 edition I cited in *Blacks, Whites and Blues*, and a clutch of regional studies, books or monographs have been published on Jimmie Rodgers (Porterfield, 1979), Charlie Poole (Rorrer, 1982) and Milton Brown (Ginell, 1994), as well as on Fiddlin' John Carson, the Stoneman Family and others.

Yet writing on the core subject of *Blacks, Whites and Blues*, the interaction of black and white music makers, remains oddly sparse. Histories of popular music since the Second World War, especially those focusing on rock 'n' roll, routinely acknowledge the influence of black music on Elvis Presley and his contemporaries, and the blending role played by record companies like Sun and King. Essayists like Peter Guralnick, Greil Marcus and Colin Escott need no direction from me or any other musico-archaeological pilot to plot their courses expertly through the vortices of the 1940s and 1950s. The period before rock 'n' roll on which I narrowed my gaze in *Blacks, Whites and Blues* attracted far less study, and what there is tends to be found in scattered essays and CD booklets. I draw the reader's attention to a couple of informative articles on the blue yodel (Coltman, 1976; Abbott and Seroff, 1993), to the extraordinary story of the 'jake leg' epidemic and the songs it elicited from white and black musicians (Morgan and Tulloss, 1978) and to an intricate study of the highly mobile song *Corrine Corrina* (Waterman, in press). These aside, the huge subject of white blues, a genre eminently suited to comparative textual and musical analysis, has a bibliography consisting of little more than a competent short survey by Charles Wolfe (Wolfe, 1993).

In recent years I have taken the opportunity offered by Johnny Parth's Document Records not only to select and organise reissues of early country recording artists but to use the notes to ask again, reformulate and add to some of the questions posed in *Blacks, Whites and Blues*, especially the matter of how and why white musicians have used the blues form.

Document's collections of the Allen Brothers, Herschel Brown and Sam McGee – to take three artists who were mentioned in *Blacks, Whites and Blues* – offer opportunities for case studies of artists for whom blues were a significant, even dominant, part of their repertoire.

For the Allens, whose extensive recorded output is replete with blues – or at least with pieces *called* blues, a distinction touched upon in a moment – it appears to be the format most appropriate to first-person narratives with comic, suggestive or topical themes. For Herschel Brown, on the other hand – a figure, incidentally, who tenaciously resists biographical unwinkling – playing with the blues seems to have been an opportunity to play at crossing the racial line, putting on blackface like Amos 'n' Andy. His *Talking Nigger Blues* might be read as a joke at the African American's expense, although the narrative is delivered against a backdrop of guitar-playing that might well have been learned from black musicians. To complicate the issue, this and its companion pieces are not, in their musical or textual architecture, blues at all but humorous narrations in the manner of Chris Bouchillon, an idiom that came to be called 'talking blues', probably after the title of Bouchillon's first hit. Then again, one could argue that Brown's meandering stand-up-comedian rap ('Sure am glad to get back down in this here country. Whenever I get back down here in the Old South it makes me feel good. It remind me of back when I was a kid. You know, back in the good old days. Back when women wore clothes') is essentially a looser form of the discursive, observational blues lyric.

By contrast again, while Sam McGee's *Railroad Blues* enshrines the kind of joke that would have appealed to Brown or the Allens ('I met a little gipsy in a fortune-telling place. She read my mind, then she slapped my face'), his instrumental inventions for guitar or banjo-guitar like *Knoxville Blues* and *Easy Rider* are in part *hommages* to obscure or forgotten African American players from whom he learned.

Of these three approaches the Allen Brothers' is the most typical. Like them, most of the recorded white blues singers of the 1920s and 1930s, the period at the core of *Blacks, Whites and Blues*, seem to have regarded the blues as a medium for particular sorts of narrative and performing styles inappropriate to and unsanctioned by the other expressive forms available to them. Blues frees the artist alike from the disengagement of the ballad, the fervour of the hymn and the melodrama of the Victorian songbook. There are no little whitewashed cabins in the world of the blues, no grey-haired mothers, no churches in the wildwood: it is not that sort of landscape at all. Slipping into the blues, the white artist signals an interlude, a shift in the tone of the performance, as if he (or, much more rarely, she) were slipping on a new costume, or a mask. To step out in the guise of the blues is to step out of line. Blues confers a licence to break rules and taboos, say the unsayable, create its own dark carnival.

All of which, to a young and imaginative white Southern musician of the 1920s or 1930s, would have been enormously seductive. (It's not as if we lack later examples of white ears being bewitched by, and retuned to, the sound of black America.) Nor should we overlook the simple fact that blues was *new*. Only the most solipsistic of musicians ignored the ebb and flow of fashion in what was coming to be seen more and more widely not just as 'music' but as 'the music business'. Some might decline a seat on the blues bandwagon because of their age, or others out of religious disapproval, but for the majority it was a journey into the future.

So far did the record business share that view that it became quite silly about the term, pasting 'Blues' into the titles of songs or tunes on the flimsiest of musical excuses (and on African Americans' recordings no less than those of their white contemporaries). Musicians did likewise, though sometimes for their own reasons. According to the white Mississippi fiddler Hoyt Ming, numerous tunes came to be called 'blues' simply because their original titles were lost in transmission: 'Sometimes a fiddler would learn to play a certain piece . . . but he didn't know what [his source] called it . . . Well, he'd just name it some kind of blues' (Russell, 1976). Certainly the titular coupling of a place-name (town, county, state) and 'Blues' very often heads a tune of undeniable blues structure or arguable blues character, such as Narmour and Smith's *Carroll County Blues*, which was in Ming's mind as he reflected on this matter, or indeed Ming's own *Tupelo Blues* – which, by the bye, was given that local name by the recording supervisor Ralph Peer, who preferred it to the more (or less, or differently) exotic title by which Ming knew it, *Florida Blues*. Frequently, too, however, the place/*Blues* combination merely informs us that the tune belonged, in some sense, to that locality, or to someone who lived there, and might as easily have been called wherever-it-is *Rag* or *Stomp* or *Breakdown*.

As Hoyt Ming went on to observe, 'When it got started, why, it just began to spread, you know. And of course all the blues didn't sound alike. Maybe some of the blues didn't sound so haunting or lonesome like. But it became so popular that some of them would name it the blues anyway.' It was a confusion that could be profitable. When the Cauley Family, a stringband from Florida, recorded the popular composition *I Don't Love Nobody*, it was issued as *Duplin County Blues*. Were the musicians cannily diverting a payment that would otherwise have been due to the copyright-holder? Or did their record company hope to sell the public an old tune in the guise of a new one?

As I said earlier, any study headed in the direction that *Blacks, Whites and Blues* aimed to take needed to look beyond what was documented, to identify musical interactions of which recordings offered little or no evidence. I was reminded of that talking to the country musician Stan Clements (brother of the more famous Zeke), who had passed much of his professional life in playing contexts, such as The Milton Berle Show, where he would not often have been thrown into the ambit of black musicians. Yet in his youth, he said, he had been greatly impressed by an African American fiddler and guitarist whom he saw on a visit to central Mississippi, and when he came across their recording of *The Jazz Fiddler* – for it turned out that they were Lonnie Chatman and Walter Vincson, alias the Mississippi Sheiks – he was at pains to learn it.

A more ramified example is the relationship between the white banjo player Virgil Anderson, from the Tennessee/Kentucky border country of the Cumberland Plateau, and the African American Bertram family, with whom he associated in his youth, in the 1920s, and from whom he learned numerous blues. The Bertrams never formally recorded, and Anderson's connection with them was revealed only when he made his own first recordings in the late 1970s. As it turned out, fiddler Cuje Bertram had other rememberers in the region: the white musician Dick Burnett of Monticello, Kentucky, recalled him as a notable player, though only one of several black fiddlers he knew. Some home recordings of Bertram in later life reveal intriguing similarities between his playing and that of Burnett's recording partner Leonard Rutherford. (They also incidentally reveal an African American musician with no taste for the blues.)

Annotating those home recordings for a Document CD I wrote: 'There is a good deal of evidence that the Upper Central Southern states of Tennessee and Kentucky have a complex and fascinating history of African-American fiddling. In central Kentucky, for example, around Richmond, Owen Walker and Jim Booker were older associates of the prolifically recorded white fiddler Doc Roberts . . . Wayne County, in south Central Kentucky, had several black fiddlers' (Russell, 1998). Such spidery networks of African American music-making in the nineteenth and early twentieth centuries may be traced in other areas and on other instruments. Studying the history of black banjo music in Appalachia, Cece Conway and Scott Odell concluded that:

> Black and White banjo players together created the five-string banjo and its music. Their ability to interact with each other through song and dance allowed them to cross class and racial borders. During the Civil War this musical exchange intensified and contributed to fiddle and banjo string bands in the mountains and along the rivers . . . Musical interaction remained important after the war in railroad crews, in coal camps, and in traveling circuses and medicine shows. (Conway and Odell, 1998)

It is hard to resist the conclusion that African American musicians had a crucial role in the transmission of repertoire and playing styles not merely within their own community, nor just in the larger arena of racially shared music – what in *Blacks, Whites and Blues* was described as the 'common stock' – but even on musical terrain where one might not expect to spy their footprints. I now think it probable that most of the Southern fiddle and stringband music loosely categorised by terms like 'old-time' – music that for three generations has been almost wholly practised by Whites – is in fact of mixed ancestry.

When *Blacks, Whites and Blues* was written, such a view was highly speculative. Less than twenty years later Peter van der Merwe could write:

African and European fiddles have much in common, both in themselves and in playing technique, making it easy for an Afro-American fiddle style to develop. But they also have many differences which continue to present the fiddler with the choice: European or African? The same is true of modal systems, rhythms, melodic contours, form, and harmony. Conveniently for the growth of the popular style, the peculiar history of the American South has ensured that the sum of such moments of choice has been unusually great.   (Van der Merwe, 1989)

Another ten years on, Marshall Wyatt observes in notes to a CD compilation of recordings by African American fiddlers that 'Although most American fiddlers today are white, it is the black influence that distinguishes their music from Irish and English predecessors' (Wyatt, 1999). Statements like those, once potentially controversial, now cause nobody to turn a hair. Where speculation may still rule is about how the lineage became so murky: why, around the beginning of the twentieth century, the African American began to fade from it, and within a couple of decades was all but invisible.

The 1970 text of *Blacks, Whites and Blues* has been republished almost without change. I have corrected one or two misprints but done nothing to paper over the cracks of error or repair the rot of bad guesswork. Still, if only to reassure the reader that I am aware of them, I feel I should plug some of the more damaging leaks in this old building. It is now known for certain that the Baxters – fiddling father Andrew and guitar-playing son Jim – were black (and from around Calhoun, Georgia) and the Carver Brothers, despite a reported association with Josh White, white. Frank Hutchison was from West Virginia, not Virginia (and we now know a good deal more about the black influences on his music), while the Allen Brothers were from Chattanooga in East Tennessee (but the oft-told story that they sued Columbia Records for issuing one of their discs in a 'race' series remains unconfirmed). Blind Blake did not record with the white Kentucky Thorobreds, though one of the latter group, fiddler Doc Roberts, did record with members of the African American Booker family.

In my 1970 Foreword I expressed the hope that *Blacks, Whites and Blues* would help to bring recognition to some of the almost forgotten musicians it celebrated. Today figures like Frank Hutchison, Jimmie Davis, Darby and Tarlton or Cliff Carlisle are securely located in the history of American vernacular music and their recordings widely available. Whether my book played any part in this is not for me to guess, but I do know, because they have been kind enough to tell me so, that many people over the years have been prompted by it to open their ears and change their minds, and I could not ask for anything more.

Tony Russell

BIBLIOGRAPHY

Abbott, Lynn, and Seroff, Doug. 1993. 'America's Blue Yodel', *Musical Traditions*, 11 (Late), 2–11.

Coltman, Robert. 1976. 'Roots of the Country Yodel: Notes Toward a Life History', *JEMF Quarterly*, 12:42 (Summer), 91–4.

Conway, Cece, and Odell, Scott. 1998. Notes to *Black Banjo Songsters of North Carolina and Virginia* (Smithsonian Folkways SF CD 40079), Washington, DC: Smithsonian Folkways Recordings.

Ginell, Cary. 1994. *Milton Brown and the Founding of Western Swing*. Urbana: University of Illinois Press.

Marcus, Greil. 1997. *Invisible Republic: Bob Dylan's Basement Tapes*, New York: Henry Holt and Co., Inc.

Morgan, John P., and Tulloss, Thomas C. 1978. 'The Jake Walk Blues', *Old Time Music*, 28 (Spring), 17–24.

Porterfield, Nolan. 1979. *Jimmie Rodgers: The Life and Times of America's Blue Yodeler*. Urbana: University of Illinois Press.

Rorrer, Kinney. 1982. *Rambling Blues: The Life and Songs of Charlie Poole*. London: Old Time Music.

Rosenberg, Neil V. 1974. *Bill Monroe and his Blue Grass Boys: An Illustrated Discography*. Nashville: The Country Music Foundation Press.

Russell, Tony. 1976. 'Pep-Stepping with the Mings', *Old Time Music*, 20 (Spring), 11–16.

    1998. Notes to *Black Fiddlers* (Document DOCD-5631), Vienna: Document Records.

Sallis, James. 1982. *The Guitar Players*. Lincoln: University of Nebraska Press.

Townsend, Charles R. 1976. *San Antonio Rose: The Life and Music of Bob Wills*. Urbana: University of Illinois Press.

Van der Merwe, Peter. 1989. *Origins of the Popular Style*. Oxford: Oxford University Press.

Waterman, Christopher A. in press. '*Corrine, Corrina*, Bo Chatmon, and the Excluded Middle', in Bohlman, P., and Radano, R. (eds.) *Music and the Racial Imagination*. Chicago: University of Chicago Press.

Wolfe, Charles. 1993. 'A Lighter Shade of Blue: White Country Blues', in Cohn, Lawrence (ed.) *Nothing But the Blues*. New York: Abbeville Press, 233–63.

Wyatt, Marshall. 1999. Notes to *Violin, Sing the Blues for Me* (Old Hat CD-1002), Raleigh, NC: Old Hat Enterprises.

RECOMMENDED RECORDINGS

This selective list includes much of the source material recommended in the original edition, and a good deal more besides, but substituting for long-deleted LPs currently (or recently) available CDs. Many of the anthologies will be found to include work by the lesser-recorded artists referred to in the text. I have excluded from this list African American artists whose work is abundantly available both complete on Document and selectively elsewhere, such as Blind Lemon Jefferson, Leadbelly or Blind Willie McTell; information on their recordings may readily be found in Document's catalogues and on various internet sites. I have also been more selective than I was in 1970 with old-time/hillbilly recordings, since far more are available, and have focussed upon those with particular relevance to the subject.

Special rosettes of recommendation are attached to the Yazoo anthologies *Before the Blues* and their several twin-volume successors, which in their wayward blending of recordings from all the Southern traditions, black and white, embody something of the spirit of *Blacks, Whites and Blues* and its own (also long-deleted) companion album.

Allen Brothers
Vols. 1–3 (1927–1934) (Document DOCD-8033-35)

Clarence Ashley [and others]
Doc Watson & Clarence Ashley – The Original Folkways Recordings: 1960–1962 [2CD] (Smithsonian Folkways CD SF 40029/30)

Gene Autry
Blues Singer 1929–1931 (Columbia/Legacy CK 64987)

DeFord Bailey
Harp Blowers (1925–1936) (Document DOCD-5164) [part]
The Legendary De Ford Bailey: Country Music's First Black Star (Tennessee Folklore Society TFS-122)

Andrew and Jim Baxter
String Bands (1926–1929) (Document DOCD-5167) [part]

Dock Boggs
Country Blues: Complete Early Recordings (1927–29) (Revenant RVN 205)
His Folkways Years 1963–1968 [2CD] (Smithsonian Folkways SF 40108)

Herschel Brown
Herschel Brown (1928–1929) (Document DOCD-8001)

Blind James Campbell
Blind James Campbell and his Nashville Street Band (Arhoolie CD 438)

Gus Cannon
Cannon's Jug Stompers – The Complete Works 1927–1930 (Yazoo 1082/3)

Cliff Carlisle
Blues Yodeler & Steel Guitar Wizard (Arhoolie/Folklyric CD 7039)

Dallas String Band
Texas: Black Country Music (1927–1935) (Document DOCD-5162) [part]

Jimmie Davis
Nobody's Darlin' but Mine [5CD boxed set] (Bear Family BCD 15943)

Delmore Brothers
Brown's Ferry Blues (County CCS-CD-116)
Freight Train Boogie (Ace CDCH 455)

Nap Hayes and Matthew Prater
String Bands (1926–1929) (Document DOCD-5167) [part]

Roscoe Holcomb
The High Lonesome Sound (Smithsonian Folkways SF CD 40104)

Peg Leg Howell and Eddie Anthony
Vol. 1 (1926–1928) (Matchbox MBCD-2004)
Vol. 2 (1928–1930) (Matchbox MBCD-2005)

Frank Hutchison
Vol. 1 (1926–1929) (Document DOCD-8003)
Old-Time Music from West Virginia (1927–1929) (Document DOCD-8004) [part] [+ Dick Justice]

John Jackson

Don't Let Your Deal Go Down (Arhoolie CD 378)

Country Blues & Ditties (Arhoolie CD 471)

Sam McGee

Sam McGee (1926–1934) (Document DOCD-8036)

Uncle Dave Macon

Go Long Mule (County CO-CD-3505)

Travelin' Down the Road (County CCS-CD-115)

Memphis Jug Band

Vols. 1–3 (Frog DGF 15–17)

Mississippi Sheiks

Show Me What You Got (Catfish KATCD 124)

Vols. 1–4 (1930–1936) (Document DOCD-5083-86)

Stop and Listen (Yazoo 2006)

Bill Monroe

The Essential Bill Monroe and his Blue Grass Boys (1945–1949) [2CD boxed set] (Columbia/Legacy C2K 52478)

The Music of Bill Monroe from 1936 to 1994 [4CD] (MCA MCAD4-11048)

The Essential Bill Monroe & the Monroe Brothers (RCA 07863 67450-2)

Charlie Poole

Old Time Songs (County CO-CD-3501)

Vol. Two (County CO-CD-3508)

The Legend of Charlie Poole – Vol. 3 (County CO-CD-3516)

Jimmie Rodgers

The Singing Brakeman [6CD boxed set] (Bear Family BCD 15540)

also on eight individual CDs (Rounder 1056–63)

Spark Plug Smith

East Coast Blues & Gospel: Spark Plug Smith & Tallahassee Tight (Document DOCD-5387)

Stovepipe No. 1

Stovepipe No. 1 & David Crockett (1924–1930) (Document DOCD-5269)

Jimmie Tarlton

Darby & Tarlton – Complete Recordings [3CD boxed set] (Bear Family BCD 15764)

Steel Guitar Rag (HMG 2503)

Taylor's Kentucky Boys

String Bands (1926–1929) (Document DOCD-5167) [part]

Henry Thomas
  Texas Worried Blues (Yazoo 1080/1)
The Two Poor Boys [Joe Evans & Arthur McClain]
  The Two Poor Boys (Document DOCD-5044)
Casey Bill Weldon
  Vols. 1–3 (1935–1938) (Document DOCD-5217-19)
  The Hokum Boys & Bob Robinson Vol. 2 (1935–1937) (Document DOCD-5237)
Bob Wills
  The Essential Bob Wills (1935–1947) (Columbia/Legacy CK 48958)
Oscar Woods
  Texas Slide Guitars (1930–1938) [+ Black Ace] (Document DOCD-5143)
  I Can Eagle Rock: Library of Congress Recordings 1940–1941 (Travelin' Man TM CD 09) [part] [+ Joe Harris, Kid West]

ANTHOLOGIES

Sounds of the South [4CD boxed set] (Atlantic 7 82496-2)
White Country Blues (1926–1938) [2CD] (Columbia 472886 2)
Old-Time Mountain Guitar (County CO-CD-3512)
Great Harp Players (1927–1936) (Document DOCD-5100)
Kansas City Blues (1924–1929) (Document DOCD-5152)
Georgia Blues & Gospel (1927–1931) (Document DOCD-5160)
Alabama: Black Country Dance Bands (1924–1949) (Document DOCD-5166)
Black Fiddlers (1929-c. 1970) (Document DOCD-5631)
Cajun: Louisiane 1928–1939 [2CD] (Frémeaux FA 019)
Hillbilly Blues 1928–1946 [2CD] (Frémeaux FA 065)
Country Boogie 1939–1947 [2CD] (Frémeaux FA 160)
Violin, Sing the Blues for Me (Old Hat CD-1002)
Hillbilly Fever! Vol. 1: Legends of Western Swing (Rhino R2 71900)
Altamont: Black Stringband Music from the Library of Congress (Rounder CD 0238)
Deep River of Song: Black Texicans (Rounder 1821)
Deep River of Song: Black Appalachia (Rounder 1823)
Black Banjo Songsters of North Carolina and Virginia (Smithsonian Folkways SF CD 40079)
Anthology of American Folk Music [6CD boxed set] (Smithsonian Folkways SW CD 40090)

From Where I Stand: The Black Experience in Country Music [3CD] (Warner Bros. 9 46428-2)

American Pop: An Audio History – From Minstrel to Mojo: On Record, 1893–1946 [9CD] (West Hill Audio Archives WH-1017)

Before the Blues Vols. 1–3 (Yazoo 2015–17)

The Roots of Rap (Yazoo 2018)

Harmonica Masters (Yazoo 2019)

Times Ain't Like They Used to Be Vol. 1 (Yazoo 2028), *Vol. 2* (Yazoo 2029)

The Rose Grew Round the Briar Vol. 1 (Yazoo 2030), *Vol. 2* (Yazoo 2031)

Ruckus Juice & Chittlins: The Great Jug Bands Vol. 1 (Yazoo 2032), *Vol. 2* (Yazoo 2033)

Hard Times Come Again No More Vol. 1 (Yazoo 2036), *Vol. 2* (Yazoo 2037)

My Rough & Rowdy Ways Vol. 1 (Yazoo 2039), *Vol. 2* (Yazoo 2040)

The Cornshucker's Frolic Vol. 1 (Yazoo 2045), *Vol. 2* (Yazoo 2046)

Times Ain't Like They Used to Be Vol. 3 (Yazoo 2047), *Vol. 4* (Yazoo 2048)

❸ RECORDING THE BLUES

Robert M. W. Dixon
and
John Godrich

FOREWORD

Early in 1920 the General Phonograph Corporation issued, for the first time, popular songs performed by a black girl. The success of this record made the industry aware of a vast, untapped market: black Americans were eager to buy records by artists of their own race. Two or three record companies immediately began systematic recording of blues singers, gospel quartets and the like, numbering the discs in special series that came to be called 'Race Series'. They sold so well that other companies entered the field and soon every blues singer who had ever appeared on a theatre stage had also made her contribution in the recording studios. The companies began to look further afield. Many made field trips to the South, recording itinerant rural blues singers, guitar evangelists and shouting black preachers. By the late twenties these 'Race Records' – which sold to an entirely black market – were about as far removed as is possible from white America's popular music of the day.

Gradually, the style of Race Records changed. In the thirties, when more and more of the black audience had migrated to northern cities, they preferred performances by urban musicians – with a full rhythm section laying down a strong beat – to the more delicate guitar-only accompaniments of country singers. Blues and pop moved closer together during the forties and fifties; today it is often difficult to distinguish them. Records that are now normal pop fare would have been considered blues performances, for a strictly minority audience, in the 1950s.

Pop music has drawn on blues material, on tunes and styles that were featured in the race series. In this book we examine the content of these race series during the period 1920–45; the ways in which the companies discovered talent, how they recorded the singers and how they marketed the records. We deal only with blues and gospel records, leaving aside instrumental jazz, novelty numbers and other items that from time to time appeared in the race series.

15 · BIRTH OF AN INDUSTRY

Thomas A. Edison's first phonographs, in 1877, were novelties; people paid to hear an approximation of their own voice played back to them at a phonograph exhibition. It was not until 1888 that instruments were manufactured in quantity, for home entertainment; and musicians and celebrities began to be lured into the studios, to record their talent for posterity. Edison established the North American Phonograph Company to handle sales, and this in turn set up thirty regional subsidiaries. The most promising of these was the Columbia Phonograph Company, covering Maryland, Delaware and the District of Columbia. Although the parent company failed, Columbia prospered, partly due to its exclusive contract with John Philip Sousa. By the turn of the century two companies were competing for the expanding market in phonographs and cylinders: Columbia and Edison's new National Phonograph Company.

But there was competition from another quarter. The National Gramophone Company had, since 1897, been manufacturing disc records. Through astute management, and because of the greater appeal of the flat record, discs were soon gaining ground on cylinders. By purchase of a vital patent, Columbia were also able to begin manufacture of discs, in 1902.

In 1901 the National Gramophone Company was reorganised as the Victor Talking Machine Company. It was, and remained, the undisputed leader of the industry. In 1902 Victor issued records by actors, music-hall entertainers and after-dinner speakers, as well as by the great opera stars of the day. In that year it also issued six single-sided records by the

41 Lucille Hegamin and her Blue Flame Syncopators

Dinwiddie Colored Quartet, a group that sang in a quite authentic Negro style, without the European influence that marked the work of other early gospel groups, such as the Pace Jubilee Singers. It was to be eighteen years before another recording of authentic black music appeared on the market.

Victor and Columbia controlled all the patents for lateral recording, in which the needle moved from side to side in the groove. When Edison, faced with a dwindling market for cylinders, decided to enter the disc business in 1912, he had no choice but to make 'hill-and-dale' records, in which the needle moved vertically in the groove, as on cylinders. Hill-and-dale records could not be played on Victor or Columbia gramophones; anyone who bought an Edison gramophone could only buy Edison records for it. Columbia ceased manufacture of phonograph cylinders in 1917 but Edison continued until his company finally discontinued making records of all types, in 1929.

Pathé-Frères, the leading European manufacturer of cylinders and records, began recording and issuing discs in America in 1914. In 1915 the General Phonograph Corporation – financed by the Lindström Company, a successful German record concern – issued discs on the OKeh label. And in 1916 the Aeolian Company, who had been manufacturing gramophones for two or three years, began the Vocalion label. All these new companies had to be content with producing hill-and-dale records.

In 1915 the Starr Piano Company of Richmond, Indiana, decided to enter the record market. Hill-and-dale discs issued between 1915 and 1918 – first on the Starr label and then on Gennett – sold badly. Who was going to buy records that could not be played on Victor or Columbia machines? In 1918 Starr produced lateral-cut discs, and Victor immediately brought suit for patent infringement. In the subsequent protracted litigation Starr were supported by, amongst others, the General Phonograph Corporation, the Aeolian Company, and the Canadian Compo Company, who all stood to gain if Victor's patent were upset. Eventually, the Supreme Court pronounced in favour of Starr. Any company was now free to make lateral-cut records.

16 · THE NEW MARKET, 1920–1922

A few items by black performers had been issued in the early years of recording but they were intended for white audiences. These minstrel routines and orchestrated spirituals generally reinforced the traditional image of the Negro. But black citizens were increasingly buying talking machines, and with them recordings by the white artists of the day. In January 1916 the *Chicago Defender* – a weekly newspaper with a circulation of a quarter of a million, that reached black communities in all parts of the country – commented that its readers had, in the course of their Christmas spending, 'paid to hear Tettrazini, Caruso . . . But how many of our race ever asked for a record of Mme Anita Patti Brown, Mr Roland Hayes, Miss Hazel Harrison, Miss Maude J. Roberts, Mr Joseph Douglas . . . ?' The *Defender* campaign intensified; in October 1916 they announced that 'records of the Race's great artists will be placed on the market' once the record companies had ascertained 'how many Victrolas are owned by members of our Race'. Each black owner of a talking machine was asked to send his name and address to the *Defender* office. But the *Defender* did not mention the matter again, and no records by black concert artists were forthcoming.

When the breakthrough came it was from a quite different direction. In 1920 Fred Hager of the General Phonograph Company, who had started issuing lateral-cut discs on the OKeh label the previous year, wanted to record *That Thing Called Love* and *You Can't Keep A Good Man Down*, composed by Perry Bradford, a black music-store proprietor from Chicago.

Hager had intended to use Sophie Tucker but Bradford eventually persuaded him to use Mamie Smith, a black girl. The tunes were recorded on the second Saturday in February and issued on OKeh 4113 in July 1920. The record was listed as 'Mamie Smith, Contralto' in the catalogue and OKeh made no attempt to draw special attention to it. But the black press proclaimed 'Mamie made a recording' and sales were unexpectedly high. Mamie was called back to the studio in August to record *Crazy Blues* and *Its Right Here For You (If You Don't Get It . . .'Tain't No Fault Of Mine)*. This time OKeh advertised widely in black communities and when the disc was issued in November it was an instantaneous success. OKeh had tapped a vast potential market – tens of thousands of black enthusiasts were willing to pay $1 each (a considerable sum by the standards of the day) to buy a record by a black singer. It may not be coincidental that the first record by a black concert artist – Mme Anita Patti Brown – was cut in September of that year.

The other companies were not slow to notice the success of *Crazy Blues*. In 1921 Emerson featured two blues records by Lillyn Brown, while Pathé-Frères issued four by Lavinia Turner on their Pathé and Perfect labels, and Starr one by Daisy Martin on the Gennett label. Recordings by coloured singers were being issued at an average of about one per week during 1921 and 1922. In January 1922 *Metronome* declared that 'every phonograph company has a colored girl recording blues'.

Although the *Talking Machine World* of 13 October 1920 bore an advertisement for Mamie Smith, now an exclusive OKeh artist, describing her as 'singer of "Blues" – the music of so new a flavor', she was in fact more of a pop singer. And there was in any case nothing new about blues – 'Ma' Rainey had been stomping the South for a dozen years, singing the most classic of blues. In November 1920 Arto, a small company from Orange, New Jersey, recorded a popular light-skinned singer named Lucille Hegamin. *The Jazz Me Blues* and *Everybody's Blues*, accompanied by Harris's Blues and Jazz Seven, released in February 1921 on Arto Universal Record number 9045, could be considered the first real blues disc. Retailing at 85 cents, it sold well, but the great hit of the year was Miss Hegamin's follow-up: *I'll Be Good But I'll Be Lonesome* – a promise to be faithful during a lover's absence – and *Arkansas Blues*. The latter had trite words:

QUARTETS—MEN'S VOICES

Negro Shouts by DINWIDDIE COLORED QUARTET
These are genuine Jubilee and Camp Meeting Shouts sung as
only negroes can sing them.

1714 **Down on the Old Camp Ground**
1715 **Poor Mourner**
1716 **Steal Away**
1724 **My Way is Cloudy**
1725 **Gabriel's Trumpet**
1726 **We'll Anchor Bye and Bye**

42 Dinwiddie Colored Quartet, from the Victor catalogue, 1903

Ain't got no time to lose
I'm tired and lonely, I'm tired of roaming
I long to see my mammy in my home-in . . .
I've got the Arkansas blues

but the catchy tune, the vibrant jazz accompaniment by the Blue Flame
Syncopaters (spelt thus) and the singer's bluesy, syncopated style combined to produce a performance that was hard to resist. Despite Arto's
poor standard of recording other companies fell over each other to lease
the masters and the Hegamin version of *Arkansas Blues* was eventually
issued on eleven different labels. OKeh called Mamie Smith into the
studios in early September to record her own version of *Arkansas Blues*,
issued on OKeh 4445.

Arto issued six records by Lucille Hegamin in 1921, and three in the
early months of 1922. But despite her success the company was failing
and went into bankruptcy in 1923. Lucille had been signed to a one year's
exclusive contract by the Cameo Record Corporation on 4 October
1921. Cameo produced a cheap 50-cent record and they put out a new
Hegamin disc every other month until 1926. In fact this was almost
all they did issue for the black market – of the twenty-six blues
records released by Cameo over a four-year period, twenty-three were
by Lucille.

Of the major companies, only Victor stood aloof from the blues craze. They had heard and rejected Mamie Smith in January 1920, and Lucille Hegamin (singing *Dallas Blues*) in October. Victor decided to concentrate on trying to sell its prestigious Red Seal classical records to Negroes. The other major company, Columbia, could not afford to ignore any new market; they had overproduced in 1921 and were heavily in debt. Columbia signed up Mary Stafford, a cabaret artist, and she recorded *Crazy Blues* in January and *Arkansas Blues* late in September 1921. Six Mary Stafford records were issued in 1921 but her contract was not renewed, Columbia turning to Edith Wilson the following year. During this period Columbia showed little initiative, trailing behind the other companies and having no inclination to break new ground or issue more than just one blues disc every other month. Indeed it is said that after Mamie Smith's *Crazy Blues* became a hit, a Columbia executive heard Mary Stafford singing the song in a Harlem cabaret; she was recording it in the Columbia studio the next morning. The story may be an exaggeration but it is certainly true that at this period the companies made little effort to seek out good or new talent. They relied on contacting singers who happened to be performing in the New York area or, in many cases, on the singers contacting them.

In January 1921 Harry Pace left the Pace and Handy Music Company, in New York, to form his own company, the Pace Phonograph Corporation. It began with a staff of one clerk in a small basement room. In May, Pace announced his Black Swan records, which would feature only coloured artists and be produced by a company whose stockholders and employees would all be coloured. He stated, 'Black Swan records are made to meet what we believe is a legitimate and growing demand. There are 12,000,000 colored people in the US and in that number there is hid a wonderful amount of musical ability. We propose to spare no expense in the search for and developing of the best singers and musicians among the 12,000,000.' Bandleader Fletcher Henderson was engaged as musical director and recording manager and one of the first three records issued was by singer Katie Crippen, accompanied by Henderson's orchestra. It has been suggested that the label name was derived from a coloured singer called Elizabeth Taylor Greenfield, who was known as 'the Black Swan'.

43 Harry H. Pace, of Black Swan Records

Pace was critical of other concerns which only recorded blues numbers by black artists; he announced his intention of covering the whole
range of 'colored performances' – including quartets, glee clubs,
vaudeville acts and concert singing. But, economically, Pace was forced
to fall back on blues. Ethel Waters was paid $100 for her *Down Home*

Blues in mid-1921. This, together with *How Long, Sweet Daddy, How Long* by Alberta Hunter, is said to have pulled the company out of the red. By October, Black Swan announced that they had 'moved to larger premises, employing fifteen clerks, an eight-man orchestra, seven district managers, were represented by 1,000 dealers and agents throughout the country and were shipping 2,500 records from their plant each day to as far afield as the Philippines and the West Indies'. By the end of 1921, Pace had signed Ethel Waters to a contract, stipulating that she did not marry within the year, which was said to make her the highest-paid coloured recording star in the country. It was announced that $104,628 had been paid for Black Swan records in the past eleven months.

On Friday, 20 January 1922, a blues singing contest was held in the Manhattan Casino, New York, as part of 'the 15th Infantry's First Band Concert and Dance'. Four singers were featured: Miss Lucille Hegamin, 'Harlem's Favorite' singing *Arkansas Blues*; Miss Alice Leslie Carter with *Decatur Street Blues*; Miss Daisy Martin with *If You Don't Believe I Love You*; and 'The Southern Nightingale', Miss Trixie Smith, who was pronounced winner and presented with a silver loving cup for her own composition *Trixie Blues*. Harry Pace signed the winner and soon released *Trixie's Blues* on Black Swan 2039, the singer's high-pitched, infectiously rhythmic vocal admirably backed by a small anonymous jazz group:

> Now if you don't want me, daddy, you have no right to lie, hey, hey
> Now if you don't want me, that's no right to lie
> 'Cause the day you quit me, daddy, that's the day you die

April 1922 was an important month for Black Swan. Harry Pace, in partnership with one John Fletcher, purchased the Olympic Disc Record Company. The Olympic plant was now used for pressing Black Swan records, and items by white singers from the Olympic catalogue were reissued on Black Swan – thus breaking Pace's pledge to use only black artists. Black Swan stepped up releases from three to ten a month, and reduced the price of its popular records to 75 cents. They also introduced comic, hillbilly and operatic Red Label series. A Red Label release, by a coloratura soprano of the Chicago Grand Opera, Antoinette Garnes, was advertised as 'The First Grand Opera Record Ever Made by a Colored Singer'; it sold for $1. Maybe because he felt a little ashamed of breaking his 'all-black policy', in August Pace began a new 14100 series restricted, with one exception, to black singers, and featuring mainly blues items. However, the records cannot have sold quite as well as Pace had anticipated for in December 1922 he advertised 'Exchange your old, worn or damaged phonograph records for new Black Swan Records at Kelly's, 2289, Seventh Avenue. 15 cents allowed on records of any make, on each new record purchased', and by April of 1923 Black Swan were appealing 'We Want Live Agents Everywhere! Music stores, drug stores, furniture dealers, news stands, cigar stores, manicuring and hairdressing parlors, confectionary stores, shoe shining parlors, delicatessen shops and all other places of business catering to retail trade.'

There were several small record ventures at this time. Over in Los Angeles, black music-store proprietors Johnny and Reb Spikes began an 'all-colored' label called Sunshine in June 1922. Only three issues appeared – one each by blues singers Roberta Dudley and Ruth Lee, accompanied by Kid Ory's Jazz Band, and an instrumental by Ory. The music was recorded in the West, 5,000 copies of each issue were pressed over in the East and these were then shipped back and sold over the counter of the brothers' own shop in Los Angeles. It was to be more than twenty years before any further blues recordings were made on the west coast.

In March 1922 the black vaudeville team of Thomas Chappelle and Juanita Stinnette produced at least a dozen records, at least nine of which featured themselves, on their own label C & S Records; after this no more was heard of the company. The same year W. C. Handy, the black composer and Pace's erstwhile partner, decided to form his own record company and advertised two items in the *Chicago Defender*; however, none seem to have appeared. And in March 1922 there was an advertisement for Echo Records – the name being more-or-less OKeh reversed – which was said to be 'a new concern owned and operated by the Negro people. Shelton Brooks, Lucille Hegamin, Lena Wilson and other stars will record for the Echo as soon as their present contracts expire . . . agents are wanted everywhere.' But, as far as is known, no Echo records were ever issued.

OKeh, who had unwittingly started it all, continued to be leader of the new trend. Mamie Smith continued to be featured (twenty-three more Mamie Smith records were issued by OKeh in 1921 and 1922) and in the early months of 1921 other, more bluesy, singers were summoned to the OKeh studios. In the summer of 1921 General Phonograph became the first company to issue a special brochure describing releases by black artists. It listed six records: a new Mamie Smith, unaccompanied singing by the Norfolk Jazz Quartet, two discs by Tim Brymn's Black Devil Orchestra (including an instrumental version of *Arkansas Blues*), and the first records by blues singers Daisy Martin and Gertrude Saunders. OKeh advertisements toted the special 'colored supplement' but they did not draw attention to the fact that, although the Mamie Smith and Norfolk Jazz Quartet discs bore numbers in the general 4000 series (these items being perhaps expected to sell to white as well as to black customers), the other four records were numbered 8001 to 8004 in a special series that was to be reserved for black talent. In fact it was January 1922 before OKeh drew attention to the new series: new releases 8018 to 8020 were then advertised 'for the Colored Catalog'.

A name was needed to describe records intended for black consumption, but there was no obvious term. The description 'colored records' was used most frequently in advertising in 1921. In January 1922 the OKeh advertisement in the *Chicago Defender* said 'All the greatest Race phonograph stars can be heard on OKeh records' and in March they invited readers to 'ask your neighborhood dealer for a complete list of OKeh race records'. But 'race', a term of common identification used within the black community, was not yet the recognised name; the word was not mentioned in OKeh advertisements during the remainder of the year. Then in May 1923 OKeh announced 'The World's Greatest Race Artists on the World's Greatest Race Records' and thereafter the term was used regularly in *Defender* advertising. It had taken almost two years to evolve a name for the 8000 series. Even so, OKeh were for a while cautious about using the name in all contexts – their advertisement in the *Talking Machine World* in August 1923 mentioned the company's 'Negro records'. Soon, however, 'Race Records' became, within and without the industry, the established name for black records intended for the black market; it remained so for twenty years.

OKeh had issued forty records in the 8000 series by the end of 1922 – half-a-dozen jazz instrumentals, eleven records by male quartets, and a couple of dozen blues discs by Daisy Martin, Gertrude Saunders, Josephine Carter, Esther Bigeou and a singer from New Orleans, Lizzie Miles (they also put one of Mamie Smith's couplings into the race series – all other records by Mamie were put out in the general series until she was dropped by OKeh, at the end of 1923). With the demise of Arto, Black Swan was the only serious competitor for the race market, and that company was beginning to find itself in financial difficulties. But in 1922 a new and powerful rival emerged.

The Wisconsin Chair Company at Port Washington was interested in all types of home furniture and it was a natural step, a few years after it had begun production of phonographs and cabinets, to form a subsidiary to manufacture records. The New York Recording Laboratories began issuing records on the Paramount label in 1917. Their initial blues releases were Lucille Hegamin's first two hits, which were leased from Arto and numbered 20052 and 20053 in the Paramount popular series, in mid-1921. Early in 1922 they recorded *Daddy Blues* and *Don't Pan Me* by Alberta Hunter, who had had two records released on Black Swan the previous year, and when the record was issued in mid-1922 it was numbered 12001, the first disc in a special Paramount series that was to be reserved for black talent. The series was priced at 75 cents, but Paramount's advertisement in the *Defender* contained a special offer: five records – the first three in the 12000 series, 20151 by Lucille Hegamin and 20143 by Specht's Society Entertainers – for $3. By then OKeh had reduced their price to 75 cents – the standard sum charged for 10-inch records by Victor, Columbia and the other major companies throughout the twenties. The Paramount race series started slowly – only nine records were issued in 1922 – but by 1923 it was competing fiercely with OKeh. OKeh described its 8000 series as 'The Original Race Record' and Paramount responded by dubbing the 12000 series 'The Popular Race Record'.

The companies were reaching wider and wider audiences with their race releases; a November 1922 OKeh advertisement listed twenty stockists outside New York: four in Chicago, three in St Louis, two each for Detroit, Cleveland and Pittsburgh, and one in each of Milwaukee; Wellsville, Ohio; Indianapolis; Knoxville, Tennessee; Poor Fork, Kentucky; Lexington, Kentucky; and Bessemer, Alabama. It was becoming obvious that the fifty blues records per year issued during 1921 and 1922 went nowhere near satisfying the demands of the market.

17 · THE CLASSIC BLUES, 1923–1926

In 1923 race records came into their own. OKeh and Paramount were putting out an increasing number of records, and just about every other company began searching for black talent. In 1923 and 1924 blues and gospel items were being issued at an average of 4 per week. The figure increased to 5 a week in 1925 and went up again the following year; more than 300 blues and gospel discs appeared on the market in 1926. These were the years of the classic blues singers – professional vaudeville and cabaret performers, almost exclusively female, who sang 12-bar blues interspersed with a few traditional and pop numbers. Sometimes their accompaniment was just a pianist but often it was a small hot jazz band. Altogether race records were issued on more than fifteen different labels during this four-year period. However, three companies – OKeh, Paramount and Columbia – dominated the market and together accounted for more than two-thirds of the total blues and gospel releases.

The main event of 1923 was the emergence of Columbia as a major race label. Frank Walker, a white impresario who was an enthusiast for both hillbilly and blues, had heard Bessie Smith singing at a gin-mill in Alabama several years before. When Walker was put in charge of Columbia's race list the first thing he did was to send for Bessie, one of the most popular singers of classic blues in the South. At first Walker played safe, getting Bessie to record numbers that were already well known through the recordings of other singers. Her first disc, recorded in New York in February 1923, featured *Down Hearted Blues* – already selling well on Paramount 12005, by Alberta Hunter – and the second coupled *Aggravatin' Papa* with *Beale Street Mamma*, selections that were on Cameo 270, by Lucille Hegamin.

After a four-line introduction, *Down Hearted Blues*, on Columbia A3844, goes into the traditional 12-bar form, Bessie's voice rich, deep and clear over Clarence Williams' piano accompaniment. The memorable final verse –

> I've got the world in a jug, the stopper's in my hand (*twice*)
> I'm going to hold it until you men come under my command

– and the power of Bessie's singing combined to make it a hit. Bessie was soon back in the studios, recording her own material; and indeed Lucille Hegamin was called by Cameo in August to make her own version of *Down Hearted Blues*, in the hopes of cashing in on some of Bessie's success. Bessie Smith was soon established as the biggest-selling blues artist of the period; many consider her to be the greatest blues singer of all time.

At the end of June, Walker recorded another fine singer – Clara Smith (no relation to Bessie). Clara's voice was thinner than Bessie's but she had a delicacy and feeling that made her records sell only slightly less well than Bessie's. In 1922 Columbia had issued seven blues records; in 1923 they put out three dozen, including fourteen by Bessie and eight by Clara. Towards the end of 1923 Columbia decided to number race records in a special series – 13000D and 13001D were by Bessie Smith, 13002D was by Clara. But this series was scrapped after eight issues – through fear of the unlucky number thirteen influencing sales – and just before Christmas the 14000D series was begun (naturally enough, with a record by Bessie Smith).

Although Columbia's race catalogue was flourishing, the company found it impossible to extricate itself from its financial troubles. Bankruptcy was acknowledged in 1923 and the company was then run by a consortium of bankers, its biggest debtors. The pattern set in 1923 was maintained over the next three years. Blues and gospel releases averaged about three per month in 1924, and increased to four each month in 1925 and 1926. Monthly advertisements in the *Chicago Defender* in 1923 gave way to weekly insertions the following year. In 1925 everybody's advertising increased; like its main rivals – OKeh and Paramount – Columbia had a dozen full-page advertisements in the *Defender* that year. But, under the conservative policy imposed on the company by the bankers' consortium, there was little attempt to diversify the race list – with Bessie's and Clara's records making up half the total number of releases it was essentially a two-artist catalogue.

Matching Columbia's fourteen records by Bessie Smith, in 1923 Paramount issued twelve by Alberta Hunter and OKeh no less than seventeen by a new singer, Sara Martin. In 1923 there were too many record companies chasing too few singers: eleven artists each had more than six records issued that year, between them accounting for more than half the total releases. The best singers were under contract to one or other of the three big companies. Lesser performers made the best of the situation, recording for whoever would have them – and almost everyone would. In 1924 Rosa Henderson had records issued on six different labels – Vocalion, Ajax, Perfect, Brunswick, Emerson and Banner (and this was no isolated instance: Lena Wilson came out on six in 1923, Hazel Meyers on six in 1924, and Edna Hicks on no less than seven different labels in 1923). More talent was urgently needed, and OKeh and Paramount were out to find it.

The 1924 Paramount catalogue bore a picture of J. Mayo Williams, black recording manager for Paramount's 'Race Artist Series.' In a paragraph headed 'What does the public want?' Paramount asked 'What will you have? If your preferences are not listed in our catalog, we will make them for you, as Paramount must please the buying public. There is always room for more good material and more talented artists. Any suggestions or recommendations that you may have to offer will be greatly appreciated by J. Mayo Williams, Manager of the "Race Artists Series".' Williams lost no time in signing well-known but previously unrecorded artists. In 1924 a Paramount advertisement bore a large headline 'Discovered at Last – "Ma" Rainey'. In the 1924 catalogue she was described thus: 'Recognised as the greatest blues singer ever known. Her records are breaking all records for popularity. "Ma" is the Mother of the Blues, because she really taught many of the younger stars how to sing Blues.' Most notably she had trained Bessie Smith, who as a girl had toured with 'Ma'

44 Paramount announces 'Ma' Rainey, 1924

in the Rabbit Foot Minstrels show. 'Ma' Rainey was to be a mainstay of the Paramount 12000 series for the next seven years.

When, in May 1924, Paramount decided on a promotional stunt, it centred on 'Ma' Rainey. 'Ma' Rainey's sixth release – numbered 12200 – was labelled *Ma Rainey's Mystery Record*; the performance was said to be so moving that no one in the Paramount offices could think of a suitable name for it. Prizes of phonographs and records were offered for the most apt title, to be judged by Mayo Williams and Harry Pace. The winning entry was *Lawd, I'm Down Wid De Blues* by Ella McGill of Jefferson, Indiana – but the labelling on the record was never changed.

In 1923 Paramount issued just over fifty blues and gospel items (their advertisements claimed 'A New Hit Record Released Every Week'), half-a-dozen or so more than OKeh. Then in April 1924, when Black Swan's financial position became impossible, it leased its masters to Paramount; numbers 12100/99 in the Paramount race series were reserved for re-issue of Black Swan material. The newspaper announcement talked of a 'merger' but the details made it clear that Black Swan had had little option: 'The Black Swan catalogue of several hundred master records is the most valuable of its kind in existence. Instead of the company operating that catalogue, the Paramount company will manufacture and distribute Black Swan records, from which the Black Swan Co. will receive a definite amount each month. After the Black Swan Co. has paid its accounts and obligations, such as every operating company must have, it will be in a position to pay its stockholders a substantial and continuous dividend, or it can retire its capital stock at a substantial premium.' It was a sad end for the only company with 'all colored stockholders' but Black Swan assured the Race that 'by Black Swan's combination with the Paramount company – a white organisation devoted to the interests of the Race and specializing in Race records – the continuance of high class Race music is assured'. By and large, Black Swan's confidence in Paramount was justified. Mayo Williams was constantly on the lookout for new talent that could be brought to Chicago to record. Unlike the bigger companies – who sold exclusively through record stores – Paramount did a good mail order business. Every advertisement and supplement had a triangular blank at the bottom; all one had to do was tick the records required and fill in one's name and address – and then pay the postman 75 cents per selection. There must have been a good chance that if there were some marketable singer or band of whom Paramount had never heard, then some rural customer would scrawl a recommendation on the back of the order slip.

In addition to digesting Black Swan, Paramount issued an average of almost 4 new blues and gospel discs a month in 1924; the next year it was just over 5 a month and this figure was maintained through 1926. But OKeh was the market leader during the classic blues period. Each year the company issued 20 more blues and gospel items than it had the previous year until in 1926 just over 100 new records were released. Of these, 80 or so were classic blues in the finest tradition – including Sara Martin, the vaudeville team of Butterbeans and Susie, Alberta Hunter (who had been dropped by Paramount in 1924) and two singers from Houston, Texas: Sippie Wallace and the teenage Victoria Spivey. In June 1926 OKeh organised an 'OKeh Race Record Artists' Ball' in Chicago, featuring half-a-dozen of their most popular singers, in addition to the bands of King Oliver, Louis Armstrong and many others; the *Chicago Defender* produced an extra 'Music Edition' to celebrate the event.

Ralph Peer, son of a white Missouri storekeeper, was in charge of the 8000 series and he was always on the lookout for new talent. In 1923 Polk Brockman, a white man who was OKeh's wholesale distributor in Atlanta, persuaded Peer to bring his equipment to Atlanta to record Fiddlin' John Carson, a favourite hillbilly singer. The 15 June edition of the *Atlanta Journal* advertised Peer's visit, and by the time a make-shift recording laboratory was set up in an empty loft on Nassau Street quite a lot of local talent had assembled. The *Chicago Defender* gave news of the trip, saying that Peer had made a 'record by Lucille Bogan, a popular blues singer from dear old Birmingham, Alabama, and an original blues by Fannie Goosby, amongst others'. OKeh 8079 coupled Lucille Bogan's *Pawn Shop Blues* with *Grievous Blues* by Fannie Goosby, the first race record to have been recorded outside the main centres of New York and Chicago. Lucille Bogan was called to New York almost immediately to record four more titles, and Miss Goosby followed a month or two later. At the end of 1923, OKeh advertisements were able to boast not only that 'OKeh made the first 12-inch blues Race record' (by Eva Taylor, one side being *Gulf Coast Blues*, a 'cover' of one of the tunes on Bessie Smith's first record) and that 'the first duet record by colored artists was on OKeh' but also that 'new OKeh Race Artists have been discovered by special recording expeditions into the South'.

Peer visited each of Atlanta, New Orleans and St Louis several times during the next few years, primarily to record hillbilly talent, but he normally also recorded one or two blues singers at each location. Polk Brockman was the talent scout in Atlanta and would advertise in the local paper and scour the countryside looking for likely talent, which he would audition himself, ahead of the arrival of the OKeh unit. Brockman claimed that he would often go to a town and find 200 people waiting to see him. In St Louis, Jesse Johnson, black proprietor of the De Luxe Music Shop and husband of blues singer Edith Johnson, was talent scout at various times for a number of companies including both OKeh and Paramount. Field trips were well advertised: in May 1926 Victoria Spivey's brothers, hearing that OKeh were to be in St Louis, sent their sister there, to audition for Jesse Johnson. Two or three days later she recorded four tunes for the OKeh field unit (including the haunting *Black Snake Blues*). These

WOW~but
BESSIE SMITH
spills fire and fury
in
"HATEFUL BLUES"
on Columbia Record 14023 D
it's Bessie singing on the other side, too —
"FRANKIE BLUES"

Having a phonograph without these records is like having pork chops without gravy—Yes, indeed

45 Bessie Smith recorded exclusively for Columbia

were so successful that she was called to the New York studios in August; OKeh issued six Victoria Spivey discs that year.

During the classic blues period, the three major companies advertised extensively. They would describe the content of the record, the qualities of the singer, the exceptional dedication of the company – all in the most lowdown imitation-jive-talk prose. A full-page Columbia advertisement in the *Chicago Defender* for 19 July 1924 said 'Wow – but Bessie Smith spills fire and fury in *Hateful Blues*, on Columbia record 14023D'. The smaller print went on 'Talk about hymns of hate – Bessie sure is a him-hater on this record. The way she tells what she is going to do with her "butcher" will make trifling fellows catch express trains going at sixty miles an hour. The music is full of hate too. You can almost see hate drip from the piano keys. Fury flies off the violin strings. Every note is a half-note. No quarter for anyone.' And above a list of other Columbia releases the copywriter declared, 'Having a phonograph without these records is like having pork chops without gravy – Yes, indeed!' A full-page OKeh advertisement in the 1925 *Defender* lauded Sippie Wallace, 'The Texas Nightingale': readers were invited to 'catch those Sippie Wallace notes as they float sky high or deep down low. Hear her as she sounds those ice cold words with their red hot meaning. Do it now with her up-to-the-second OKeh blues, "He's The Cause Of My Being Blue", on OKeh.'

In 1921 Victor had auditioned at least four black singers before deciding not to issue any blues records for the time being. With the expansion of the race market in 1923 – and Columbia's great success with Bessie Smith – Victor could no longer afford to remain aloof. Serious recording commenced in April 1923 and Victor's first three blues issues were numbered 19083 to 19085 in the popular series – they advertised 'A Special List of Blues' in the *Chicago Defender* during August. But the best singers were under contract to OKeh, Paramount or Columbia and the artists Victor were able to secure – Rosa Henderson, Edna Hicks, Lena Wilson, Lizzie Miles – were not in the same class as Bessie and Clara Smith, or Ida Cox, Paramount's new star. It may have been poor sales, or perhaps some general change in company policy, that caused Victor to cease blues recording as suddenly as they had begun. The last session involved Gertrude Saunders – who had had a single record in the OKeh 8000 series in 1921 – on Monday, 27 August 1923. Victor had issued seven blues records in 1923; they did not release a single selection for the race market during the following two years.

Thomas Alva Edison, who still confined himself to cylinders and hill-and-dale discs, was finding times increasingly hard. In 1923 he issued two blues records by Helen Baxter and in 1925 he put out a batch of three race records – 51476 to 51478 – by Rosa Henderson, Viola McCoy and Josie Miles. Four blues titles even found their way on to Edison's Blue Amberol cylinders. But Edison's next race release was not until 1929 – Eva Taylor singing *Have You Ever Felt That Way?* and *West End Blues* – issued just a few weeks before the company discontinued all record production.

After the conclusion of Gennett's successful battle in the courts with Victor in 1921 a close friendship arose between them and OKeh,

Aeolian-Vocalion and Compo due to their support in the fight. This led to a pooling and leasing of Gennett and other masters, which was later extended to other companies, such as Paramount. Also part of the arrangement was that H. S. Berliner of Compo would make pressings for Gennett and the others in Montreal.

At first Gennett did not appear to see eye-to-eye with the general trend towards race records and this may well have been an important factor in their steadily declining sales in the early twenties. Although they conceded the Daisy Martin record in 1921, they didn't enter the market proper until 1923, with twenty issues by such minor singers as Viola McCoy, Edna Hicks and Josie Miles. Gennett's interest (or the public's interest in Gennett's choice) appeared to wane again after this and an average of less than one blues record a month was maintained until the end of 1926, with little of note among them. Gennett records originally sold for 75 cents – maybe even 85 cents in 1921 – but when their 3000 series appeared in 1925 the price was cut to 50 cents, probably in an effort to boost sales. Recordings alternated between their studios in Manhattan, and Richmond, Indiana, where the pressing plant was situated.

Ajax records, first advertised as 'The Superior Race Record' and later 'The Quality Race Record', made their appearance in October 1923 and sold for 75 cents. They were manufactured in Canada by the Compo company in their Lachine, Quebec, plant. Of Ajax records, 90 per cent were by black artists, the blues masters being specially recorded for them in New York and marketed through the Ajax Record Company of Chicago. By August 1925 they had disappeared from the scene, but at least 137 records had been issued over a period of two years, including items by Rosa Henderson, Viola McCoy, Monette Moore (under the pseudonym Susie Smith), Mamie Smith and their own exclusive artist Helen Gross.

Late in 1925 another black record company was promoted, this time in Kansas City by the singer and entertainer Winston Holmes, who had his own music store on 18th Street. Meritt records sold at 75 cents and were pressed in batches of 400 according to demand; they only achieved seven issues in three years. Lottie Kimbrough's *City Of The Dead* and *Cabbage Head Blues*, labelled as Lena Kimbrough, was Meritt's best seller, closely followed in popularity by two sermons from Rev. J. C. Burnett, *The Downfall Of Nebuchadnezzar* and *I've Even Heard Of Thee*. These

46 The Kansas City label Meritt recorded sermons by Reverend Gatewood

so appealed to Columbia that they persuaded Burnett to record for them; Holmes sued for breach of contract, but lost. The Winston Holmes Music Company finally went out of business about 1929.

The Aeolian Company issued just over two dozen race records on its Vocalion label in 1923 and 1924 – by minor artists, such as Lena Wilson, Viola McCoy, Rosa Henderson and Edna Hicks, who went the rounds of the smaller companies. Towards the end of 1924, Aeolian's record division was bought by the Brunswick-Balke-Collender Company of Chicago (BBC) – makers of billiards and bowling alley equipment – who had issued half-a-dozen discs by exactly the same group of artists on their own Brunswick label in the autumn of 1923 and the spring of 1924. There was little race activity at BBC in 1925 – six or so issues on the Vocalion label and none at all on Brunswick. Then in March 1926, BBC announced the formation of a Race Record Division, which would be headed by Jack Kapp, formerly Columbia's representative in Chicago. The Vocalion 1000 series – the fourth major race series – was inaugurated the following month. BBC tried to develop an image for the new series; reacting against the *double-entendres* of many current songs, they announced 'Better and Cleaner Race Records', a description that was retained until May 1928. Two dozen blues records were issued before the end of the year – as well as a fair amount of jazz – but they were mostly by the minor classic blues singers (those that had not been snapped up by the main companies). It was an uninspiring start for the new series.

Between 1923 and 1926 the great majority of blues records were by women, professional singers who sang mostly for city audiences, using fairly standard song material. There were exceptions: in 1924 OKeh issued two tunes recorded in Atlanta, *Barrel House Blues* and *Time Ain't Gonna Make Me Stay*, by Ed Andrews, accompanying himself on his own guitar. However the record cannot have been a great success, for Andrews never made another. Then, late in 1924, the Paramount talent scouts brought in Papa Charlie Jackson, a minstrel show entertainer who accompanied himself on the banjo. His first record – *Papa's Lawdy Lawdy Blues* and *Airy Man Blues* on Paramount 12219 – sold well, and Paramount's batch of releases for the New Year of 1925 included Papa Charlie's second record: the traditional *Salty Dog Blues* backed with *Salt Lake City Blues* (Papa Charlie's woman has left him and he declares he's going to jump on a freight train and go to Salt Lake City where 'you have a wife in the morning, another wife at night'). Papa Charlie had eight records in the 12000 series in 1925 – only Ida Cox and 'Ma' Rainey had more – and was one of Paramount's most successful artists for a further five years. In 1927 a Paramount advert asked 'have you heard about the twitching, twisting, shaking, shimmying, throbbing, sobbing – sensational new dance, "Skoodle Um Skoo"? Papa Charlie Jackson, the one and only "Papa Charlie", tells about it in his latest Paramount record. It's a torrid record with some mean banjo picking with it. Ask your dealer for Paramount 12501 or send us the coupon.'

Paramount, because of their mail order service, had more rural customers than the other companies and some of these were requesting recordings by country blues singers. In 1925 Sam Price – later to become a well-known race artist in his own right, but then working in a music store in Dallas – wrote to Mayo Williams recommending Blind Lemon Jefferson, a rough itinerant singer and guitar-picker from Texas. He was at once called to Chicago; Paramount – overall a smaller company than OKeh and lacking the justification provided by an extensive hillbilly catalogue – made no field trips to the South. Blind Lemon's first two selections, on Paramount 12347, were *Booster Blues* and *Dry Southern Blues*:

> The train's at the depot with the red and blue lights behind (*twice*)
> Well, the blue light's the blues, the red light's a worried mind

They were unlike anything that had appeared on record before. Blind Lemon's expressive, whining voice and his fluent guitar – complementing and sometimes replacing the voice – were an unbeatable combination. Paramount issued eight records by Lemon in 1926 and he was their major artist for the rest of the decade. Realising the demand for country blues performers – men who, unlike the classic blues singers, wrote almost all their own material – Paramount began looking for more talent of this type. In September 1926 they recorded Blind Blake from Georgia, a slightly more sophisticated performer whose records sold almost as well as Lemon's. Observing Paramount's success with Blind Lemon and Blind Blake, other companies were soon recording country blues, and in the closing years of the decade were competing as fiercely for this new market as they had over the classic blues singers a few years before.

In 1925 Bell laboratories perfected the technique of electric recording, and the rights to this new process were offered – at a highish price – to Victor and Columbia. But the consortium controlling the bankrupt Columbia company was reluctant to make so heavy an investment. English Columbia, which had been owned by the American company until 1922, had a go-ahead management who were determined to secure rights to electric recording. When it turned out that this was only possible through an American affiliate, English Columbia bought a controlling interest in its erstwhile parent.

PARAMOUNT

THE POPULAR RACE RECORD

♪♪ **My Lord's Gonna Move this Wicked Race**

A wonderful, inspiring, spiritual song that will never grow old. Beautifully rendered by the perfectly blended voices of the famous Norfolk Jubilee Quartette. It's a song that is sure to inspire you. Everyone who hears it will feel uplifted—just a little bigger and better in heart and spirit. Every Christian home will prize this record.

12035—MY LORD'S GONNA MOVE THIS WICKED RACE Vocal Quartette
Norfolk Jubilee Quartette
FATHER PREPARE ME Vocal Quartette   Norfolk Jubilee Quartette

PARAMOUNT JUBILEE SINGERS

12072—STEAL AWAY TO JESUS Mixed Quartette Paramount Jubilee Singers
MY SOUL IS A WITNESS TO MY LORD Mixed Quartette
Paramount Jubilee Singers
12073—WHEN ALL THE SAINTS COME MARCHING IN Mixed Quartette
Paramount Jubilee Singers
THAT OLD TIME RELIGION Mixed Quartette
Paramount Jubilee Singers

ELKINS-PAYNE JUBILEE SINGERS

12070—STANDING IN THE NEED OF PRAYER Male Quartette
Elkins-Payne Jubilee Singers
I COULDN'T HEAR NOBODY PRAY Mixed Quartette
Paramount Jubilee Singers
12071—GONNA SHOUT ALL OVER GOD'S HEAVEN Male Quartette
Elkins-Payne Jubilee Singers
DOWN BY THE RIVERSIDE Male Quartette
Elkins-Payne Jubilee Singers

MME. M. TARTT LAWRENCE

12092—HIS EYE IS ON THE SPARROW Piano Acc.   Madame Lawrence
STAND BY ME Piano Acc.   Madame Lawrence

MME. HURD FAIRFAX

12040—I'M SO GLAD TROUBLE DON'T LAST ALWAYS Mezzo Solo, Piano Acc.
Madame Hurd Fairfax
SOMEBODY'S KNOCKING AT YOUR DOOR Contralto Solo, Piano Acc.
Madame Hurd Fairfax

BLACK SWAN
THE RACE'S OWN RECORD

47 Jubilee singers were promoted by Paramount, 'The Race's Own Record'

It may have been this change of management early in 1926 which was responsible for the widening of the Columbia race series. Previously Columbia had done some recording in the field, like OKeh, mainly of hillbilly material, although just one blues disc in the 14000D series had been recorded outside New York – 14106D by 'Doc' Dasher, made in Atlanta in September 1925. In April 1926 the Columbia field unit made some race recordings in New Orleans and then went on to Atlanta, where they recorded a gospel quartet and a preacher.

Since 1921 OKeh and Paramount had been recording unaccompanied male quartets singing novelty and jazz numbers, which were often issued in the popular series (having a considerable white sale). From the early days of the 12000 race series Paramount had been featuring quartets singing spirituals – the most popular was the Norfolk Jubilee Quartet – and was the only one of the major race companies to make regular issues of this type of music. Now, in Atlanta, Columbia recorded the Birmingham Jubilee Singers. Their first record, *He Took My Sins Away* and *Crying To The Lord* on Columbia 14140D, sold nearly 5,000 copies and their second more than 13,000; the group recorded prolifically for Columbia, and then for Vocalion, over the next four years. Soon all the companies were looking for gospel quartets – over seventy records of this type of music were issued in 1927 and its popularity has continued to the present day. Except for the lean years of 1932–4 a minimum of thirty gospel quartet records was put out each year until 1941.

But the most important item from Columbia's Atlanta visit was four 'sermons with singing' by a local preacher, Rev. J. M. Gates, assisted by two unidentified female members of his congregation. On *Death's Black Train Is Coming*, Rev. Gates announces: 'I want to sing a song tonight, and while I sing I want every sinner in the house to come to the angel's feet and bow, and accept prayer – you *need* prayer. Subject of this song, Death's Black Train Is Coming – it's coming, too.' The unaccompanied voices then sing about the hell-bound train, that will bring judgement to all transgressors:

48 Reverend Gates recorded for several companies, including Vocalion

Some men and some women, they care nothing for the gospel life,
Till the bell ring and the whistle blows, for the little black train's in sight
Refrain:
The little black train is coming, get all your business right,
You better get your house in order, for that train may be here tonight

The singing had a compelling rhythm; the song concerned a metaphor popular amongst black Christians, and the Columbia engineers had arranged for a train whistle to sound several times in the background. When the selection was issued in July 1926 on Columbia 14145D, backed with a slow dirge *Need Of Prayer*, it was an instantaneous success. The previous year Columbia had issued some sermons by Calvin P. Dixon, nicknamed 'Black Billy Sunday', and Paramount a couple by Rev. W. A. White, but the Gates coupling contained the first sermons *with singing*. The advance pressing order for 14145D was 3,675; when the remaining two sides from Gates' Atlanta session were issued in October, on Columbia 14159D, the advance order was 34,025.

As soon as he saw how well Gates's first disc was selling, Polk Brockman – the Atlanta talent scout who had engineered the first OKeh field trip three years earlier – visited the preacher at his home and signed an exclusive contract with him (Columbia had neglected to do so). Every record company was wanting to issue sermons, preferably sermons by Rev. Gates. Brockman took Gates and some members of his congregation up to New York about the beginning of September and had him record for no less than five different record companies – OKeh, Victor, BBC's Vocalion, Pathé and Banner. Gates recorded forty-two sides within the space of two or three weeks and although he did not record any one sermon for all five companies there was plenty of repetition. *The Dying Gambler* was put on wax in the OKeh, Victor and Banner studios, and new versions of *Death's Black Train Is Coming* were made for Victor and Pathé. Gates was recorded again by OKeh when they came to Atlanta in November, and later that month Brockman took him back to New York to make eight sides for Gennett and seven, including yet another version of *Death's Black Train*, for Banner. By this time other preachers were being discovered – OKeh had got hold of Rev. H. R. Tomlin (whose first record was *his* version of *Death's Black Train*); Columbia lured Rev. J. C. Burnett away from Meritt and discovered Rev. W. M. Mosley; Victor recorded Rev. Mose Doolittle. In a nine-month period – from September 1926 to June 1927 – sixty records of sermons were put out by the various companies, and no less than forty of them were by Rev. J. M. Gates!

18 · INTO THE FIELD, 1927–1930

The years 1927 to 1930 were the peak years of blues recording. There were in 1927 just 500 blues and gospel records issued, an increase of 50 per cent on the already high 1926 figure. This rate of release – an industry average of almost 10 new records each week – was steadily maintained until the end of 1930. The companies were able to maintain the flow of music only through exhaustive searches for new talent. Paramount – the market leader during the peak years – brought a wide variety of artists north to its Chicago studios. The other companies made frequent excursions to the major towns in the South: during these four years Atlanta was visited seventeen times by field units in search of race talent, Memphis eleven times, Dallas eight times, New Orleans seven times, and so on. (Full details of all these field trips are included in the authors' comprehensive discography: Dixon, Godrich and Rye *Blues and Gospel Records, 1890–1943*; fourth, revised and expanded edition, Oxford University Press, 1997.)

During the peak years there were five main companies manufacturing records for the coloured market. General Phonograph had been unable to secure rights to electrical recording and – feeling that they could not, using the old acoustic method, compete effectively with Victor and Columbia – sold their OKeh-Odeon record division to Columbia in October 1926. It was continued as the OKeh Phonograph Corporation, a Columbia subsidiary. For three years after the take-over, the Columbia and OKeh labels were run by quite separate managements, but care was taken that they did not compete for the same artists (Rev. Gates' first records were on Columbia, but Columbia was the only label not to record him during the 'sermon boom'; he eventually became an exclusive OKeh artist). And the Columbia 14000D series was enlarged, at the expense of the OKeh 8000s. In 1926 only about 50 blues and gospel records had appeared on Columbia, compared with over 100 on OKeh. The Columbia releases gradually increased and the OKehs dwindled until in 1929 about 85 blues and gospel items were put on the 14000D series as against only around 65 in the OKeh 8000 series. OKeh was still a major race label – and it always bore far more good jazz than Columbia – but it was not the power it had been in the classic blues period. The other major race companies during the peak years were Paramount, Brunswick-Balke-Collender with its Vocalion and Brunswick labels, the small Gennett concern, and Victor.

The record industry as a whole had not been in too healthy a state during the early twenties. After the boom year of 1921, in which for the first time 100 million discs were sold, sales declined slowly but steadily. Eventually even Victor began to feel the squeeze – their sales fell from $51 million in 1921 to $44 million in 1923, and then dropped to $20 million in 1925. Something had to be done, and one obvious move was for Victor to begin large-scale production of race records, and compete for a market that had been growing at an enormous rate during the period when overall sales had been falling. In July 1926 – almost three years since the last race session in a Victor studio – blues singers Mike Jackson and Mabel Richardson were recorded. Victor's first efforts were not too promising – they included Elizabeth Smith, a minor singer in the classic style; a gospel quartet called the Taskiana Four; Mamie Smith (who had been dropped by OKeh at the end of 1923 and then briefly featured on Ajax in 1924); and the inevitable sermons by Rev. Gates. There was little else they could do – the best artists were under contract to Paramount, OKeh or Columbia.

Then Victor hired Ralph Peer, who had been largely responsible for building up OKeh's fine race and hillbilly catalogues. Peer realised that Victor was several years too late to be able to get a substantial share of the classic blues market and decided to concentrate his efforts on the country blues field. In February 1927 Peer set out with the Victor field unit, calling first at Atlanta where he recorded thirty titles by white hillbilly performers and four selections by country blues singer Julius Daniels. After six days in Atlanta the unit moved on to Memphis where, between 24 February and 1 March, they recorded thirty titles by black jazz bands, preachers, guitar evangelists and blues singers. Peer had visited Memphis ahead of the field unit and – on the recommendation of Charlie Williamson, black bandleader and talent scout – had auditioned the Memphis Jug Band, a group consisting of a kazoo player, a jug-blower and two guitarists, one of whom doubled on harmonica. Peer thought the group had market potential and they were the first artists recorded, on the morning of Thursday 24 February, in the temporary studio set up in the McCall building.

The final call was New Orleans, and Victor again concentrated on black performers – including Louis Dumaine's Jazzola Eight, Rev. Isaiah Shelton and Richard 'Rabbit' Brown, a guitar-picking ferryboat man, who recorded *James Alley Blues* and *I'm Not Jealous* (on Victor 20578) as well as two long ballads *The Mystery Of Dunbar's Child* and *The Sinking Of The Titanic* (issued on a 12-inch disc, 35840). Of the blues recorded on this tour the big successes were the titles by the Memphis Jug Band. *Sun Brimmer's Blues* and *Stingy Woman Blues*, on 20552 in the general series, sold so well that Peer asked leader Will Shade to bring the group to Chicago to record four more titles, on Thursday 9 June.

Early in 1927 Mayo Williams, who had done so much to build up the Paramount race list, resigned in order to start his own Chicago Record Company. In May the *Chicago Defender* carried the first advertisement for Williams's Black Patti records. All the titles had been recorded for Williams by Gennett, and at least half the material was also issued on Gennett's own labels. Black Patti featured jazz bands, choirs, some fine blues singers (including Sam Collins from Mississippi) and – despite the label name – two white crooners. Black Patti adverts appeared in thirteen successive weekly editions of the *Defender* and then suddenly stopped; the last issue was *You Heard Me Whistle* and *Boll Weavil* by harmonica-playing Jaybird Coleman, on Black Patti 8055.

Meanwhile, Brunswick-Balke-Collender were still struggling to establish their Vocalion race series. Spurred by the success of records by unaccompanied gospel quartets, and sermons in the Rev. Gates style,

BBC pioneered a third type of religious record – gospel songs by itinerant guitar-playing evangelists. In November 1926 they recorded Blind Joe Taggart performing numbers like *Take Your Burden To The Lord* and *Just Beyond Jordan* (issued on Vocalion 1061) and in December Edward W. Clayborn, a powerful singer who played a singing bottle-neck guitar, made *The Gospel Train Is Coming* and *Your Enemy Cannot Harm You (But Watch Your Close Friend)*. When these titles were first issued, on Vocalion 1082, the artist credit was just 'The Guitar Evangelist'; however the record sold so well that it was re-pressed many times during the next few years and the label seems to have been printed afresh each time – copies have been found labelled Edward W. Clayburn, Edward W. Clayborn and even Rev. Edward W. Clayton! Religious singers like Taggart and Clayborn sang in the same general style and led the same sort of life as country blues singers like Blind Lemon Jefferson; they were distinguished only by their choice of material. Taggart in fact recorded one secular number – *C & O Blues* on Vocalion 1116 – making sure that this appeared under the pseudonym of 'Blind Amos'.

But, successful as were their religious issues, BBC were not doing at all well on the blues side. They needed someone to search out likely talent. When Mayo Williams's Black Patti venture folded in August 1927, Vocalion had no hesitation in hiring him as talent scout for the 1000 series. In October, Mayo Williams brought an old medicine show entertainer called Jim Jackson to BBC's Chicago headquarters and recorded six minutes of *Jim Jackson's Kansas City Blues*:

> I woke up this morning feeling bad
> Thought about the good times I once have had
> *Refrain.*
> I'm gonna move to Kansas City, I'm gonna move to Kansas City
> I'm gonna move baby, honey where they don't like you

It was released, on the two sides of Vocalion 1144, on 8 December 1927 and was an immediate hit. Vocalion had found an artist whose appeal matched that of Victor's Memphis Jug Band. Jim Jackson was called back to Chicago in January to record eight more selections, including Parts 3 and 4 of *Jim Jackson's Kansas City Blues*.

The first country blues singer to appear on the Columbia 14000D series was Peg Leg Howell, recorded in Atlanta in November 1926 and again the following April. Atlanta was a centre for white folk music and – like all other record companies – Columbia went there mainly for hillbilly talent; but they also kept a lookout for good country blues singers. The field unit was in Atlanta from 25 March to 8 April 1927 and although only about 30 of the 200 titles recorded were by black artists, they included 2 tunes by Robert Hicks, a versatile singer who accompanied himself on the 12-string guitar. *Barbecue Blues* and *Cloudy Sky Blues* were put out under the name Barbecue Bob on Columbia 14205D; 10,850 copies were pressed and the record issued on 10 May. Initial sales were so good that Hicks was called to New York in the middle of June to record 8 more numbers. And when Columbia returned to Atlanta in November they recorded not only a further 8 selections by Barbecue Bob, but also 6 by his brother Charley Lincoln, who sang the same sort of songs in very much the same style.

In December 1927 Frank Walker took the Columbia field unit to Dallas and Memphis. Nearly all the time in Dallas was devoted to race artists – three or four blues singers and two popular gospel singers: Washington Phillips, who accompanied himself on the dulceola, an unusual instrument of the dulcimer family, and Blind Willie Johnson, a singer with an incredibly rough, powerful voice that was perfectly complemented by his virtuoso guitar. In Memphis, Columbia recorded a couple of preachers and two blues singers, Reubin Lacy from Mississippi and Lewis Black from Arkansas. They issued a record by Lewis Black in March 1928 but it must have sold badly for Black's other two sides were not released until June 1929; none of the Lacy titles were issued. Columbia did not return to Memphis.

Since late 1925, OKeh had been issuing a new record every six weeks by singer–guitarist Lonnie Johnson. Johnson was not exactly a country blues singer but his material and style were on the outer edge of the country blues idiom. After the take-over by Columbia, OKeh made no field trips for a while. Then, in February 1928, they visited Memphis to record a number of hillbilly and race artists, some of whom (like Rev. Gates) had travelled west from Georgia and others (such as blues singers Tom

49 The cover of the 1930 Victor Records catalogue

Dickson and John Hurt) had come north from Mississippi. Lonnie Johnson went with the unit, himself recording in both Memphis and San Antonio. In San Antonio he also provided the guitar accompaniment for Texas Alexander, a shouting rural singer who had been recorded in New York by OKeh the previous August.

The pattern was now set for the next few years. Columbia visited Atlanta each spring and autumn to replenish the hillbilly catalogue, and also made a few race recordings; the late autumn of each year they went to Dallas, to make further titles by Blind Willie Johnson and Washington Phillips, and some by the accomplished Texas pianist–singers – men like Whistlin' Alex Moore and Texas Bill Day. OKeh paid regular visits to Atlanta and San Antonio for hillbilly material, and usually recorded a few black artists at each location. Victor went to Atlanta once or twice a year for hillbilly material, and also recorded a few titles for the race catalogue (generally including 4 new numbers by the Atlanta blues singer and twelve-string guitarist Blind Willie McTell, who also contrived to be recorded by Columbia under the pseudonym 'Blind Sammie').

Victor was the only company systematically to exploit the gold mine of black talent in and around Memphis. Their second visit there, in January and February 1928, yielded three times as much material as the initial visit in early 1927 – and again black artists greatly outnumbered white hillbilly performers. Besides more titles by the Memphis Jug Band, Victor recorded the Cannon's Jug Stompers, Vocalion's popular artist Jim Jackson, and a fine group of Mississippi blues singers – Tommy Johnson, Ishman Bracey and Frank Stokes. Stokes was an oldish man, his voice had a pronounced vibrato and his style of singing and guitar playing were distinctly archaic. His *Downtown Blues* and *Bedtime Blues* on Victor 21272 sold well and when Victor returned to Memphis in August 1928 they recorded 10 further selections by Stokes.

The August visit was Victor's most extensive to date. Between Monday 27 August and Monday 24 September they recorded 180 titles, three-quarters of them by race artists. They would normally record between 6 and 8 tunes each day (the most they ever managed in a day was 12), recording two takes of each item, or three if there had been something amiss with either of the first two. All the singers they had tried

Stevedore Stomp—Fox Trot *The Dicty Glide—Fox Trot*	Ellington's Cotton Club Orchestra *Ellington's Cotton Club Orchestra*	V- 38053	10	.75
Stingy Woman—Blues *Sun Brimmers—Blues*	Memphis Jug Band *Memphis Jug Band*	20552	10	.75
St. James Infirmary *with Vocal Refrain* *When You're Smiling—Fox Trot*	King Oliver and His Orch. *King Oliver and His Orchestra*	22298	10	.75
St. Louis Blues *Piano Duet* *After You've Gone*	"Fats" Waller-Bennie Paine *"Fats" Waller-Bennie Paine*	22371	10	.75
St. Louis Blues *I'm a Broken-Hearted Blackbird*	Leroy Smith and His Orchestra *Leroy Smith and His Orchestra*	21472	10	.75
St. Louis Blues *Pipe Organ* *Lenox Avenue Blues*	Thomas Waller *Thomas Waller*	20357	10	.75

STOKES, FRANK—with Guitar

Bedtime Blues	21272
Bunker Hill Blues	V-38548
Downtown Blues	21272
How Long?	V-38512
I Got Mine	V-38512
It Won't Be Long Now	21672
Mistreatin' Blues	21672
Nehi Mamma Blues	21738
South Memphis Blues	V-38548
Stomp That Thing	21738
'Taint' Nobody's Business	V-38500
Take Me Back	V-38531
What's the Matter Blues	V-38531

Frank Stokes

Stompin' On Down—Fox Trot *Tiny's Stomp—Fox Trot*	"Tiny" Parham and His Musicians *"Tiny" Parham and His Musicians*	V- 38060	10	.75
Stomp That Thing *with Guitar* *Nehi Mamma Blues*	Frank Stokes *Frank Stokes*	21738	10	.75
Stop Dat Band *Creep Along Moses*	Taskiana Four *Taskiana Four*	20184	10	.75

50 Frank Stokes appeared with King Oliver and Duke Ellington in the Victor catalogue

out in February were recorded again, and new ones besides. Jim Jackson recorded 12 more items, including a two-part *I'm Gonna Move To Louisiana*, that had the same tune and almost the same words as his *Kansas City Blues*. The autumn trip to Memphis now became an annual event for Victor – it was here that they recorded most of their race material.

Although Vocalion had become a major producer of race records at about the same time as Victor, they were slower to take recording equipment into the field. Then in 1928 they recorded some not-too-exciting blues artists in Dallas, New Orleans and Atlanta, and several gospel performers in Birmingham, Alabama; although they did stop at Memphis, only 2 race titles were recorded, fairly dull tunes by a singer who styled himself 'Keghouse'. Not until 1929 did they do any significant recording in the South.

It is difficult to know whether it was by luck or guile that the Vocalion field unit arrived in Memphis – in mid-September 1929 – just about a week before Victor was due. The Memphis Jug Band and Cannon's Jug Stompers were under contract to Victor, and Vocalion could not use them; but they did manage to snatch a number of worthwhile performers from under Victor's nose, including blues singer Robert Wilkins (whom Victor had recorded the previous autumn) and Speckled Red, whose raucous piano number *The Dirty Dozens* became one of Brunswick-Balke-Collender's most successful releases.

During the peak years there were fewer small companies producing just half-a-dozen or so race records each year. They either dropped out of the market altogether, or increased their output, like Vocalion and Gennett. In 1926 Pathé decided to compete more seriously for this expanding market and announced a race series on their Perfect label. Perfect 101 and 102 – by Rosa Henderson, under the pseudonym 'Mamie Harris', and Mary Stafford, the singer Columbia had dropped at the end of 1921 – were released in July 1926. In a period when the market was crying out for country blues, Perfect put out second-rate selections by minor classic blues singers, like Rosa Henderson, seasoned with a few sermons by Rev. Gates. Although Perfect records sold for only 39 cents, the public evidently preferred to pay 75 cents for the more up-to-the-minute material on Paramount, Victor, OKeh, Columbia or Vocalion. The Perfect race series had reached number 136 by the end of 1927; only two or three more records appeared on it in the next three years.

January 1927 saw the emergence of Gennett as a major race label. Of all the major producers it was the only one never to have a separate race series; yet strangely enough it was the only company to print the words 'Race Record' on the record label (and it had been doing so since late in 1924). Gennett's first electric recording had appeared in 1926, on the 50-cent 3000 series. However, the high royalty which had to be paid for the privilege of using electric recording techniques made a price increase necessary; a new 6000 'Electrobeam' general series was started in 1927, selling at 75 cents. Some first-class blues artists appeared in this series, including the honkytonk pianist Cow Cow Davenport and Cryin' Sam Collins, the earliest of the great Mississippi blues singers to record.

51 Electrobeam Gennett record labels bore 'Race Record' and the month of issue

Nevertheless, the volume of sales continued to be poor, and Gennett only managed to keep their heads above water by paying low artist fees. For example, in 1925 Baby Bonnie was paid $15 per title for *Longing Blues* and *Home Sweet Home Blues* on Gennett 3041, the pianist $10 and the trumpeter $5. And the same year singer John Henry Howard was paid $30 for nine titles! After 1925 royalties were offered rather than a flat fee – average payment was 1 cent, less 10%, per side sold.

Although talent scouts were regularly employed, only one field trip was made: to Birmingham, Alabama, where a temporary studio was rigged up in the local Starr Music Store (probably the reason Birmingham was chosen). Recording lasted from July to the end of August 1927 and included a preacher, a quartet, harmonica-player Jaybird Coleman (on no less than eighteen titles) and a number of blues singers. Only one of the two titles recorded in Birmingham by William Harris was issued, on Gennett 6306; but Harris' high-pitched voice, competent guitar and his original treatment of traditional material must have sold for he was called to Gennett's headquarters in Richmond, Indiana, in October 1928 to record fourteen more numbers.

In order to compete with cheap labels such as Pathé's Perfect, in September 1925 Gennett initiated the Champion label, at 35 cents each or three for $1. Almost everything that appeared on Gennett was also put out on Champion. Later they also issued some blues material on the cheap Superior label, selling exclusively through chain stores. In addition, the mail-order firm of Sears Roebuck put out Gennett race items on its established cut-price label Silvertone and also, from 1928, on Supertone. All issues on these cheap labels were under pseudonym, in order to hide the fact that identical material was being issued on Gennett for 75 cents and on the other labels for less than half the price. Thus Lottie Kimbrough – a massive singer who was billed as Lottie Beaman, 'The Kansas City Butter Ball', by Paramount – appeared under her own name on Gennett, as Lottie Everson on Champion, as Lottie Brown on Supertone, and as Martha Johnson on Superior. Sam Collins was labelled Jim Foster on Champion and Silvertone.

In December 1925 a most interesting label made its appearance. Called Herwin, and produced by *Her*bert and Ed*win* Schiele of the St Louis Music Company, it was sold mainly through advertisements in farm journals, for 75 cents, an exceptionally high price for mail-order records. Three companies – two of whom were Gennett and Paramount – were known to have pressed, labelled and shipped these records for Herwin, which accounts for the same issue number being used twice, for quite different couplings, in some instances. To save costs, the quality of material used for pressing was very poor and the records wore out quickly. Owing to these factors sales were bad and in 1930 Herwin was sold to Paramount after 73 issues – almost all pseudonymous – over four years.

The only race company that made no field trips whatever during the peak years was Paramount. Yet, both in number of records released, and in the range of singers recorded, Paramount was the market leader. During each of the peak years Paramount issued more than 100 blues and gospel records (in addition to a fair amount of jazz and some novelty numbers). Gennett issued around 40 each year; Columbia altogether 150 in their two established series – OKeh 8000 and Columbia 14000D. And although the Victor race catalogue was of a high quality, the quantity was not great – about 60 a year. The main emphasis in the peak years was on the country blues, but the best of the classic singers still sold well; Sara Martin and Sippie Wallace were dropped by OKeh at the end of 1927, but Bessie Smith, 'Ma' Rainey, Victoria Spivey and Clara Smith continued to have a new record issued about every other month.

The great gospel boom had been in late 1926; Rev. J. C. Burnett's first record on Columbia – *Downfall Of Nebuchadnezzar* and *I've Even Heard Of Thee,* exactly the same titles as on his earlier Meritt release – sold 80,000 copies soon after its release in November 1926; this was four times as many as the normal sale of a Bessie Smith record, and Bessie was still outselling just about every other blues singer. But the bubble soon burst and Burnett's fourth record, in March 1927, had initial sales in the region of 15,000. However this was still rather more than for the average blues record, and sermons continued to be a worthwhile proposition throughout the peak years. Besides Gates and Burnett, two Chicago preachers were well represented in the catalogues. Victor had secured Rev. F. W. McGee, who accompanied himself on the piano and often included a cornet, guitar and drums as well – his records had a swinging, jazzy flavour. Vocalion had Rev. A. W. Nix, whose *Black Diamond Express To Hell* was perhaps the best-known sermon of any period: Parts 1 and 2 appeared on Vocalion 1098 in May 1927, Parts 3 and 4 on Vocalion 1421, released in November 1929, and Parts 5 and 6 on Vocalion 1486, in June 1930. The theme was basically the same as that of the record that started it all – *Death's Black Train Is Coming* by Rev. J. M. Gates. The Vocalion advert announced 'Here she comes! The *"Black Diamond Express To Hell"* with Sin, the Engineer, holding the throttle wide open; Pleasure is the Headlight, and the Devil is the

Conductor. You can feel the roaring of the Express and the moanin' of the Drunkards, Liars, Gamblers and other folk who have got aboard. They are hell-bound and they don't want to go. The train makes eleven stops but nobody can get off . . .'; and they appended a map of the express's route, marking the stops: 'Liars' Ave', 'Dance Hall Depot', 'Stealing Town' and so on.

In 1927 one third of the 500 releases were gospel items; the figure dropped to about a quarter in 1928 and remained at this level for the next two years. There was an annual output of around 50 sermons, 50 records by unaccompanied quartets, and 20 or so by guitar evangelists. Besides the regular evangelists – Blind Joe Taggart, Blind Willie Johnson, Edward W. Clayborn and Paramount's Blind Willie Davis – quite a few blues singers tried their hand at gospel numbers, the records often being issued under a pseudonym. Thus Barbecue Bob assumed his real name – Robert Hicks – for religious numbers, and the two gospel issues from Blind Lemon Jefferson were labelled 'Deacon L. J. Bates', the 'L. J.' being a rather obvious clue.

Paramount issued almost twice as many blues and gospel items in 1927 as they had in 1926. Their best-selling artists were recorded at a tremend-ous rate, reminiscent of the overissuing of classic blues singers in 1923 and 1924. New Blind Lemon and Blind Blake discs appeared just about every month. (Victor, in contrast, were considerably more cautious – even Memphis Jug Band releases were held at 6 a year.) So successful was Blind Lemon that a special yellow and white label was produced for Paramount 12650 *Piney Woods Money Mama* and *Low Down Mojo Blues*, bearing his picture and the legend 'Blind Lemon Jefferson's Birthday Record'.

Paramount's New York studio having closed down in 1926, artists continued to record in Chicago until, in 1929, new studios were opened in Grafton, Wisconsin; by the end of the year all recordings were made here. This was the era of the very best in blues and gospel recording. Paramount had issued material by Frank Stokes and his partner Dan Sane, under the name Beale Street Sheiks, and by Gus Cannon, under the name Banjo Joe, in 1927, before Victor signed them. Full credit must go to the talent scouts, foremost of whom was Henry C. Spier, a music-store owner from Jackson, Mississippi, who searched the South for talent to send up to the Paramount studios. Among the artists Spier unearthed were Son House, who had an unforgettable ringing guitar style, Skip James, an original singer who transferred his guitar technique wholesale to the piano, and the great Charley Patton. Paramount asked Gennett to record 14 tunes by Patton at their Richmond, Indiana, studio in June 1929; the first issue was *Pony Blues* and *Banty Rooster Blues*, on Paramount 12792. Patton was a light-skinned man with curly blond hair, but his appearance was deceptive. Patton's deep rough voice blurred over the lyrics and often descended into incomprehensibility – it was perfectly complemented by his clear-toned fluent guitar; as with Blind Lemon, the guitar often took over the vocal line. Patton's whole performance produced a riveting, hypnotic effect, perhaps comparable to that of an African witch-doctor.

Realising that they had a star in Patton, Paramount labelled his second blues release – *Screamin' And Hollerin' Blues* on Paramount 12805 in September 1929 – 'The Masked Marvel'. The advert bore a drawing of a blindfolded singer – looking nothing like Patton – and the clue that this was an exclusive Paramount artist. Anyone correctly guessing the Masked Marvel's identity would get a free Paramount record of their choice. There must have been many records claimed, for no one else could be mistaken for Patton. Eager to exploit all angles, Paramount also put out 2 gospel items by Patton under the pseudonym 'Elder J. J. Hadley'. In 1930 he had 13 records issued – more than any other blues artist.

Paramount also had a number of cheap, three-for-a-dollar, subsidiary labels. One of these, Broadway, featured a race series – pseudonymously as usual, to disguise the fact that it merely duplicated material from the higher-priced label. 'Ma' Rainey appeared on Broadway as Lila Patterson, Ida Cox as Kate Lewis and as Velma Bradley; Blind Lemon, however, was issued on Broadway without a pseudonym.

In January 1928 Paramount's recording manager, Arthur E. Satherley, left to work for QRS records (no one has yet discovered what – if anything – these initials stand for), taking with him those masters to which he had personal rights. Most of these items, already issued on Paramount in many cases, appeared in the QRS 7000 race series, but the series

52 Q.R.S. label – the letters probably had no meaning

mainly consisted of material recorded by QRS at Long Island City – including 10 titles by Clifford Gibson, a mellow singer from Louisville who was afterwards signed by Victor. However, QRS soon lost interest in the 7000 series and it was discontinued after number 7092, in 1929.

The year 1927 had been a glorious one for all types of recording, with industry sales exceeding 100 million for the first time since 1921. Victor's receipts had climbed back to $48 million, more than double what they had been in 1925. Exact figures are not available, but it seems probable that race records were making up 5%, or a little more, of total industry sales. The average blues or gospel record had sales in the region of 10,000. In 1928 the figure was 1,000 or so lower; but it was still a thriving market and the future looked rosy. In January 1929 Victor decided to inaugurate a special race series (race releases had until then been mingled into the general series). The V38000 series at first contained both jazz and vocal issues, but after V38035 it was decided to reserve it for instrumental performances, and the V38500 series – begun in April 1929 – carried the blues and gospel items.

Benefiting from Mayo Williams's know-how, Vocalion were steadily increasing their share of the market. Their 3 releases a month in 1926 gave way to 4 the next year and 5 in 1928. Brunswick-Balke-Collender started a second race series, the Brunswick 7000s, in May 1927 but only issued a handful of miscellaneous records on it in the following eighteen months. Then, in 1929, BBC issued around 90 blues and gospel records in the Vocalion 1000 series and also put out 50 in the Brunswick race series; these figures were repeated the following year. The sudden expansion was made possible partly through intensive recording activity in the field, and partly through Mayo Williams's discovery of three new and extraordinarily popular artists.

In June 1928 Vocalion took a unit to Indianapolis to record Leroy Carr, an urban singer who accompanied himself on the piano – a welcome contrast to the rural singer–guitarists who could now be heard by the dozen on all the major labels. The lead side on Carr's first record – released on Vocalion 1191, in mid-August 1928 – was *How Long How Long Blues*, a lament for a girl friend who had travelled away up the railroad:

> How long, how long, has that evening train been gone
> How long, how long, baby how long

The tune was as unforgettable as Jim Jackson's *Kansas City Blues* of the year before. Carr's full, mournful singing, and the brilliance of his piano and the guitar of his partner Scrapper Blackwell combined to make a runaway hit. He was called to Chicago to record 6 more tunes in August, and in December he returned to make *How Long How Long Blues* Parts 2 and 3 (on Vocalion 1241 and 1279 respectively). Vocalion issued 10 records by Carr in 1929, and the same number the following year.

In May 1928 Vocalion finally dropped their tag 'Better and Cleaner
Race Records'. This was an honest thing to do, since their releases had
been as full of innuendo as anyone else's. But it also showed considerable foresight, for the artists Mayo Williams brought to the studio in
September that year specialised in the most suggestive lyrics in the
business. Hudson Whittaker, otherwise known as Tampa Red 'The Guitar
Wizard', and pianist Georgia Tom Dorsey recorded *It's Tight Like That*,
released on Vocalion 1216. The gradually accelerating tempo, Tampa Red's
open bottle-neck guitar playing and the sly humour with which the
simple lyrics were delivered produced an irresistibly erotic effect. Soon
the record was being played and copied everywhere. Tampa Red was in
such demand that in 1929 he had 17 new records issued, all on Vocalion

53 Pianist Leroy Carr was highly influential in the 1930s

(numerically, his nearest rivals were Blind Blake and Leroy Carr, with 10 apiece, and Blind Lemon Jefferson and Lonnie Johnson, who had 9 each).

Victor and Columbia continued to concentrate on their country blues artists, and gave no signs of noticing that a new urban style was sweeping Chicago. But Paramount, as always, lost no time in exploiting the new craze. They created a group called 'The Hokum Boys' (first recorded in December 1928, only a week or two after *It's Tight Like That* was released) that had a variable personnel and specialised in Tampa-Red-type numbers – tunes like *Beedle Um Bum, Somebody's Been Using That Thing* and *It's All Worn Out*.

In February 1930 the OKeh field unit called at Shreveport, Louisiana, to do some recording at the request of the local radio station. While there, they also recorded a white singer called Blind Andy and a small black group who called themselves the Mississippi Sheiks. The Sheiks sang – often as vocal duets – catchy numbers like *Lonely One In This Town* and *Bootleggers Blues*, and accompanied themselves on a violin and one or two guitars. Their records went down so well that OKeh recorded 14 more numbers at San Antonio in August and a further 16 in Jackson, Mississippi, just before Christmas. The Sheiks – with their vaguely hillbilly sound – were producing, within a rural idiom, the same type of music that Tampa Red and Georgia Tom had perfected in Chicago; it was probably no coincidence that one of the selections recorded in San Antonio was *Loose Like That*, issued on 8820. Their most popular title was *Sitting On Top Of The World* – words heavy with irony, sung at slow tempo against a mournful mocking violin accompaniment:

> Was all the summer, and all the fall
> Just trying to find my little all and all
> *Refrain.*
> But now she's gone, I don't worry
> I'm sitting on top of the world

At the end of 1930 the record companies were anything but sitting on top of the world. Columbia, for instance, had pressed an average of 11,000 copies of each new blues and gospel record in 1927; in the latter half of 1928 the figure was down to 7,000, and by the end of 1929 it had fallen to 5,000. By May 1930 – in the wake of the Stock Market crash – the company was pressing an average of 2,000, and that figure was halved by the end of the year. As 1931 dawned, race records were selling about a tenth as well as they had four years previously. And the situation continued steadily to worsen; 350 or 400 copies were pressed of each of the last twenty-two discs in the Columbia 14000D series, issued between May and October 1932, and Columbia – still pricing the records at 75 cents – couldn't even sell this small number; all twenty-two were still in catalogue in November 1934.

Paramount was the first company to succumb; their last advertisement in the *Chicago Defender* had been on 26 April 1930 (for 12917, *Mississippi Blues* and *Got To Have My Sweetbread*, by piano bluesman Charlie Spand). Over 100 blues and gospel items were issued in 1930 but in 1931 the number was down to about three dozen. In 1932 they brought the popular Mississippi Sheiks to Grafton, Wisconsin, to record twelve titles (including one called *The New Sittin' On Top Of The World*). The Sheiks sang and played as they never had before but even they could not save Paramount from financial ruin; the last record in the 12000 series – which altogether bore more issues than any other race series – was *She's Crazy*

'Bout Her Lovin' and *Tell Her To Do Right* by the Sheiks, issued on Paramount 13156 in late 1932.

At the end of 1930 the Starr Piano Company discontinued their 75 cent Gennett label but continued to issue some race titles on the cheap Champion and Superior, including records by Scrapper Blackwell, Leroy Carr's guitarist, and by Georgia Tom, Tampa Red's partner (Carr and Tampa Red were both firmly under contract to Vocalion). The Superior label was discontinued in July 1932; the following month a few sides were recorded by members of the Memphis Jug Band but, after that, recording virtually ceased. In 1933 only seven race titles were recorded – four piano solos by Turner Parrish in January, and three blues with guitar accompaniment by Archie Lewis, in March. Champion still managed to release about a dozen blues discs in 1933, half what they had put out in each of the two previous years, by using rejected titles from earlier years. They continued in this way into 1934 and then, in August, made some new race recordings – four blues by Frank James, accompanying himself on the piano. James was promised a $\frac{1}{2}$-cent royalty per side sold, but just nineteen copies of Champion 16809 – *Snake Hip Blues* backed with *Frank's Lonesome Blues* – had been shipped out of the factory when the company went into liquidation at the end of 1934. It is doubtful if James ever received the 19 cents he was due.

After its take-over of OKeh, the Columbia company had continued to run the two labels quite independently, with each having its own studio and field unit. In the autumn of 1929 – with sales running at half the 1927 level – they effected some degree of rationalisation and used a single field unit to cover both labels. But the Columbia and OKeh catalogues were still kept as separate as possible. The joint unit went in late 1929 to the old OKeh stomping ground of San Antonio, where it recorded just for OKeh issue; then it went to Dallas, Columbia's regular centre, where all recordings were earmarked for Columbia issue. The third stop was New Orleans: Columbia artists – including Blind Willie Johnson – were recorded on 10 and 11 December, and then OKeh artists – amongst them Rev. Gates, called down from Atlanta – from 13 until 17 December.

Blind Willie Johnson's first records had sold no better than the average disc in the Columbia 14000D series – in early 1929 they would manage about 5,000 as against Barbecue Bob's 6,000 and Bessie Smith's 9,000 or 10,000. But in mid-1930 the blind evangelist became the star of the list – his records were *still* selling 5,000 copies, although Barbecue Bob was down to 2,000, Bessie Smith to 3,000, and the average release had initial sales of only just over 1,000. Columbia issued seven records by Blind Willie in 1930, but, as times became harder the following year, even his appeal waned. In 1931, like Barbecue Bob, Bessie Smith and the rest, Blind Willie's records were selling in hundreds rather than thousands.

The Columbia label had no new artists, and its releases were cut by over a third in 1931. OKeh was in a slightly better way. They not only had the fast-selling Mississippi Sheiks, but had also been issuing solo records by Bo Carter, a guitar-playing member of the group. Carter gave perfectly straight country blues renditions of songs with simple, risqué lyrics – *Ants In My Pants, Same Thing The Cats Fight About* and *Ram Rod Daddy*. His first records went so well that late in 1931 OKeh put out a special batch of three Bo Carters – numbers 8887 to 8889 in the race series. Thanks to the Sheiks and Bo Carter, OKeh managed to issue marginally more blues and gospel than they had the previous year.

But times *were* getting harder. Columbia-OKeh made one field trip in 1931, to Atlanta in October/November. This time the principle of keeping the labels separate was forgotten. The first day they recorded two tunes by Blind Willie McTell which were marked in the ledger 'Blind Sammie' and allocated matrix numbers from the Columbia series; then McTell was recorded singing two more tunes, but this time the name 'Georgia Bill' was entered and the selections given OKeh matrix numbers. A month or two later Blind Willie appeared – under the two different pseudonyms – on Columbia 14632D and OKeh 8936.

That was the last field trip Columbia made. In December 1931 English Columbia sold the American company to Grigsby-Grunow, which had grown fat on the profits of its Majestic radio sets and was seeking to diversify. The new management decided at first to concentrate on Columbia – to the exclusion of OKeh – and continued to release two new items each fortnight in the 14000D series for most of 1932. Bo Carter and Mississippi Sheiks items – originally earmarked for OKeh issue – appeared on Columbia 14671D and 14672D. Then in October they decided that sales did not justify any more releases; 681 discs had appeared in the series, over a period of nine years. The last glimpse of the 14000Ds is in the November 1934 Columbia catalogue, which still lists a few choice items – four by Barbecue Bob, ten by Blind Willie Johnson, fifteen by Bessie Smith (out of the sixty-six discs she had had issued in the 14000Ds) and just one – out of a grand total of fifty-three issued – by Clara Smith. Grigsby-Grunow continued with the OKeh 8000s, issuing a couple of records every other month. They did just a little recording in 1932: four tunes by Clara Smith, twelve by Lonnie Johnson and – surprisingly – two by Lucille Hegamin, her first for six years. In 1933 they recorded the Mississippi Sheiks and, after a two-year absence from the studio, Bessie Smith. But this was not because they imagined Bessie would still sell well among her own people – the session was organised at the request of English Parlophone, who were building up a jazz catalogue.

In 1930, when most companies were considering cutting back on their race issues, the American Record Corporation entered the field. ARC had been formed in August 1929 by the merger of three small companies: the Cameo Record Corporation, with labels Cameo and Romeo, the Plaza Music Company, whose labels included Banner and Oriole, and the Pathé Phonograph and Radio Corporation, owners of Perfect. These were all cheap labels, selling at prices much below the regular 75 cents charged by the big companies. Perfect – the most popular of the bunch – had been 39 cents but was reduced to 25 cents at about the time ARC was formed.

The Depression, with the massive unemployment it brought, had a shattering effect on the pockets of black record buyers. Race records probably accounted for only about 1 per cent of total industry sales in 1931, as against around 5 per cent four years earlier. There was a clear opening for cut-price race discs. In 1930 ARC decided to revive the Perfect race series, and this time they made sure that they used currently popular artists singing up-to-the-minute material. In April 1930 ARC recorded some solo blues by Georgia Tom, and some Tampa-Red-type numbers by a group called The Famous Hokum Boys that included Georgia Tom and a guitarist called Big Bill Broonzy. Big Bill had had two rather disappointing records issued by Paramount in 1928, and now ARC recorded five solo items by him, and issued them under the name

54 Blues singer 'Georgia Tom' became the successful gospel song writer, Thomas A. Dorsey

ORIOLE RECORDS

Old Familiar Tunes—Sacreds and Race

(Ready for Shipment November 1st)   Oct. 22, 1931.

OLD TIME SINGING and PLAYING

8100 (TWENTY-ONE YEARS   Vocal-Nov.Acc.   Carson Robison Trio
     (IN THE CUMBERLAND MOUNTAINS   Vocal-Nov.Acc.   Carson Robison Trio
This is a national hit, TWENTY-ONE YEARS - the prison song of the south, the song that
everyone is singing. "I've Counted The Footsteps, I've Counted The Stars, I've Counted A Million Of These Prison Bars." It happened in Nashville, Tenn. A real master-
piece. Buy this record in quantity lots -- you'll sell plenty. It is coupled with
"In The Cumberland Mountains", another wonderful number, a song that speaks for itself.

8101 (DARLING NELLIE GRAY   Vocal Duet-Nov.Acc.   Martin & Roberts
     (SUNNY TENNESSEE   Vocal Duet-Nov.Acc.   Martin & Roberts
These numbers are nationally known and are recorded by genuine southern talent. A
title strip announcing this record and proper demonstration will result in sales.

8102 (THE LITTLE OLD JAIL HOUSE   Vocal   Asa Martin
     (THE ROVING MOONSHINER   Vocal   Asa Martin
The "Jailhouse" and the "Moonshiner" are two subjects that will always sell. They are
recorded by talent who lives with them and renders them in their own inimitable style.
Don't overlook Martin's story about the Jailhouse and the Moonshiner.

8103 (I SHALL NOT BE MOVED   Vocal Duet   Frank & James McCravy
     (METHODIST PIE   Vocal-Nov.Acc. Gene Autry
Two songs that are known by everyone and recorded by artists who have a tremendous
following.

8104 (THE WAGGONER   Old Time Fiddling   Fiddling Doc Roberts Trio
     (SHORTENIN' BREAD   Old Time Fiddling   Fiddling Doc Roberts Trio
Two 'hot' fiddle tunes that are sure-fire. Doc Roberts, the champion old time fiddler,
puts these numbers over in a style that is pleasing to all lovers of old time dance
tunes. You'll sell plenty of this record -- keep a supply on hand.

BLUES by COLORED ARTISTS

8105 (AIN'T GOING THERE NO MORE   Vocal-Inst.Acc.   'Famous' Hokum Boys
     (PIE EATING STRUT   Vocal-Inst.Acc.   'Famous' Hokum Boys
Every colored person knows the Famous Hokum Boys. This record is true to their style.
It has plenty of snap and just the type the negro looks for.

8106 (SLOW MAMA SLOW   Vocal with Guitar   Salty Dog Sam
     (NEW SALTY DOG   Vocal with Guitar   Salty Dog Sam
These two songs are recorded by a new artist "just from the South". Genuine negro
blues in the style the negro likes. There is a big demand for this type of selection.
This is your chance to clean up. A down home record by a down home artist. Be sure
to demonstrate this record to every negro that comes to your counter. Tell them it is
made by a real negro. This is a real big opportunity.

8107 (BLACK CAT CROSSED YOUR PATH   Sermon   Rev. Jordan Jones & Cong.
     (HELL AND WHAT IT IS   Sermon   Rev. Jordan Jones & Cong.
This record will be bought by white people as well as negroes. The subject is true to
negro superstition, they will like it and the white people will buy it for the kick
they get out of it.

American Record Corporation   **1776 Broadway, N.Y.**

55 An ARC advance release sheet sent to record dealers

Sammy Sampson. Bill sang straight country blues numbers, with less recourse to *double-entendre* than most singers of the period, and provided complex, rhythmic guitar accompaniments. In September 1930 ARC had a second race recording session – involving once again Georgia Tom, Sammy Sampson and the Famous Hokum Boys. The next year they went slightly further afield, and recorded twenty-one gospel numbers by the Famous Garland Jubilee Singers, ten sermons by former Paramount artist Rev. Emmet Dickinson, twenty blues by Gennett's Sam Collins (including *I'm Still Sitting On Top Of The World*) and eighteen numbers by Joe Evans and Arthur McClain, guitarist–singers from Alabama who affected a Mississippi Sheiks style, and even added a violin for *their* version of *Sitting On Top Of The World*. In 1931 and into 1932 ARC issued a steady two records or so each month by their limited group of artists, in the Perfect 100 series. All the records were also simultaneously issued on Oriole, Romeo and – from the end of 1931 – on Banner. Thus Perfect 0189, by the Famous Garland Jubilee Singers, was also on Oriole 8088, Romeo 5088 and Banner 32266; Perfect 0193 by Sam Collins (labelled as Salty Dog Sam) came out on Oriole 8106, Romeo 5106 and Banner 32311. While the Perfect series contained only race records, Romeo and Oriole bore hillbilly as well, and Banner featured a full range of popular material, in addition to race and hillbilly. All the labels were priced at 25 cents, but sold through different retail outlets – Romeo could only be bought in S. H. Kress's dime stores, Oriole only in McCrory's stores, and so on. They became known, collectively, as 'the dime store labels'.

In April 1930, Brunswick-Balke-Collender's record division had been bought by Warner Brothers Pictures. The name was changed to the Brunswick Radio Corporation and the headquarters moved from Chicago to New York, but otherwise everything was as it had been. With the gradual rundown of Paramount, BRC was undisputed leader of the race market. Not only did they have Tampa Red and Leroy Carr: in Memphis, in February 1930, Vocalion had recorded some solo blues and some duets by singer–guitarists Memphis Minnie and her husband Kansas Joe McCoy. Columbia had recorded them in New York in 1929, but didn't even issue all the titles they had made. Now, Vocalion made a big thing of Minnie's earthy singing and classic guitar accompaniment. Her big tune was *Bumble Bee*, issued on Vocalion 1476 about May 1930; when Columbia saw how well it was selling they belatedly – in August 1930 – issued the version they had recorded fourteen months previously. Vocalion followed up with *Bumble Bee No. 2*, on Vocalion 1556 in January 1931, and *New Bumble Bee*, on 1618 in July. The theme was simple:

I've got a bumble bee
Don't sting nobody but me
And I tell the world
He's got all the things I need

Memphis Minnie and Kansas Joe appeared on fourteen records in 1931 – there were six solo blues by Joe, six duets, and sixteen solos by Minnie.

BRC were the only company to issue as many blues and gospel items in 1931 as they had the previous year. In addition to nearly 100 in the Vocalion 1000 series, they produced around 40 on Brunswick. The 7000 series had the slogan 'Get 'em – cause they're HOT!', but it contained nothing as hot as Memphis Minnie. Lucille Bogan – the first singer to have been recorded on location – now had regular releases on Brunswick; she had improved enormously since 1923 and on two records her full voice and perfect phrasing were admirably complemented by Tampa Red's guitar. Warner discontinued field trips at the end of 1930, and about the same time they started a cheap label – Melotone. The 500 records put out on Melotone in its first two years only included a score of race items, amongst them 3 popular religious items that had appeared on Vocalion in 1927 – a Blind Joe Taggart, Edward W. Clayborn's first record, and Rev. A. W. Nix's *Black Diamond Express To Hell*, Parts 1 and 2.

In October 1930 Consolidated Film Industries had bought ARC; then, in December 1931, they purchased the Brunswick Record Corporation from Warner Brothers. ARC and BRC maintained separate identities on the surface – as sister subsidiaries within the CFI organisation – but they were effectively run as one concern. The Brunswick 7000 race series was discontinued (it had reached 7233) and although the Vocalion 1000s were continued, the price was reduced from 75 cents to 35 cents. New titles from Tampa Red and Memphis Minnie were put out both on Vocalion and on ARC's four dime-store labels, selling at 25 cents. Big Bill was

ROMEO RECORDS
by
AMERICA'S BEST RACE ARTISTS
BLUES — SACREDS — SPIRITUALS

BIG BILL

5494 { I Wanta See My Baby / Hobo Blues

5-11-67 { Rising Sun, Shine On / Let Her Go — / She Don't Know

5433 { Prowlin' Ground Hog / C-C Rider

5347 { Mistreating Mama Blues / Long Tall Mama

35-10-31 { Dirty No-Gooder / Dying Day Blues

— FOR SALE BY —

S. H. KRESS 5, 10 and 25c Stores

56 Big Bill (Broonzy) records were sold by the Kress stores on the Romeo label

now being issued under his own name, but just on the dime-store labels. ARC–BRC's control of the market can be seen from the fact that in 1932 they had three of the four most popular artists (in terms of number of releases) – Tampa Red, Memphis Minnie and Big Bill; the one they didn't have was the Mississippi Sheiks, who appeared that year on OKeh, Columbia and Paramount.

But sales were *still* falling. In April 1932, $100 was paid for twenty tunes from Joshua White, a singer who had been Blind Joe Taggart's lead boy at the age of thirteen, and who had recorded with him for Paramount. This was ARC–BRC's last race recording of the year. Even when the field unit visited San Antonio in November only hillbilly artists were used. Material that had already been recorded continued to be put in the Vocalion 1000 series until it ran out in November. In mid-1933 a few items by ARC artists were issued on Vocalion under pseudonym – Joshua White became 'Tippy Barton', for instance – and the series finally finished with number 1745, by Big Bill.

Regular issues continued to be made on Perfect, Romeo, Oriole and Banner – and from November 1932 all material was also issued simultaneously on Melotone. Some recording was done in 1933 – a group of Georgia singers including Buddy Moss, Curly Weaver and Blind Willie McTell, Lucille Bogan, and a few more. Surprisingly, no recordings were made in 1933 of the most popular singers from the immediately preceding years: Tampa Red, Leroy Carr, Memphis Minnie and Big Bill. In the late summer of 1933 BRC started a new Vocalion general series, the 2500s. At first there were few race issues – the Blind Willie McTell titles, and some numbers by Lucille Bogan's guitarist, Sonny Scott. However, by the end of the year sales were improving and in 1934, for the first time since 1931, ARC–BRC recorded race artists in Chicago – including Tampa Red and Memphis Minnie. And they also travelled to St Louis to record Leroy Carr and Scrapper Blackwell. Things were getting back to normal at Vocalion.

But not so at Columbia. Although ARC–BRC were finding a market for their 35-cent and 25-cent discs, people were still loth to spend 75 cents on a Columbia or OKeh record. Finally Grigsby-Grunow went into liquidation and in late 1934 BRC bought its subsidiary, the Columbia

Phonograph Company. In 1923 there had been a dozen independent labels issuing race records. Through an eleven-year sequence of merger and take-over, seven of these – Brunswick, Vocalion, Cameo, Banner, Perfect, OKeh and Columbia – were now owned by Consolidated Film Industries.

Victor, who had been taken over by the Radio Corporation of America in January 1929, were the only company successfully to weather the Depression years without change of ownership. Their sales were as low as anyone else's – and in 1932 industry sales were 6 million discs, as compared with 104 million in 1927. But Victor's resources were more solid and, as hard times worsened, they effected a policy of ruthless economy. At first, the company had tried to fight off falling sales. Although Victor had issued race catalogues and supplements in the peak years they had not advertised in the black press. Then, in March 1930 there was a Victor display in the *Chicago Defender*, the first since August 1923; this was in fact the month before Paramount stopped advertising in the *Defender*. However, sales continued to fall and the nineteenth Victor insertion – on 27 December 1930 – was the last.

Like the other major companies Victor had always made at least two 'takes' of each title. This was an obvious point for economy, and on 16 June 1931 Raymond R. Sooy, the chief recording engineer, sent round a memorandum 'Starting with this date, only one wax to be processed, unless wax becomes defective.' In 1931, with country blues selling less and less well, Victor decided to dispense with their annual visit to Memphis. In May they called at Charlotte, North Carolina, mainly for hillbilly material, and went on to Louisville, where they recorded the white singer Jimmie Rodgers, and also a number of blues piano sides by Walter Davis and Roosevelt Sykes. Sykes had been discovered by talent scout Jesse Johnson in 1929, and taken to New York to record, as OKeh's answer to Leroy Carr. Since he was under contract to OKeh, Sykes told Victor that his name was Willie Kelly, and his records were issued thus. Walter Davis's mellow vocal style and Carr-like material were liked, and he was again recorded by Victor in Chicago in September.

In 1931 Victor cut their blues and gospel releases by a third, to about forty. They had discontinued the V38500 series – at V38631 – the previous year and in January 1931 started a 23250 blues and gospel series (there was also a 23000 series for jazz, and a 23500 one for hillbilly material). The only race recordings Victor made in 1932 were in the course of their single field trip, to Dallas and Atlanta in February. They went to Dallas for Jimmie Rodgers, and also recorded Walter Davis and a few local blues singers; in Atlanta there were four tunes from the inevitable Blind Willie McTell and four blues duets from the Sparks brothers, issued as 'Pinetop and Lindberg'. Most of the material from this trip had been issued by the middle of the year, and thereafter Victor continued to put out race records simply by using titles that they had recorded three or four years before, and rejected at the time. Three-quarters of the selections issued between summer 1932 and summer 1933 had been recorded at least two years earlier – there was a Frank Stokes from 1929, a Robert Wilkins from 1928, a Memphis Jug Band from 1929, and so on.

In 1931 total blues and gospel releases had averaged eight a week, only 20 per cent below the level of the peak years. In 1932 they were half that, and the following year there were less than 150 new issues – the lowest level since 1922. In 1933 Victor were still charging 75 cents – and that for material that they had considered below par years before. With unemployment running high few black or white customers could afford this price. In order to survive, Victor were forced to follow ARC–BRC and enter the cheap record market. Their 35-cent label, Bluebird, was launched in the summer of 1933. The first race discs on Bluebird were reissues of old Victor material – by Walter Davis, the Memphis Jug Band, Cannon's Jug Stompers and Revd Gates. But Victor needed new material, and they decided to go to Chicago to find it.

In the twenties, Victor had seldom recorded more than eight titles in a day, whereas most companies had averaged twice as many. There was time for an artist to discuss his material with the recording manager, rehearse it thoroughly, and then record it twice at a leisurely pace. Even after the company started making one and not two takes of each tune, in 1931, ten titles was a good day's work. Now, as a further economy, engineers were told to make maximum use of the studio facilities and their own time. Thus, on Wednesday 2 August 1933, no less than thirty-five race titles were recorded in Chicago, by a dozen artists including Roosevelt Sykes (once more as Willie Kelly), the Sparks brothers, and

Walter Davis. The Walter Davis items were put out simultaneously on Bluebird, at 35 cents, and in the Victor 23250 series, at 75 cents. However, it soon became apparent that there was little point in continuing to produce 75-cent race records and at the end of 1933 the Victor race series – which had reached 23432 – was withdrawn.

By the beginning of 1934 there were, besides the ailing and barely active Gennett and Columbia concerns, only two companies competing for the race market: ARC–BRC and Victor. But that year there emerged a strong new competitor. In the middle of the year, English Decca financed an American company of the same name and put in charge Jack Kapp, who had run Brunswick-Balke-Collender's race series. Even more important, Jack Kapp brought with him Mayo Williams, as race talent scout. They began recording in New York and Chicago in August and before the end of the year had issued two or three dozen items in their new race series, the Decca 7000s. Whereas the other two companies still maintained 75-cent labels (Victor and Brunswick respectively) in addition to the cheap Bluebird and Vocalion, Decca priced all their records at 35 cents; to cut overheads they began by making just one take of each title. Decca intended to grab as large a share as it could of the once more expanding record market.

From 1934 until 1945 there were three main race labels, all selling at 35 cents: Decca, the Brunswick Record Corporation's Vocalion, and RCA-Victor's Bluebird. Whereas Decca had a special race series, Bluebird and Vocalion numbered blues and gospel material in their general series. However, Vocalion added a 0- prefix to the number of each hillbilly and race item in the 2500 series. And although the Bluebird B5000 series at first featured all types of music, after B7950 (at the end of 1938) this series was reserved for hillbilly and race material, with popular records transferred to the new B10000 series.

Gennett had failed at the end of 1934. On 28 June 1935 Decca bought the Champion trademark, and rights to certain Gennett material. Late that year they started their second race series, the Champion 50000s; it featured some reissues of Gennett blues – including the final four sides by Frank James – and some reissues from Paramount – including all twelve tunes from the Mississippi Sheiks' 1932 session – as well as original material recorded by Decca. However, the series cannot have been a success, for it was discontinued after only seventy-eight issues. After BRC bought the Columbia Phonograph Corporation, in late 1934, they put out a further thirteen records in the OKeh 8000 series – newly recorded selections by Papa Charlie Jackson and the Memphis Jug Band, favourites of seven years before. Papa Charlie recorded a new version of *Skoodle-um-skoo*, on OKeh 8954. The Memphis Jug Band's *Jug Band Quartette* and *Little Green Slippers*, on OKeh 8966, was the last issue in the 8000 series; it had lasted for fourteen years, longer than any other race series.

Besides its regular Vocalion issues, BRC–ARC were also putting out race records on the five 'dime-store labels' – Perfect, Oriole, Romeo, Banner and Melotone – still selling at 25 cents. Generally, the dime-store labels did not duplicate material that had appeared on Vocalion. In late 1935, ARC replaced the complicated numbering system (which had been different for each label) with an extremely simple system. The first part of the number indicated the year, the second part the month, and the third part the number of the individual record in that month's batch of releases, popular records being numbered from 1 and hillbilly and race from 51. Every, or almost every, number appeared on each of the five labels. Thus Big Bill's *C & A Blues* was on 5–12–65; it was the fifteenth hillbilly/race disc issued in December 1935.

There was one change of company ownership in the late thirties. In February 1938 the Columbia Broadcasting System bought BRC–ARC. Within two months they had discontinued the five dime-store labels; before the end of the year they followed Victor's example of 1931 and told their engineers to make one, and not two, takes of each title; then, in 1940, they changed the name of their expensive label from Brunswick to Columbia, and of the cheaper one from Vocalion to OKeh. All records after 5621 were put out as OKeh; some of the better-selling earlier records in the 2500 series – originally put out as Vocalion – were re-pressed as OKehs.

There were two other labels that featured a fair quantity of race material during the thirties. The store group Montgomery Ward, with a label of the same name, drew at various times on Gennett, Decca and Bluebird. And Sears Roebuck used ARC material on its Conqueror label; the Sears catalogue priced Conqueror records at 21 cents each in 1934, at two for 45 cents in late 1935, and at the bargain price of six for 55 cents in the autumn of 1936.

The urban style of music that had appeared – notably on BBC's Vocalion – at the very end of the twenties dominated the market from 1934 on. Tampa Red, Memphis Minnie, Big Bill, Roosevelt Sykes and Walter Davis each continued to have a new record issued every few weeks until the beginning of the Second World War. Leroy Carr died in 1935, and the following year Decca issued nine records by Bill Gaither, a black radio store proprietor from Louisville, under the name 'Leroy's Buddy'. Gaither played guitar, and sang very much in Leroy's style; his piano player, Honey Hill, imitated Leroy, and Gaither's records sold well for half-a-dozen years.

In 1934 Mayo Williams was managing two artists who had been briefly featured in the Vocalion 1000 series a few years earlier: Amos Easton, who wasn't very proficient on any instrument but sang well in the easy, relaxed manner of Leroy Carr, and Peetie Wheatstraw, who was as fluent on guitar as he was on piano and whose singing had more bite and vigour than Easton's. The race labels were anxious for new talent and in 1934 Williams arranged for Easton to record for all three of the major labels; most of his records appear under the pseudonym 'Bumble Bee Slim'.

Both Victor and BRC–ARC sent out field units in 1934. Victor contacted the perennial Rev. Gates in Atlanta, but otherwise the race activity was in Texas. BRC–ARC recorded the old OKeh singer Texas Alexander in San Antonio in April and again in Fort Worth in September; in March Victor visited San Antonio to record Bo Carter and the Mississippi Sheiks and a new artist called Joe Pullum. Pullum didn't play any instrument but he sang, in an almost falsetto voice, with incredible control and feeling; he was perhaps the most technically accomplished of all blues singers. Rob Cooper's barrelhouse piano accompaniment perfectly reinforced and complemented Pullum's vocal. Their first record, on Bluebird B5459, was *Black Gal What Makes Your Head So Hard?*:

> Black gal, black gal
> What makes your head so hard?
> Black gal, woman what makes your head so hard?
> Lord, I would come to see you
> But your man has got me barred

Pullum's record was such a success that Vocalion had no less an artist than Leroy Carr record *Black Gal*, in New York in August. Within a few weeks of opening their Chicago studio, Decca got Mary Johnson to record the tune (issued on Decca 7014); then, as Bluebird exploited their success by putting out Pullum singing *Black Gal*, nos. 2, 3 and 4 (on

B5592, B5844 and B5947), Decca recorded another version by a rather mediocre singer called Jimmie Gordon. When Decca issued Gordon's *Black Gal* on 7043 the label read 'Joe Bullum'! However, they afterwards repented of the subterfuge and relabelled the record as by Jimmie Gordon.

Pullum's popularity waned fairly soon and Bluebird stopped recording him in 1936. Record buyers preferred the rocking beat of the Chicago artists to Pullum's quiet, introspective approach. Even Big Bill was now using a piano player, and a drummer or bass player, and gradually forsaking his country blues origins for a swinging, urban sound. Will Weldon, who had been on the Memphis Jug Band's first records, came back in 1935 to make his first recordings in eight years; Weldon, styling himself 'Casey Bill', played a steel guitar with panache and sounded very much like Tampa Red. Vocalion even got Big Bill and Casey Bill together, and labelled the records 'The Hokum Boys'. Casey Bill was managed by Lester Melrose, the brother of Frank Melrose (a white pianist who played in such a Negroid manner that he had had a record in the old Paramount race series). Melrose also managed Lil Johnson, whose full voice and controlled phrasing were reminiscent of the best of the classic blues singers. The only other popular woman singer – apart from Memphis Minnie – was Georgia White, who was also a lively pianist and was billed by Decca as 'The World's Greatest Blues Singer'.

When the companies began full-scale recording again, in 1934, they were each after the most popular artists; and the singers sometimes took advantage of the situation. In 1934 Amos Easton had twelve records issued, on Bluebird, Decca and Vocalion. His popularity was at its height and the following year, still contriving to record for all the companies, he had no less than twenty-nine releases (including some, under the pseudonym 'Shelley Armstrong', on Decca's second-string Champion label) – twelve more than any one blues singer had ever had issued in one year before. In 1935 half the best-selling artists were recording for at least two companies. But the companies soon introduced some order, by insisting on exclusive contracts; by 1938 each of the most popular artists was firmly tied to just one label. Of course people sometimes tried to get around it. Lester Melrose managed several of the major blues singers and many minor ones. In 1937 he took over, from Mayo Williams, a new rough-voiced singer from Mississippi called Johnnie Temple. Melrose arranged a Decca contract for Temple and then, in October 1937, took him to the Vocalion studio. However, soon after the session Vocalion noticed that Decca were making regular issues of Temple's records. Decca confirmed that their contract with Temple did not expire until 21 May 1939; Vocalion made a file memorandum against the four Temple titles 'do not release', and – on 6 June 1938 – Melrose refunded the $84 he had received for the session the previous October.

Industry sales were steadily rising: 37 million discs were sold in 1937, six times as many as five years before. More and more blues and gospel records were released every year. From a less-than-3-a-week average in 1933, with many of these being titles recorded years before, issues gradually increased until in 1937 the average was 9 a week. The total for 1937 was 50 less than the annual output during the peak years, but in fact the number of blues records was about the same (just under 400); the difference was in the number of gospel releases.

Gospel issues had been cut back even more than blues in the hard years of 1932 and 1933; and there was no big increase in religious recordings from 1934 onwards, as there was with blues. Sermons were virtually out. Bluebird recorded Rev. Gates in 1934 and then not again until 1939; Decca brought back Rev. J. C. Burnett for eight titles in 1938. But this was almost all; there were usually only about half-a-dozen sermon records in any year after 1931. In fact, of the 370 sermon discs issued in the period covered by this book – nearly 100 of these being by Rev. Gates – more than 300 were put out between mid-1926 and the end of 1931.

In 1934 there was some recording of guitar evangelists. Joshua White made a number of sacred items, and after a while ARC kept his own name for religious records, putting out blues numbers under the pseudonym 'Pinewood Tom'. In 1934 Decca brought back Blind Joe Taggart and the following year they recorded a number of gospel songs from Blind Willie McTell, and even persuaded Memphis Minnie to sing *Let Me Ride* and *When The Saints Go Marching Home* – issued on Decca 7063 as by Gospel Minnie. But there were fewer records by guitar evangelists being released than during the peak years, and soon even these faded away; in 1938 there was not a single new issue.

The main religious activity in the thirties concerned gospel quartets. In 1934 there had only been eight quartet records, but the number gradually built up until in 1938 there were over fifty, the level of the peak years. Every label had its regular quartet – Mitchell's Christian Singers on Vocalion, the Heavenly Gospel Singers on Bluebird, and Paramount's Norfolk Jubilee Quartet on Decca.

The companies had three main ways of unearthing new talent: by placing advertisements in local papers, especially just before a field unit was due in a nearby town; by just relying on chance comments from singers, concerning others who might be good recording propositions; and by employing their own talent scouts, who would carry out steady, systematic searches. The last method was intensively employed in the thirties – Roosevelt Sykes, for instance, would find likely artists for Decca (or, sometimes, for Lester Melrose). But despite this, race catalogues in the thirties relied more heavily on a small nucleus of popular singers than they had in the twenties. In 1937, sixteen singers had more than six records issued in the year, accounting altogether for more than a third of all race releases; in the peak years there had usually been about ten artists with more than six records out in a year, and they altogether accounted for less than a fifth of the total releases.

There was far less recording in the field in the thirties; in view of the popularity of the Chicago singers there was less need. Decca appear to have recorded blues and gospel artists at just three locations in the South – Walter Vinson, of the Mississippi Sheiks, and Oscar Woods, 'The Lone Wolf', at New Orleans in March 1936; pianist Alex Moore and other Texas artists at Dallas in February 1937; and a number of gospel groups and blues singers at Charlotte, North Carolina, in June 1938. Victor made about four field trips a year, mainly for the hillbilly catalogue. They dropped the Mississippi Sheiks in 1935 but continued to record a dozen new titles by Bo Carter every year, or every other year, calling him to San Antonio, New Orleans or Atlanta. In 1935 Victor recorded four titles in New Orleans by Little Brother Montgomery, an original and versatile pianist with a highly personal whining vocal style. He sang one of his own compositions, that had been featured on his single Paramount release, in 1930:

57 The cover of the 1940 Decca Race Records catalogue

I've got the Vicksburg blues, and I'm singing them everywhere I go (*twice*)
Now the reason I sing them, my baby says she don't want me no more

Vicksburg Blues, on Bluebird B6072, was a success and the following year
Victor returned to New Orleans to record more titles by Brother, and
some by other local singers.

Whereas in the twenties Victor had normally recorded eight titles a
day in the field (while the competition would do fifteen to twenty), they
now aimed at twenty-five or more (the competition still stuck to between
fifteen and twenty). In the St Charles Hotel, New Orleans, on Thursday
15 October 1936, they began with twelve duets from the Chatman Brothers
(who were in fact two of Bo Carter's brothers, Chatman being his real
name); then four from Matilda Powell, calling herself 'Mississippi Matilda'.
Between 4.45 and 6 p.m. they recorded six tunes by Eugene Powell (presumably some relation of Matilda), under the name 'Sonny Boy Nelson'.
Then, into the evening, they recorded ten harmonica blues by Robert
Hill, with Eugene Powell providing guitar accompaniment; and then
twelve blues from Bo Carter. Bo Carter received 20 per cent of Sonny
Boy Nelson's royalty – presumably he acted as Nelson's agent – and his
address was recorded as c/o Matilda Powell, Anguilla, Mississippi, showing the close connections between all these artists. The next day the unit
began with twelve blues from Tommy Griffin; then four from Annie
Turner, with Little Brother Montgomery accompanying on the piano;
then no less than eighteen tunes, one after another, from Little Brother;
after that a sentimental song from Creole George Guesnon, again accompanied by Little Brother; and finally two numbers from Walter Vinson
(going under the name Walter Jacobs). They had recorded eighty-one
tunes in two days – what would have been a normal two weeks' work
six years earlier. The New Orleans session in 1936 was Victor's last
substantial race field recording; in subsequent years they recorded a fair
number of gospel quartets in the field, but only one or two unimportant
blues singers.

By and large Victor visited the same towns over and over again – New
Orleans, San Antonio, Atlanta and Charlotte, North Carolina. BRC–ARC,
however, took pains to seek out talent in unusual places. In 1935 they

visited Jackson, Mississippi; in 1936 Augusta, Georgia and Hattiesburg, Mississippi; and in 1937 Hot Springs, Arkansas and Birmingham, Alabama. They recorded about 100 titles at each location, of which rather more than half were generally by black artists. Some fine country blues singers were recorded, including Robert Wilkins, who had been featured on Brunswick and Victor in the twenties (this time he gave his name as Tim Wilkins). But there was really little demand for country blues in the thirties, and the company didn't even bother to issue a large proportion of the material they collected.

BRC–ARC made regular visits to San Antonio and Dallas (though never to Atlanta) for hillbilly material, and also did some useful blues recording there. In 1935 and 1936 they recorded a group of artists put forward by local talent spotter Lester Hearne, including pianist Black Boy Shine and singer Bernice Edwards. In 1937 the white singer Jimmie Davis (who later became Governor of Louisiana) suggested Kitty Gray and her Wampus Cats, a Texas group with something of a Chicago sound, but featuring the Shreveport guitarist Oscar Woods. At the same session – in San Antonio – Vocalion recorded six sides each by Son Becky and Pinetop Burks; the latter especially was a brilliant pianist–singer in the best Texas tradition. And in San Antonio the company recorded a young country blues singer whose records did sell well – Robert Johnson, from Mississippi, who brought an unusual tortured intensity to his singing and bottleneck guitar playing. BRC–ARC recorded sixteen tunes by Johnson in November 1936, and then a further thirteen in Dallas the next June. This was Johnson's last session; he was said to have been poisoned by his girl friend soon after it.

There were two other country blues singers who could hold their own against Tampa Red, Bumble Bee Slim and the rest in the race lists of the thirties: Sleepy John Estes, who had been a Victor artist in 1929 and 1930 and now had regular releases in the Decca 7000 series, and Blind Boy Fuller, an itinerant singer–guitarist from Carolina. Fuller was first recorded by Vocalion in 1935 and his clear, mean-sounding voice and accomplished, rhythmic guitar style gradually became more and more popular. In July 1937 Decca recorded twelve blues by Fuller and immediately issued four of them on Decca 7330 and 7331. But Vocalion protested that he had an exclusive contract with them and Decca were forced to withdraw the records; they were finally able to release them in 1942, after Fuller had died. In 1938 Blind Boy Fuller had fourteen records issued, more than any other artist – one more in fact than Big Bill, who had a new release each month throughout the thirties. The following year Columbia, who had bought the Vocalion label, got him to sing some religious numbers and issued them as by 'Brother George and his Sanctified Singers'; the Sanctified Singers were harmonica player Sonny Terry and Oh Red, Fuller's regular washboard accompanist. After Fuller's death, Columbia continued to use the name 'Brother George' for records by another Carolina singer, Brownie McGhee, some of whose secular items were labelled – much to his annoyance – 'Blind Boy Fuller #2'.

In 1937, the best year for blues since 1930, Lonnie Johnson returned to recording. And Bluebird began regular issues by two new Chicago stars: harmonica player and singer Sonny Boy Williamson, and Robert Brown, who went under the name 'Washboard Sam'. Brown was a Lester Melrose protégé, and in 1935 and 1936 had had records issued on Vocalion under the names 'Ham Gravy' and 'Shufflin' Sam' as well as 'Washboard Sam'. Bluebird had issued one record in 1935 and three in 1936. Then, in 1937, they put out Bluebird B7001, *We Gonna Move* coupled with *Back Door*:

> Oh, tell me mama, who's that a while ago (*twice*)
> Yes, when I come in, who's that went out that back door

Sam did everything the Chicago singers had been doing for the past few years; and he did it better. His powerful rhythmic vocal – backed by Big Bill's guitar, Black Bob's piano, Sam's own agile washboard and Arnett Nelson's fluid clarinet – was irresistible. Bluebird arranged an exclusive contract and Washboard Sam, too, had a new release every month.

Tampa Red was still recording steadily for Bluebird, and Memphis Minnie for Vocalion. Minnie was paid at the flat rate of $12.50 per side. And she could reckon to be doing well: another Vocalion artist, pianist Curtis Jones, received only $7.50 per side. When the company took a field unit to Memphis, in July 1939, their rates were even lower. The company files show total expenses of $67.55 for ten tunes by singer–guitarist Little Buddy Doyle – $5 per side for Doyle, $10 overall for

58 Washboard Sam, perhaps the most popular blues singer of the late 1930s

Hammie Nix, who accompanied on the harmonica, and $7.55 for expenses. Victor's rates at this time are not known, but they probably paid a little more. Decca's remuneration would have been about the same as Vocalion's. It appears in fact that singers were now being paid rather less than they had been ten years before; when Mississippi John Hurt

LONNIE JOHNSON, Blues Singer

B-8322	{ Nothing But a Rat She's My Mary
B-8338	{ Four O Three Blues The Loveless Blues
B-8363	{ Why Women Go Wrong She's Only a Woman
B-8387	{ Trust Your Husband Jersey Belle Blues
B-8530	{ Get Yourself Together Don't Be No Fool
B-8564	{ Be Careful I'm Just Dumb

59 Lonnie Johnson as advertised by Bluebird

– a fairly unknown singer – was asked to come to New York to record by OKeh in 1928 he was paid $20 per side, in addition to all his expenses.

From 1934 to 1936 blues and gospel releases made up about 20 per cent of the total issues of the three companies. With sales of pop records still disappointing, it was a worthwhile effort to cultivate the race market. Then pop interest revived; in 1937 there were twice as many pop issues as in the previous year. Race releases were about 15 per cent higher – Decca and Bluebird each put out around 120 items whilst BRC–ARC issued almost 100 on Vocalion, and another 100 on the dime-store labels. When CBS bought BRC–ARC in early 1938 they stopped production of the dime-store labels, and, although a few more race records appeared on Vocalion than previously, there was an overall loss – blues and gospel releases in 1938 averaged less than 8 a week, one a week down on 1937. But in 1938 pop issues again doubled, and the companies began devoting more and more of their time to popular material, to the detriment of the race catalogue. Decca shut down their permanent studio in Chicago in May 1937, and thereafter just went there once or twice a year, for a few days of intensive recording activity; CBS went to San Antonio in May 1938 and – for the first time since 1932 – did not record a single black artist. Blues and gospel releases were down to 6 a week by 1940. And an increasing proportion were gospel items – mostly unaccompanied quartets; a quarter of the total race releases in 1939 were sacred, as against an eighth two years earlier. Taking advantage of the boom, Victor recorded Revd Gates again in Rock Hill, South Carolina, in February 1939, and then in Atlanta in 1940.

In the post-1937 years most releases were by established artists: Blind Boy Fuller, Big Bill, Washboard Sam, Tampa Red, Bill Gaither, Walter Davis, Peetie Wheatstraw, Sonny Boy Williamson and so on (Bumble Bee Slim had been dropped in 1938). But there were a few innovations. For instance, four of the classic blues singers reappeared briefly – Black Swan's Trixie Smith and Paramount's Alberta Hunter recorded a few titles for Decca and Bluebird; Lester Melrose was instrumental in getting Victoria Spivey back into the studios; and jazz enthusiast John Hammond – who had arranged Bessie Smith's last session in 1933 – supervised a session involving Ida Cox and her All Star Orchestra, in the Columbia studios in 1940.

And two fine country blues singers were dug out by the talent scouts. Bukka White had made fourteen sides, of which only four were ever issued, for Victor in Memphis in 1930; and then – through Lester Melrose – two for Vocalion in Chicago in 1937. White's intense throaty singing and driving guitar appealed to black record buyers and Vocalion asked him to return to make some more titles; but by then he had been committed to the Mississippi State Penitentiary. It wasn't until Melrose secured his parole in 1940 that he was able to travel north and record twelve more numbers, mostly blues about prison life. CBS paid him well, by their standards: $17.50 per selection, and $20 overall for accompanist Washboard

Sam; with $33.50 payment for expenses the twelve tunes cost the company $263.50.

In November 1939 Bluebird recorded Tommy McClennan, a Mississippi singer with a gravelly voice and primitive but effective guitar accompaniment; he was immediately in demand, and had eight records issued in 1941. At McClennan's last session, in February 1942, he recorded *Bluebird Blues*, issued on Bluebird B9037, a plea to the company to come and ask him to do some more recording:

> Bluebird, Bluebird, please fly right down to me (*twice*)
> If you don't find me on the M & O, you'll find me on the Santa Fe

The race labels had always kept considerable quantities of old issues in catalogue. One of the longest-lived records was the Norfolk Jubilee Quartet's *Father Prepare Me* and *My Lord's Gonna Move This Wicked Race*, issued on Paramount 12035 in mid-1923 and still available when the company folded nine years later. Sales were so great that the original masters wore out, and the Quartet was called back at least once to re-record the titles. Even through the Depression years large catalogues were maintained. The 1935 Vocalion catalogue listed every record put out by Memphis Minnie and all but one of the forty-six items by Leroy Carr; most of these were in the Vocalion 1000 series, originally priced at 75 cents, but now available for only 35 cents. Victor did not reduce the price of any records, preferring instead to start a new label, Bluebird. Victor race issues were withdrawn and only a few of them reissued on the cheaper label, but the company kept most Bluebird blues around for a fair time – the 1937 catalogue listed 175 currently available blues and gospel discs. Decca, however, went one better and declared that *all* their issues would remain permanently available; according to the 1940 catalogue it was still possible to buy every record put out in the 7000 series since it began in 1934.

In the late thirties there were no large advertisements, or supplements with lurid drawings telling the story of a blues; no way-out copy impressing upon the customer that he could not afford to be without such-and-such a record. The companies merely listed the new releases – blues coming after hillbilly in the supplements – with specification of the instrumentation. Decca issued separate race catalogues, whereas BRC–ARC listed race records in a final section of the general catalogue. Victor had admitted hillbilly into the general catalogue in 1933, but excluded records by black artists. In 1937 the Bluebird catalogue mingled all types of music with only the pictures of some of the artists in a centre section showing their colour. However, by the end of the thirties there was a separate Bluebird catalogue for non-pop items: the first section dealt with hillbilly (under the name 'Old Familiar Tunes'), then came 'Race Records', followed by 'Children's', 'Cajun' and finally 'Irish' items.

From 1934 on, the three companies had played fairly equal parts in supplying black record enthusiasts. Then, in 1941, with industry sales once more topping 100 million discs, there was a further cut-back in race releases; Bluebird still put out 100 new items but Decca and Columbia, for the first time in five years, fell well short of the figure. That year several Decca artists moved company – Roosevelt Sykes to Columbia, and Johnnie Temple and Sleepy John Estes to Bluebird.

Early in 1942 the government restricted the use of shellac, and blues and gospel releases – at 125 – were half what they had been in 1941. Well over half of these came from Victor, with Washboard Sam still the firm favourite, followed by Tampa Red, Walter Davis, Sonny Boy Williamson and Tommy McClennan. Columbia released only a score or so race items on their label (the renamed Vocalion), and a third of these were by Big Bill. Decca's main activity surrounded Blind Boy Fuller – the issue of material recorded five years earlier – and the Selah Jubilee Singers.

In July 1942 the president of the American Federation of Musicians, J. C. Petrillo – worried about the effects of jukeboxes on live music – announced a ban on all recording, and the studios were closed for two years. But race material that had already been recorded remained unissued by and large, and the catalogues were ruthlessly pruned. The December 1941 Victor catalogue listed 350 blues and gospel items, whereas in May 1943 there were only 75 items available, and only 2 of these had been issued before 1940 – Washboard Sam's *Diggin' My Potatoes* from 1939, and his still-popular *Back Door*, from 1937.

Between 1920 and 1942 about 5,500 blues and 1,250 gospel records had been issued, involving, all told, about 1,200 artists. Two performers – Tampa Red and Big Bill – each had more than 100 releases; sixteen more had between 50 and 100 and a further fifty-four between 20 and 50; these seventy-two most popular artists altogether accounted for almost half the total releases.

Although commercial recording of music came to a standstill with the Petrillo Ban, one recording concern was unaffected – the Music Division of the Library of Congress. Since 1933 they had been collecting all types of folk music on record to form a permanent reference library in their Archives. A dedicated group of researchers, led by John A. Lomax, had been combing the countryside with small mobile recording units, concentrating particularly on prison farms and penitentiaries. Over the course of the nine years up to 1942 they had recorded about 4,000 titles by at least 850 black singers, quite apart from their activities in hillbilly and other spheres.

The blues and ballad singer Huddie Ledbetter – better known as Leadbelly – was discovered and recorded by Lomax in the State Penitentiary, Angola, Louisiana, in 1933, and after his release continued to record for them right up to his death in 1949. In May 1939 Library of Congress field workers stumbled upon Bukka White in the State Penitentiary at Parchman, Mississippi, where he was serving a sentence for shooting a man, and recorded just two titles, *Po' Boy* and *Sic 'Em Dogs On*. In 1940 Blind Willie McTell bobbed up in Atlanta – recording activity seemed to draw him like a magnet – and recorded a long series of songs and reminiscences. A trip to Lake Cormorant, Mississippi, in 1941 unearthed the magnificent Son House, unrecorded since his Paramount days, and, realising what they had found, the researchers returned again in 1942 for more. One might say their star discovery, however, was a young country boy called McKinley Morganfield whom they recorded in Stovall, Mississippi, in 1941 and 1942. He was soon to be known to the public as Muddy Waters and to be one of the most commercially successful blues singers of the post-war period.

Before leaving the war years, two companies who played their own small part in blues recording history should not be overlooked. The first, appearing in 1939, was Varsity, the product of one-time Victor executive Eli Oberstein. The label was intended as a competitor to the big three – Bluebird, Vocalion and Decca – and Oberstein immediately instituted a race series. This featured just a little original recording but was predominantly reissues of old recordings. It began with a number of reissues of Paramount material through an arrangement with the Crown label, which had been connected with Paramount in the early thirties. This soon changed to Gennett material, either by arrangement with Harry Gennett himself, or through Decca who had acquired rights in 1935 when buying Champion. Almost all issues were under simple-minded pseudonyms – Sally Sad, Tall Tom, Big Boy Ben, Jim Jam and others. The name 'Down South Boys' concealed the identity of the Mississippi Sheiks on Varsity 6009, and of preacher Black Billy Sunday and the Norfolk Jubilee Quartet on either side of 6011. However, a general lowering of prices by Victor and Columbia in mid-1940 precipitated Oberstein into bankruptcy and by autumn 1941, after reissuing some of the rarest Champions of the Depression years, the Varsity race series had disappeared.

The second label was Joe Davis, produced towards the end of the war by the music publisher, singer and promoter of the twenties of that name, who first attempted to revive the old Gennett label. Although Harry Gennett had ceased making records for the public in 1934, he had continued with private work such as sound effects for radio stations. Joe Davis made a deal whereby he obtained Gennett's war-time shellac ration in return for loaning Gennett a lot of money to refurbish his pressing plant. Gennett sold him pressings for 20 cents each plus .02 cents excise tax, old Electrobeam sleeves were used for the records, and the legend 'Gennett Record Division, The Starr Piano Co Inc, Richmond, Indiana' appeared on the label. Rarities from 1930 by artists such as Big Bill and Georgia Tom appeared, plus newly recorded items by an artist in no way connected with Gennett: Gabriel Brown (he had been recorded in Florida in 1935 by the Library of Congress).

The idea of a Gennett revival was dropped after eight issues and the label name changed to Joe Davis. More titles by Gabriel Brown appeared together with some by pianist Champion Jack Dupree and by Columbia's Revd J. C. Burnett. By now Davis had acquired Oberstein's Varsity

60 Victor's 1943 catalogue used anachronistic imagery

masters, but, apparently deciding that race records no longer paid, the venture soon drifted into other channels.

When the Petrillo Ban ended in 1944 the big companies made a half-hearted attempt to carry on as before. A new Bluebird race series had been begun in 1943 and Decca and Columbia soon followed suit. Victor

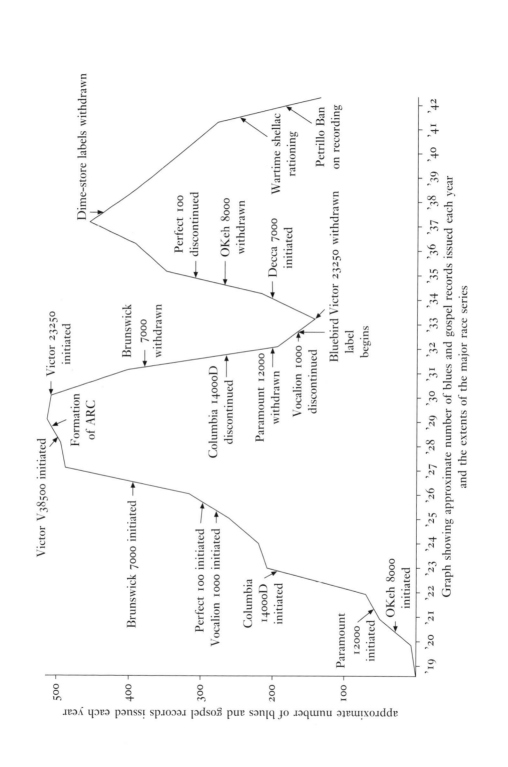

Graph showing approximate number of blues and gospel records issued each year
and the extents of the major race series

Year	Atlanta, Georgia	Dallas and Fort Worth, Texas	Memphis, Tennessee	New Orleans, Louisiana	San Antonio, Texas	Birmingham, Alabama	Bristol, Tennessee	Charlotte, North Carolina	Jackson, Mississippi	Knoxville, Tennessee	Rock Hill, South Carolina	St Louis, Missouri	Other locations
'23	OK											OK	
'24	OK			OK								OK	
'25	OK, Co			OK								OK	
'26	OK, Co			Co									
'27	Co, Vi	Co	Co, Vi	Co, Vi		Ge	Vi	Vi					Vi: Savannah, GA
'28	OK, Co, Vi, Vo	Co	OK, Vi, Vo	Co	OK	Vo	Vi			Vo			Vi: Nashville, TN; Vo: Indianapolis, IN; OK: Richmond, VA; Co: Greensboro, NC; Vo: Kansas City, KS; OK: Shreveport, LA; Vi: Cincinnati, OH
'29	OK, Co, Vi	Co, Vi, Vo	Vi, Vo	OK, Co	OK								
'30	OK, Co	Vo	Vi, Vo	Co	OK				OK	Vo			
'31	Vi	Vi						Vi					Vi: Louisville, KY
'32													
'33													
'34	BB				BB, Vo							Vo	
'35	BB	Vo		De, BB	BB, Vo			BB	Vo				Vo: Augusta, GA, and Hattiesburg, MS
'36		Vo		BB	BB, Vo			BB					Vo: Hot Springs, AR
'37	BB	Vo			BB, Vo	Vo					BB		Vo: Columbia, SC
'38	BB	Vo	Vo		BB						BB		
'39		Vo											
'40		Vo											
'41	BB	BB											
'42													

CHART OF FIELD TRIPS
Under each town are shown the record labels which recorded blues and gospel material there, year by year. The following abbreviations are used:
BB–Bluebird   Co–Columbia   De–Decca
Ge–Gennett   OK–OKeh   Vi–Victor
Vo–Vocalion (recording jointly with the chain store labels in the mid-thirties)

continued with their old favourites Washboard Sam, Tampa Red and Sonny Boy Williamson, and Columbia with Memphis Minnie and Big Bill; Decca had no big-name blues singers left. But the public mood was changing, and with it the type of music people were prepared to pay for. Sensing this, a number of small record companies sprang up in all parts of the country – in Chicago, Detroit, the South, and the West Coast — and were soon supplying public demand. Many of the new ventures were under black ownership. The large companies were swiftly left behind. When Victor discontinued the Bluebird label in 1950 they made sure to reissue Washboard Sam's two most successful tunes, *Back Door* and *Diggin' My Potatoes*, on Victor 20-2162. But these were now old and stale and not to be compared with, for example, the rousing, shouting, throbbing Muddy Waters records that were being put out by the emerging Chicago record company, Chess. It was an altogether new era in blues recording.

FURTHER INFORMATION

The reader interested in delving further into the area covered by *Recording the Blues* is recommended towards *Blues and Gospel Records, 1890–1943*, fourth edition (revised and enlarged), compiled by Robert M. W. Dixon, John Godrich and Howard Rye, and published by the Clarendon Press, Oxford (1997). This gives full recording details of every blues and gospel recording during this period, including unissued material and field recordings made by the Library of Congress and other bodies. It includes thumbnail sketches of the labels which issued 'race records' together with details of all field trips to record away from the major northern centres. There are indexes of tune titles, broadcasts and films, vocalists and accompanists.

ACKNOWLEDGEMENTS

The information contained in this book has been collected from many sources over a period of fifteen or so years; it would be impossible to list all those who have helped us. Special thanks are due to Walter C. Allen, Helene Chmura (late of Columbia Records), Derek Coller, E. C. Foreman (of RCA-Victor), Robert G. Koester, John K. MacKenzie, Dan Mahony, Paul Oliver, Tony Russell, Brian Rust, Max Vreede, Bert Whyatt and Bob Yates. Paul Oliver, Bert Whyatt and Bob Yates also read the initial draft of the book and made welcome suggestions and criticisms. Amongst our published sources are *The Columbia 13/14000D Series* by Dan Mahoney (2nd edition, 1966); *A Glimpse At The Past* by Michael Wyler (1957); and the magazines *Record Research, Jazz Journal* and *Record Changer*.

22 · AFTERWORD

Howard Rye

When the original authors of *Recording The Blues* wrote, in their foreword, that 'Early in 1920 the General Phonograph Corporation issued, for the first time, popular songs performed by a black girl', they were describing an event whose significance they had correctly assessed, but which they were describing both inaccurately and in language which three decades later appears doubly offensive. The term 'black girl' was assuredly intended to insult neither women nor African Americans, nor Mamie Smith herself, who was a mere child of thirty-seven. Paul Oliver comments elsewhere on the changes in linguistic and other sensibilities in the intervening years. The impression then generally held that the recording of African American artists began only in 1920 is as false as the language has become dubious.

That the OKeh recordings of Mamie Smith launched the 'Race Record', marketed primarily to African Americans, is beyond dispute, but this was by no means the beginning of the recording of African American music. The authors were of course perfectly well aware that a good deal of African American religious music had been recorded before 1920, but most of it belongs to the 'jubilee' tradition. This music has never much interested blues or jazz enthusiasts and in common with almost everyone else the authors believed that it was not a distinctively African American style. Furthermore, recordings of it by such groups as the Fisk University Jubilee Singers, who recorded extensively for Victor, Edison and Columbia between 1909 and 1920, were thought to be compromised by being targeted at white audiences.

In the intervening years, extensive research, notably by Doug Seroff, Ray Funk and Lynn Abbott, and also by Tim Brooks, has led to a major reassessment of the jubilee tradition. Very little of this work has been published (Seroff, 1989), but it has been available to other researchers, which made possible the inclusion of many jubilee groups in the 1997 edition of *Blues and Gospel Records*. The earliest jubilee session so far known, by the Unique Quartette on 19 December 1890 for the New York cylinder company, was discovered by Tim Brooks. Though nothing has so far been found from their twenty-one sessions for this company in 1890–3, a secular recording which they made for Edison in 1893 has been recovered.

Recording of African American music more directly ancestral to music in the later Race catalogues appears to have begun with Cousins and De Moss in 1895. Their *Poor Mourner* (Berliner 3010) is the first known record showing the rhythmic characteristics of later African American music. A second recording, *Who Broke The Lock* (Berliner 3012), was known to musicologist Harry Smith and is mentioned in the notes to his *Anthology of American Folk Music* issued by Folkways in 1952. Very little more African American music, other than vocal groups, seems to have been recorded in the United States over the next twenty years. The many recordings of comedian Bert Williams on Victor and Columbia include some material of sufficient interest, including even some actual blues, to justify inclusion in *Blues and Gospel Records 1890–1943*, but his singing style had more influence on jazz than on blues vocalists.

There is evidence that the coming of blues into the repertoire of African American vaudeville artists did not go unnoticed by the recording industry, though that movement has only recently begun to be documented (Oliver, 1984; Vincent, 1995). However, the American recording companies chose to hire white 'character' singers to pastiche the music rather than to record the creators. The 1916 issue, *Nigger Blues* by George O'Connor (Columbia A2064), makes clear that the source of the music was well known to those who sought to profit from it, however little they may have respected its creators. By the time Mamie Smith reached OKeh, similar recordings by such white artists as Nora Bayes and Marie Cahill had become numerous. It will be recalled that Mamie's first tunes had been intended for another such, Sophie Tucker.

Angela Y. Davis has observed of 'Ma' Rainey that: 'The racialized classification of her 160 recordings ensured that her part and the role played by her peers in shaping the popular musical culture of the mainstream would never have to be acknowledged.'

Whether or not this was any part of the intention in establishing segregated catalogues for African American material, it was undeniably an effect that the opportunities for direct comparison between imitators and imitated were minimised. From the viewpoint of white show-business this was doubtless a very convenient effect.

The widespread American belief, as prevalent today as in 1916, that white Americans can perform African American music as effectively as any African American, could not be shared in Europe, where audiences were already acknowledging the African American contribution as distinctive. It appears that the first recordings of African American music were actually made in 1890 in England by the Bohee Brothers, a minstrel banjo duo. Unfortunately, these are known only from literature, but they were the first of a steady stream of recordings by expatriate African Americans over the next thirty years. A great deal of research has been undertaken into the perambulations of these artists, primarily by Rainer Lotz, published in many magazines and anthologised in his *Black People: Entertainers of African Descent in Europe, and Germany* (Lotz, 1997). The recordings include a long series (1903 to 1911) by the singer and harmonica player Pete Hampton. Hampton was not a blues artist in the later sense, but no one hearing his *Dat Mouth Organ Coon* (1904, Edison Bell 6360), and especially the unaccompanied harmonica solo which follows his vocal war with a very, very earthbound English pianist, can be in any doubt that he belongs securely to the most authentic traditions.

More extraordinary still are the recordings made in London in 1916–17 by Dan Kildare's Clef Club Orchestra. The band was appearing at Ciro's Club and English Columbia chose to release the records under the very dated name Ciro's Club Coon Orchestra. They have been listed in jazz discographies from the earliest days and generally dismissed either as bad jazz (which is a matter of definitions) or as bad ragtime (which they probably are). Only in the last few years has it been noted (Rye and Brooks, 1997) that what they are in fact is very fine examples of the tradition of stringband music which was to give such groups as the Dallas String Band to the later Race catalogues.

Recognition that music belonging to the 'blues tradition' was recorded before 1920 much more extensively than the few non-jubilee gospel recordings acknowledged in 1970 does not alter the fact that there was a major change in the thrust of marketing after 1920. It is no doubt true that all the records so far noted sold mainly to Whites – in the case of those released in Europe almost exclusively so. They were certainly not aimed at the African American market in the way that the Race catalogues were to be.

Two booklength studies of Race labels have appeared since 1970, on Paramount (Vreede, 1971), and on Black Swan (Thygesen *et al.*, 1996). From the latter, we can analyse in more detail how Harry Pace sought to cater for the whole spectrum of the record market while using, originally, only African American artists. In this respect the label's aspirations were entirely different from the intentions of the various Race series operated by white-owned companies.

Black Swan was not in fact the first black-owned recording company to seek to place concert music into the drawing rooms of the African American middle class. As early as 1919, George W. Broome had founded Broome Special Phonograph Records (Sutton, 1994). As far as is known, the output is exclusively classical. Potentially of more interest to the student of vernacular music is the See Bee label, which appears to have been connected with Marcus Garvey. It is likely that most of its issues remain to be traced. A coupling by the Five Harmoniques (See Bee 200) is the only blues issue so far known.

'Blues' recording in these early years cannot be clearly distinguished from the recording of jazz singers or from the recording of popular singers who worked with jazz accompaniments. The jazz enthusiasts' portmanteau term for this eclectic field, 'classic blues', has come in for its fair share of criticism over the years and many prefer the term 'vaudeville blues' as more accurately descriptive. Undeniably much of what travelled under the blues banner during the first blues boom was far from classic and only marginally blues. Once the most studied group of blues artists, because most acceptable to jazz enthusiasts, all but the greatest of these female singers, and sometimes even Bessie Smith and 'Ma' Rainey themselves, have at times been dismissed as an irrelevance, mere popular singers, by new generations of blues lovers. Growing interest in female contributions to the arts has played a major part in reversing this trend (Harrison, 1988; Davis, 1998), as has the increasing availability of the music for study. This has enabled a reassessment of a number of previously ignored singers such as Viola McCoy, Helen Gross and Josie Miles, though argument about whether they belong to blues or jazz is likely to continue and is ultimately meaningless.

This increasing availability is perhaps the most remarkable of the changes which need to be documented since the publication of *Recording The Blues*. The second edition of *Blues and Gospel Records 1902–1942*, as it then was, published the previous year, included microgroove reissues. They took up sixty-seven pages, but the number of issues was quite manageable and by no means all of those listed were still available. Then, as now, reissues of vintage blues by the major record companies rarely remained in catalogue longer than it took the accountants to spot that they were not meeting the profit norms for popular records, and many of the issues which had been made by collectors for collectors were genuinely limited editions of as few as 100 copies.

The list also includes the first stirrings of a wind of change. Origin and Yazoo in America and Roots in Austria had already begun the task of restoring the blues legacy to wider circulation. While Yazoo set the highest standards of reproduction, and also confined its output to what its proprietor, Nick Perls, regarded as the best material, carefully arranged into anthologies, some others were concerned primarily to make the material available for study, even if the condition and reproduction precluded anyone taking much pleasure in the results. Surprisingly perhaps, the two types of issue contrived to co-exist, both in the market place and on purchasers' shelves, and both thrived through the 1970s and 1980s and into the CD era.

By the end of the 1980s, one of the former proprietors of Roots, Johnny Parth, had established Document Records in a declared attempt to re-issue everything in *Blues and Gospel Records*. Obliged to restart on CD in August 1990, he took the opportunity to systematise his catalogue and by July 1999 had issued 880 CDs, representing the quasi-totality of the blues and gospel sections of the Race catalogues and much closely related jazz. Inevitably, he has been obliged to use whatever material collectors will make available in the condition in which it is supplied, but in the reissue of vaudeville blues and other unfashionable areas, including many types of gospel music, he has enjoyed a virtual monopoly. Some gaps inevitably remain, either because the records have not actually been recovered by collectors or because rare records are in the hands of selfish people who do not want to share their treasures with others. Fortunately they are not numerous and the result has been that the proportion of the material with which *Recording The Blues* is concerned that is now available in the market place is far greater than it ever was at any one time between 1920 and 1945! In 1970, the notion that the complete works of the Rev. J. M. Gates would ever again be available for purchase by ordinary record buyers seemed so far-fetched as not even to be laughable, and those few who would belittle Johnny Parth's achievement should bear this in mind.

However much better placed we now are to make musical judgements available in 1970 only to a fortunate few, very little research has been done since 1970 which seriously affects understanding of how the music came to be recorded in the first place. *Recording The Blues* remains an accurate guide. In the intervening years, the greatest research effort has been devoted to elucidating the activities of Paramount, whose filing does not survive and must be painstakingly reconstructed. Major progress towards doing this was made by the late Max Vreede (Vreede, 1971; Vreede and van Rijn, n.d.), and more recently detailed research into African American newspapers by Laurie Wright (Wright, 1997, 1999) has provided new evidence on the dating of many Paramount sessions. The researches of Stephen Calt and Gayle Dean Wardlow (Calt and Wardlow, 1988; Calt, 1988/9; Calt and Wardlow, 1990–2; Wardlow, n.d.; Wardlow, 1998) have thrown much light on the history of the company and especially the role of the talent scout H. C. Speir and the company's recording of country blues artists in its final years at Grafton, Wisconsin.

Awareness has grown of the involvement of African American artists themselves as talent scouts for several companies. Ted Vincent (Vincent, 1995) has pointed out how ready enthusiasts have been to accept accounts of African American artists being brought to record companies on the initiative of white recording executives and in particular ridicules the notion that Frank Walker instigated Columbia's recording of Bessie Smith and sent Clarence Williams to 'find' her. He points out that Williams had already been promoting her to recording companies. Williams also worked for OKeh, as did both Lonnie Johnson and the pianist Richard M. Jones. Will Shade of the Memphis Jug Band performed similar services for Victor and his name appears on a number of recording sheets in a supervisory role. The role of J. Mayo Williams at Paramount is well known and was backed up by a publishing company, Chicago Music, which appears to have been a personal fief. In any event Williams used it also to copyright material recorded for his own Black Patti label. When he moved to Brunswick/Vocalion, he formed a new publishing house, State Street Music.

A recent study of the Gennett label (Kennedy, 1994) is not primarily concerned with the company's blues recordings, and gives an account of the Black Patti label somewhat at variance with other sources, but it throws much light on Gennett's operations, as does a study of the company's blues output published in *78 Quarterly* (Tsotsi, 1988–91). It should also be noted that although the company withdrew from recording music, it did not in fact fail and remained in business producing mainly sound effects records through the 1930s, as is noted when discussing the part it played in the life of Joe Davis's labels in the 1940s.

The operations of the ARC labels in the period after 1934 require further elucidation. The statement that 'Vocalion added a 0- prefix to the number of each hillbilly and Race item in the 2500 series', is slightly misleading since up to number 03510 the numbers were often, though not invariably, doubled up with the general series. For example, 03490 is by Blind Boy Fuller, but there is also a 3490 which is an African American jazz coupling by trumpeter Red Allen.

The notion is surprisingly widespread that records in General series were aimed exclusively at white buyers in the same way that Race series were aimed exclusively at black buyers and the various other ethnic series at those particular communities. A very cursory examination of advertisements in the African American press will establish that General series issues by African Americans were advertised alongside Race issues and so were records by other artists thought likely to interest the readers. This practice mirrors the growing number of African American jazz artists whose records were promoted to record buyers generally. Decca's decision in 1940 to start an 8500 'Sepia Series' separate from the 7000 Race series seems to have been motivated in part by a desire to segregate those records which, while primarily of interest to African Americans, were particularly likely to appeal to the growing number of jazz enthusiasts who liked their music hot.

Some technical aspects of record-company activities in the 1930s remain unexplained. Earlier discographies listed numerous 'remake' sessions at ARC, which are so described in the company's filing, at which additional takes were apparently recorded. The extended possibilities of comparison resulting from the reissue programmes of recent years have made clear that the majority of these remade takes are in fact identical to one of the takes recorded at the original session. Most though not all of these remakes were evidently done for some unknown technical reason. One type of technical remake for which the reason is known (Shor, 1994) resulted from the switch in the late 1920s from true 10-inch masters to the international 25-cm standard. The latter is slightly smaller and it was found that some 10-inch masters were too large to be pressed as 25-cm records without unacceptably short lead-in grooves. This accounts for the use of dubbed masters on, for example, many ARC series reissues from the earlier OKeh and Columbia Race series.

Surviving test pressings have yielded many alternative takes for issue and study in recent years, sometimes providing distinctly different performances for listeners' enjoyment, but always throwing light on the creative process even when the musical differences are small. When alternative takes were issued to the original audience, usually because a master broke down or because for some reason stampers of different takes were sent to different plants or used for different pressings, the customer normally remained unaware of it and it may certainly be doubted that many of the original purchasers would have wished to hear some of the strings of takes which have become available to students. By the end of the 1930s many companies were recording complete sessions, including breakdowns and studio chatter, onto safety acetates as a back up. Even some of these have become available for study.

It is not only some of the technical aspects of recording-company activity which have remained inscrutable. While the activities of researchers have recovered details of the lives of numerous artists who were still biographical blanks in 1970 (Harris, 1979), two of the most important female singers of the 1930s, Georgia White and Lil Johnson, remain mystery figures who have proved impervious to research. A very few details have emerged of the former's life outside the recording studio, but no single public appearance by Johnson seems to have been traced and she might have lived solely in the recording studios for aught that anyone knows to the contrary. It is difficult to escape the conclusion that her 'real life' must have unfolded under some other name.

While the declaration of the Petrillo Ban continues to provide a convenient cut-off point for consideration of the early years of blues recording, continuing research has made it appear less neat than it once did. The activities of Joe Davis throughout the period, including a detailed study of his labels of the war years, have been the subject of a lengthy monograph (Bastin, 1990) but Davis was not alone in providing a preview of the post-war recording industry. As early as 1940, the Bronze label of Leroy Hurte, a former member of The Four Blackbirds, had recorded Gladys Bentley, who had previously recorded for OKeh in 1928/9, and went on to record a number of gospel groups (Pickering, 1995). In 1944, Cecil Gant's *I Wonder* (Bronze BR117) became one of the first post-war blues hits, though most of the sales went to a slightly later version recorded for Gilt-Edge. One of the major players on the post-war scene, Herman Lubinsky's Savoy label, was launched in late 1942, though only jazz was recorded until the King Solomon gospel label was introduced in September 1943 (Ruppli and Porter, 1980). Singer and guitarist Saunders King made his first records for the San Francisco based Rhythm label in June 1942, though interestingly these were clearly aimed at the wider jazz market rather than at the Race market.

It may also be noted that while the major labels tended after the war to stick to their tried and trusted, but increasingly outmoded, artists, Columbia devoted considerable energy to documenting the continuing fusion of swing and blues which came to be known as rhythm and blues, making many recordings in Chicago by such artists as the singing alto saxophonist Buster Bennett, a veteran of many pre-war blues sessions, and drummer Red Saunders. These recordings had attracted little attention but are the subject of a major and scholarly documentation on the web site of the Red Saunders Research Foundation.

Despite this limited involvement in contemporary sounds, Columbia still got left behind on the 'down-home blues' scene. In September 1946, they actually recorded McKinley Morganfield, the future 'Muddy Waters'. The results were not considered worthy of issue, though fortunately they did survive to be issued in later years. The majors simply were not on the wavelength of new generations of African American record purchasers.

ACKNOWLEDGEMENTS

My understanding of the issues with which this essay is concerned has benefitted from discussions and exchanges of information and views with many people, but especially Alan Balfour, Mark Berresford, Tim Brooks, Jeffrey P. Green, Barry Kernfeld, Rainer Lotz, Tony Russell, Alyn Shipton, Chris Smith, Richard Spottswood, Laurie Wright. It should be unnecessary to say that all opinions expressed engage only myself.

BIBLIOGRAPHY

Bastin, Bruce. 1990. *Never Sell a Copyright: Joe Davis and his Role in the New York Music Scene, 1916–1978*. Chigwell: Storyville Publications.
Calt, Stephen. 1998/9. 'Paramount, the Anatomy of a "Race" Label', *78 Quarterly*, 3 (1988), 9–23; 4 (1989), 9–30.
Calt, Stephen, and Wardlow, Gayle. 1988. *King of the Delta Blues: The Life and Music of Charlie Patton*. Newton, NJ: Rock Chapel Press.
    1990–2. 'The Buying and Selling of Paramounts', *78 Quarterly*, 5 (1990), 7–24; continued as 'Paramount Part 4 (The Advent of Arthur Laibley)', *78 Quarterly*, 6 (1991), 9–26; continued as 'Paramount's Decline and Fall (Part 5)', *78 Quarterly*, 7 (1992), 7–29.
Davis, Angela Y. 1998. *Blues Legacies and Black Feminism: Gertrude 'Ma' Rainey, Bessie Smith, and Billie Holiday*. New York: Pantheon Books.

Harris, Sheldon. 1979. *Blues Who's Who: A Biographical Dictionary of Blues Singers*. New Rochelle, NY: Arlington House.

Harrison, Daphne Duval. 1988. *Black Pearls: Blues Queens of the 1920s*. New Brunswick, NJ: Rutgers University Press.

Kennedy, Rick. 1994. *Jelly Roll, Bix, and Hoagy: Gennett Studios and the Birth of Recorded Jazz*. Bloomington, IN, and Indianapolis: Indiana University Press.

Lotz, Rainer E. 1997. *Black People: Entertainers of African Descent in Europe, and Germany*. Bonn: Birgit Lotz Verlag.

Oliver, Paul. 1984. *Songsters and Saints, Vocal Traditions on Race Records*. Cambridge: Cambridge University Press.

Pickering, Ed, with Dawson, Jim. 1995. 'The Bronze Story', *Blues & Rhythm The Gospel Truth*, 105 (January), 4–9.

Red Saunders Research Foundation: <http://hubcap.clemson.edu/~campber/rsrf.html>

Ruppli, Michel, and Porter, Bob. 1980. *The Savoy Label: A Discography*. Westport, CT, and London: Greenwood Press.

Rye, Howard, and Brooks, Tim. 1997. 'Visiting Firemen 16: Dan Kildare', in Wright, Laurie (ed.) *Storyville 1996/7*, Chigwell: L. Wright, 30–57.

Seroff, Doug. 1989. 'The Original Fisk Jubilee Singers and The Spiritual Tradition "How Shall We Sing The Lord's Song In A Foreign Land?" Part One The Age of Minstrelsy', *Keskidee*, 2 (1989), 4–9, 21 [Part Two never published].

Shor, Russ. 1994. 'Silent Partners: George Avakian (Conclusion)', *VJM's Jazz & Blues Mart*, 96 (Winter), 5–7.

Sutton, Allan. 1994. *Directory of American Disc Record Brands and Manufacturers, 1891–1943*. Westport, CT, and London: Greenwood Press.

Thygesen, Helge, Berresford, Mark, and Shor, Russ. 1996. *Black Swan: The Record Label of the Harlem Renaissance*. Nottingham: VJM Publications.

Tsotsi, Tom. 1988–9. 'Gennett-Champion Blues Richmond, Indiana (1923–1934)', *78 Quarterly*, 3 (1988), 49–53; 4 (1989), 79–85; 5 (1990), 78–82; 6 (1991), 87–93; 7 (n.d.), 95–102.

Vincent, Ted. 1995. *Keep Cool: The Black Activists who Built the Jazz Age*. London and East Haven, CT: Pluto Press.

Vreede, Max. 1971. *Paramount 12000 13000*. London: Storyville.

Vreede, Max, and van Rijn, Guido. n.d. 'The Paramount L Master Series', *78 Quarterly*, 9, 67–87.

Wardlow, Gayle Dean. n.d. 'The Talent Scouts: H. C. Speir (1895–1972)', *78 Quarterly*, 8, 11–33.

1998. *Chasin' That Devil Music: Searching for the Blues*. San Francisco: Miller Freeman Books.

Wright, Laurie. 1997. 'Dating Paramount's Chicago Recordings 1923–1926', in Wright, Laurie (ed.), *Storyville 1996/7*. Chigwell: L. Wright, 58–72.

1999. 'Dating Paramount's Chicago Recordings – Concluded', in Wright, Laurie (ed.) *Storyville 1998/9* Chigwell: L. Wright, 80–7.

INDEX TO BOOK 1.

Savannah Syncopators

Italic indicates extended discussion, or illustrations.

INDEX TO BOOK 2.

Blacks, Whites and Blues

Note: page numbers in *italic* refer to photographs.

INDEX TO BOOK 3.

Recording the Blues

Italic indicates publications and books, while page numbers in italic indicate mention in the graph, and in illustration and illustration captions. Small capitals indicate record label names.